math expressions

MH

NSF

Grade 1

Volume 2

math expressions

HMH

Dr. Karen C. Fuson

Watch the frog come alive in its pond as you discover and solve math challenges.

Download the *Math Worlds AR* app available on Android or iOS devices.

Grade 1
Volume 2

This material is based upon work supported by the
National Science Foundation
under Grant Numbers
ESI-9816320, REC-9806020, and RED-935373.

Any opinions, findings, and conclusions, or recommendations expressed in this material
are those of the author and do not necessarily reflect the views of the National Science Foundation.

BIG IDEA 1 - Represent and Compare Data

BIG IDEA 2 - *Compare* Problem Types

BIG IDEA 3 - Measure and Order by Length

BIG IDEA - Add 2-Digit Numbers

Student Resources

Dear Family:

In the previous unit, your child learned the Make a Ten strategy to find teen totals. Now, your child builds on previous knowledge to use make a ten to find an unknown partner. The Make a Ten strategy is explained below.

In a teen addition problem such as 9 + 5, children break apart the lesser number to make a ten with the greater number. Because 9 + 1 = 10, they break apart 5 into 1 + 4. Then they add the extra 4 onto 10 to find the total. A similar method is used to find unknown partners with teen totals. Children look for ways to make a ten because it is easier to add onto 10.

In the *Math Expressions* program, Make-a-Ten Cards help children use this method. Each card has a problem on the front. The back shows the answer and illustrates the Make a Ten strategy using pictures of dots. Below the pictures are corresponding numbers to help children understand how to make a ten. Practice the method with your child. As you continue to practice the Make a Ten strategy with your child, your child will become more adept at using mental math.

If you have any questions about the Make a Ten strategy, please contact me.

Sincerely,
Your child's teacher

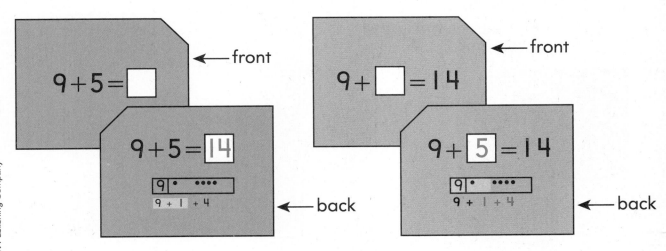

Make-a-Ten Cards

Estimada familia:

En la unidad anterior, su niño aprendió la Estrategia hacer decenas para hallar totales de números de 11 a 19. Ahora, su niño ampliará esos conocimientos previos y hará decenas para hallar una parte desconocida. La Estrategia hacer decenas se explica debajo.

En una suma con números de 11 a 19, tal como 9 + 5, los niños separan el número menor para formar una decena con el número mayor. Como 9 + 1 = 10, separan el 5 en 1 + 4. Luego suman al 10 los 4 que sobran para hallar el total. Un método semejante se usa para hallar partes desconocidas con totales de números de 11 a 19. Los niños buscan maneras de formar una decena porque es más fácil sumar con 10.

En el programa *Math Expressions* las tarjetas de hacer decenas ayudan a los niños a usar este método. Cada tarjeta tiene un problema en el frente. En el reverso se muestra la respuesta y se ilustra la Estrategia hacer decenas mediante dibujos de puntos. Debajo de los dibujos están los números correspondientes para ayudar a los niños a comprender cómo se hace una decena. Practique el método con su niño. A medida que practican la estrategia, su niño adquirirá mayor dominio del cálculo mental.

Si tiene alguna pregunta sobre la Estrategia hacer decenas, por favor comuníquese conmigo.

Atentamente,
El maestro de su niño

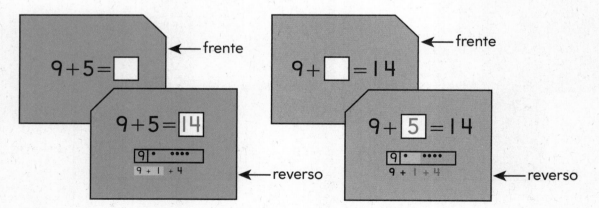

Tarjetas de hacer decenas

10-group

longest

column

number line

grid

row

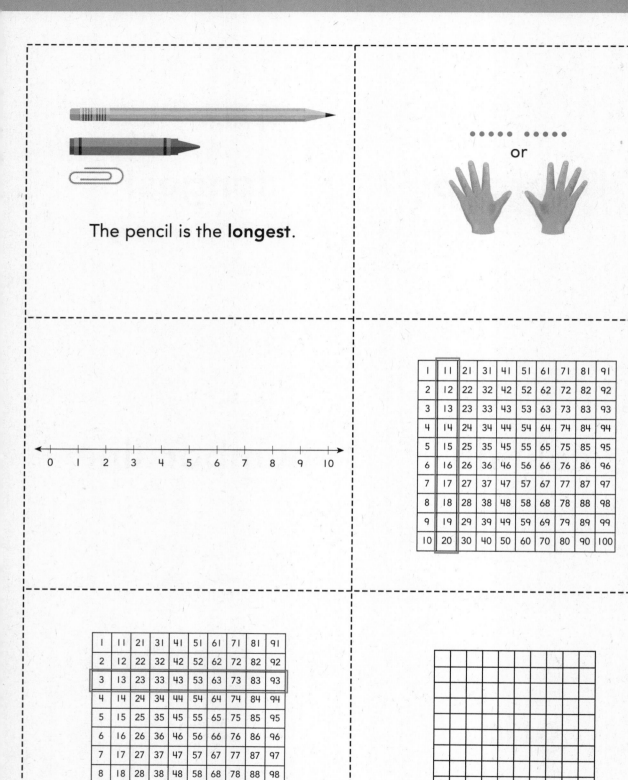

The pencil is the **longest**.

or

1	11	21	31	41	51	61	71	81	91
2	12	22	32	42	52	62	72	82	92
3	13	23	33	43	53	63	73	83	93
4	14	24	34	44	54	64	74	84	94
5	15	25	35	45	55	65	75	85	95
6	16	26	36	46	56	66	76	86	96
7	17	27	37	47	57	67	77	87	97
8	18	28	38	48	58	68	78	88	98
9	19	29	39	49	59	69	79	89	99
10	20	30	40	50	60	70	80	90	100

1	11	21	31	41	51	61	71	81	91
2	12	22	32	42	52	62	72	82	92
3	13	23	33	43	53	63	73	83	93
4	14	24	34	44	54	64	74	84	94
5	15	25	35	45	55	65	75	85	95
6	16	26	36	46	56	66	76	86	96
7	17	27	37	47	57	67	77	87	97
8	18	28	38	48	58	68	78	88	98
9	19	29	39	49	59	69	79	89	99
10	20	30	40	50	60	70	80	90	100

shortest

The paper clip is the **shortest**.

$7 + \boxed{} = 16$ $6 + \boxed{} = 15$ $7 + \boxed{} = 11$

$8 + \boxed{} = 12$ $9 + \boxed{} = 13$ $6 + \boxed{} = 11$

$7 + \boxed{} = 12$ $8 + \boxed{} = 13$ $9 + \boxed{} = 14$

$5 + \boxed{} = 11$ $9 + \boxed{} = 18$ $7 + \boxed{} = 13$

$8 + \boxed{} = 14$ $9 + \boxed{} = 15$ $4 + \boxed{} = 11$

$7 + \boxed{4} = 11$

7 + 3 + 1

$6 + \boxed{9} = 15$

6 + 4 + 5

$7 + \boxed{9} = 16$

7 + 3 + 6

$6 + \boxed{5} = 11$

6 + 4 + 1

$9 + \boxed{4} = 13$

9 + 1 + 3

$8 + \boxed{4} = 12$

8 + 2 + 2

$9 + \boxed{5} = 14$

9 + 1 + 4

$8 + \boxed{5} = 13$

8 + 2 + 3

$7 + \boxed{5} = 12$

7 + 3 + 2

$7 + \boxed{6} = 13$

7 + 3 + 3

$9 + \boxed{9} = 18$

9 + 1 + 8

$5 + \boxed{6} = 11$

5 + 5 + 1

$4 + \boxed{7} = 11$

4 + 6 + 1

$9 + \boxed{6} = 15$

9 + 1 + 5

$8 + \boxed{6} = 14$

8 + 2 + 4

Purple Make-a-Ten Cards

$5 + \square = 12$ $6 + \square = 13$ $8 + \square = 17$

$8 + \square = 15$ $9 + \square = 16$ $3 + \square = 11$

$4 + \square = 12$ $5 + \square = 13$ $6 + \square = 14$

$7 + \square = 15$ $8 + \square = 16$ $9 + \square = 17$

$3 + \square = 12$ $4 + \square = 13$ $5 + \square = 14$

Purple Make-a-Ten Cards

$8 + \boxed{9} = 17$

8 | •• •• •••••
8 + 2 + 7

$6 + \boxed{7} = 13$

6 | •••• •••
6 + 4 + 3

$5 + \boxed{7} = 12$

5 | ••••• ••
5 + 5 + 2

$3 + \boxed{8} = 11$

3 | ••••• •
3 + 7 + 1

$9 + \boxed{7} = 16$

9 | • •••••
9 + 1 + 6

$8 + \boxed{7} = 15$

8 | •• •••••
8 + 2 + 5

$6 + \boxed{8} = 14$

6 | •••• ••••
6 + 4 + 4

$5 + \boxed{8} = 13$

5 | ••••• •••
5 + 5 + 3

$4 + \boxed{8} = 12$

4 | ••••• ••
4 + 6 + 2

$9 + \boxed{8} = 17$

9 | • •••••
9 + 1 + 7

$8 + \boxed{8} = 16$

8 | •• ••••••
8 + 2 + 6

$7 + \boxed{8} = 15$

7 | ••• •••••
7 + 3 + 5

$5 + \boxed{9} = 14$

5 | ••••• ••••
5 + 5 + 4

$4 + \boxed{9} = 13$

4 | ••••• •••
4 + 6 + 3

$3 + \boxed{9} = 12$

3 | ••••• ••
3 + 7 + 2

Purple Make-a-Ten Cards

Name _____

Match the equation with the picture that shows how to use the Make a Ten strategy to solve. Write the unknown partner.

1 $8 + \boxed{} = 12$

9	• • •

2 $9 + \boxed{} = 15$

7	• • • • •

3 $7 + \boxed{} = 12$

9	• •

4 $8 + \boxed{} = 14$

8	• • • •

5 $9 + \boxed{} = 12$

8	• • • • • •

6 $8 + \boxed{} = 15$

9	• • • • • •

7 $9 + \boxed{} = 11$

9	• • • • • • • •

8 $9 + \boxed{} = 17$

8	• • • • • • •

9 $7 + \boxed{} = 11$

7	• • • •

Solve the story problem.

Show your work.
Use drawings, numbers, or words.

---

10 Some birds are in a tree. 5 more birds fly
into the tree. Now there are 13 birds.
How many birds were in the tree before?

tree

[ ] _____
label

---

11 14 cats are black or orange. 8 cats are black.
How many cats are orange?

cat

[ ] _____
label

---

12 10 kites are big. 10 kites are small.
How many kites are there?

kite

[ ] _____
label

---

13 Juan has 8 books. Meg brings more books.
Now there are 17 books. How many books
does Meg bring?

book

[ ] _____
label

 Check Understanding

Listen. Then tell how to solve the story
problem.

Unknown Partners with Teen Totals

$15 - 6 = \boxed{}$ $16 - 7 = \boxed{}$ $11 - 7 = \boxed{}$

$12 - 8 = \boxed{}$ $13 - 9 = \boxed{}$ $11 - 6 = \boxed{}$

$12 - 7 = \boxed{}$ $13 - 8 = \boxed{}$ $14 - 9 = \boxed{}$

$11 - 5 = \boxed{}$ $17 - 8 = \boxed{}$ $13 - 7 = \boxed{}$

$14 - 8 = \boxed{}$ $15 - 9 = \boxed{}$ $11 - 4 = \boxed{}$

$11 - 7 = \boxed{4}$

| 7 | ••• | • |

$7 + 3 + 1$

$16 - 7 = \boxed{9}$

| 7 | ••• | ••••• |

$7 + 3 + 6$

$15 - 6 = \boxed{9}$

| 6 | •••• | ••••• |

$6 + 4 + 5$

$11 - 6 = \boxed{5}$

| 6 | •••• | • |

$6 + 4 + 1$

$13 - 9 = \boxed{4}$

| 9 | • | ••• |

$9 + 1 + 3$

$12 - 8 = \boxed{4}$

| 8 | •• | •• |

$8 + 2 + 2$

$14 - 9 = \boxed{5}$

| 9 | • | •••• |

$9 + 1 + 4$

$13 - 8 = \boxed{5}$

| 8 | •• | ••• |

$8 + 2 + 3$

$12 - 7 = \boxed{5}$

| 7 | ••• | •• |

$7 + 3 + 2$

$13 - 7 = \boxed{6}$

| 7 | ••• | ••• |

$7 + 3 + 3$

$17 - 8 = \boxed{9}$

| 8 | •• | ••••••• |

$8 + 2 + 7$

$11 - 5 = \boxed{6}$

| 5 | ••••• | • |

$5 + 5 + 1$

$11 - 4 = \boxed{7}$

| 4 | •••••• | • |

$4 + 6 + 1$

$15 - 9 = \boxed{6}$

| 9 | • | ••••• |

$9 + 1 + 5$

$14 - 8 = \boxed{6}$

| 8 | •• | •••• |

$8 + 2 + 4$

Blue Make-a-Ten Cards

$12 - 5 = \boxed{}$ $13 - 6 = \boxed{}$ $18 - 9 = \boxed{}$

$15 - 8 = \boxed{}$ $16 - 9 = \boxed{}$ $11 - 3 = \boxed{}$

$12 - 4 = \boxed{}$ $13 - 5 = \boxed{}$ $14 - 6 = \boxed{}$

$15 - 7 = \boxed{}$ $16 - 8 = \boxed{}$ $17 - 9 = \boxed{}$

$12 - 3 = \boxed{}$ $13 - 4 = \boxed{}$ $14 - 5 = \boxed{}$

18 − 9 = 9

9 · ····· (dots)
9 + 1 + 8

13 − 6 = 7

6 ···· ···
6 + 4 + 3

12 − 5 = 7

5 ····· ··
5 + 5 + 2

11 − 3 = 8

3 ····· ·
3 + 7 + 1

16 − 9 = 7

9 · ·····
9 + 1 + 6

15 − 8 = 7

8 ·· ·····
8 + 2 + 5

14 − 6 = 8

6 ···· ····
6 + 4 + 4

13 − 5 = 8

5 ····· ···
5 + 5 + 3

12 − 4 = 8

4 · ····· ··
4 + 6 + 2

17 − 9 = 8

9 · ·····
9 + 1 + 7

16 − 8 = 8

8 ·· ·····
8 + 2 + 6

15 − 7 = 8

7 ··· ·····
7 + 3 + 5

14 − 5 = 9

5 ····· ····
5 + 5 + 4

13 − 4 = 9

4 · ····· ···
4 + 6 + 3

12 − 3 = 9

3 ····· ··
3 + 7 + 2

Blue Make-a-Ten Cards

Name _____

Match the equation with the picture that shows how to use the Make a Ten strategy to solve.

1 $12 - 8 = \boxed{}$

| 7 | ••• ••• |

2 $14 - 9 = \boxed{}$

| 8 | •• •••• |

3 $13 - 7 = \boxed{}$

| 8 | •• •• |

4 $15 - 8 = \boxed{}$

| 7 | ••• •• |

5 $14 - 8 = \boxed{}$

| 9 | • •••• |

6 $12 - 7 = \boxed{}$

| 6 | •••• •••• |

7 $11 - 8 = \boxed{}$

| 8 | •• ••••• |

8 $14 - 6 = \boxed{}$

| 9 | • • |

9 $11 - 9 = \boxed{}$

| 8 | •• • |

Subtraction with Teen Numbers **235**

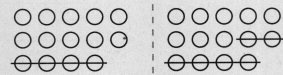

	Step 1	Step 2
$14 - 6 = \boxed{8}$	$14 - 4 = 10$	$10 - 2 = 8$

4   2

Subtract. Show your work.

10 $15 - 8 = \boxed{}$

11 $13 - 4 = \boxed{}$

12 $12 - 9 = \boxed{}$

13 $17 - 9 = \boxed{}$

✔ Check Understanding

Draw to show how to make a ten to solve $13 - 8$.

Name _____

Solve the story problem.

Show your work.
Use drawings, numbers, or words.

① 17 berries are in a bowl. 9 are red and the rest are purple. How many berries are purple?

bowl

☐ _____

label

② I draw some stars. 8 are large and 7 are small. How many stars do I draw?

star

☐ _____

label

③ There are 14 puppies. Some are brown and some are black. How many brown and black puppies could there be?
Show three answers.

puppy

☐ brown puppies and ☐ black puppies

or ☐ brown puppies and ☐ black puppies

or ☐ brown puppies and ☐ black puppies

Mixed Practice with Teen Problems **237**

Solve the story problem.

Show your work.
Use drawings, numbers, or words.

4 15 frogs are by the pond. 9 hop away.
How many frogs are there now?

pond

☐ _____
label

5 16 butterflies are in the garden.
Some fly away. There are 8 left.
How many butterflies fly away?

butterflies

☐ _____
label

6 Some grapes are in a bowl. I eat 6 of them.
Now there are 7 grapes. How many grapes
were in the bowl before?

grapes

☐ _____
label

7 There are 12 horses in a field. Some run
away. Now there are 5 horses. How many
horses run away?

horse

☐ _____
label

 Check Understanding

Listen to the story problem. Then explain
how to solve it.

Mixed Practice with Teen Problems

Name _____

Match the equation with the picture that shows how to use the Make a Ten strategy to solve.

① $8 +$ ▢ $= 14$

② $7 + 5 =$ ▢

③ $8 + 3 =$ ▢

④ $6 +$ ▢ $= 15$

⑤ $9 +$ ▢ $= 18$

⑥ $9 +$ ▢ $= 15$

⑦ $8 + 4 =$ ▢

⑧ $7 + 6 =$ ▢

⑨ Ring the picture above that shows how to use the Make a Ten strategy to solve the equation.

$13 - 7 =$ ▢

Add.

10 $9 + 3 = \boxed{}$　　**11** $7 + 8 = \boxed{}$　　**12** $7 + 5 = \boxed{}$

13 $11 + 9 = \boxed{}$　　**14** $12 + 7 = \boxed{}$　　**15** $8 + 12 = \boxed{}$

Find the unknown partner.

16 $9 + \boxed{} = 14$　**17** $10 + \boxed{} = 19$　**18** $6 + \boxed{} = 13$

19 $\boxed{} + 4 = 12$　**20** $\boxed{} + 8 = 11$　**21** $\boxed{} + 6 = 15$

Subtract.

22 $11 - 2 = \boxed{}$　　**23** $14 - 6 = \boxed{}$　　**24** $13 - 9 = \boxed{}$

25 $16 - 8 = \boxed{}$　　**26** $13 - 7 = \boxed{}$　　**27** $12 - 5 = \boxed{}$

(PATH to FLUENCY) Subtract.

1 $10 - 8 = \boxed{}$　　**2** $7 - 1 = \boxed{}$　　**3** $6 - 6 = \boxed{}$

4 $9 - 7 = \boxed{}$　　**5** $8 - 4 = \boxed{}$　　**6** $10 - 6 = \boxed{}$

 Check Understanding

Explain how to make ten to solve. $17 - 8 = \boxed{}$

　　　　Small Group Practice with Teen Problems

Name _____

1 Rosa reads 8 stories. Tim reads 5 stories.
How many stories do they read in all?

2 Rosa reads 8 stories. Tim also reads some stories.
They read 13 stories in all. How many stories
does Tim read?

3 Rosa reads some stories. Tim reads 5 stories. They read 13
stories in all. How many stories does Rosa read?

Teen Problems with Various Unknowns **241**

Some crayons are in a box.
I take 6 crayons out.
Now there are 9 crayons in the box.
How many crayons were in the box before?

Am I correct?

4 Look at what Puzzled Penguin wrote.

| 9 | – | 6 | = | 3 |

| 3 | crayons

5 Help Puzzled Penguin.

| | – | | = | |

| | crayons

✓ **Check Understanding**

Make up a story problem to find the unknown total and another story problem to find an unknown partner.

© Houghton Mifflin Harcourt Publishing Company

Teen Problems with Various Unknowns

Name _____

Model and solve the story problem.
Color to show your model.
Cross out the cubes you do not use.

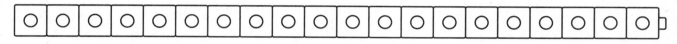

1 There are 6 red pencils, 5 yellow pencils,
   and 7 green pencils in a cup.
   How many pencils are in the cup?

pencil

| | | | | | | | | | | | | | | | | | | | |

☐ _____
      label

2 I have 4 white fish, 2 black fish,
   and 6 orange fish in my fish tank.
   How many fish are in my fish tank?

fish

| | | | | | | | | | | | | | | | | | | | |

☐ _____
      label

3 There are 3 pears on the table, 10 pears
   in a basket, and 7 pears in a bowl.
   How many pears are there?

pear

| | | | | | | | | | | | | | | | | | | | |

☐ _____
      label

Solve the story problem.

Show your work. Use drawings, numbers, or words.

4 There are 5 red crayons, 9 blue crayons, and 1 yellow crayon on the table. How many crayons are on the table?

crayon

☐ _____
label

5 Charlie sees 4 books on a desk, 6 books on a shelf, and 8 books on a cart. How many books does Charlie see?

desk

☐ _____
label

6 Gina finds 7 seashells. Paul finds 6 seashells. Lee finds 3 seashells. How many seashells do they find altogether?

seashell

☐ _____
label

 Check Understanding
Solve. Kara sees 1 lion, 3 tigers, and 9 zebras. How many animals does Kara see?

Problems with Three Addends

Add or subtract.

1 $9 + \boxed{} = 17$

2 $15 - 8 = \boxed{}$

3 $7 + \boxed{} = 16$

Solve the story problem.   Show your work.

4 There are 14 ants. There are 9 red ants, and the rest are black. How many ants are black?

$\boxed{}$ _____
                        label

5 Bailey found 4 clam shells, 5 snail shells, and 6 scallop shells. How many shells did she find in all?

$\boxed{}$ _____
                        label

Name _____ Date _____

Subtract.

1 7 − 2 = ☐

2 6 − 1 = ☐

3 7 − 4 = ☐

4 8 − 5 = ☐

5 6 − 3 = ☐

6 7 − 7 = ☐

7 8 − 7 = ☐

8 9 − 6 = ☐

9 6 − 5 = ☐

10 8 − 2 = ☐

11 10 − 2 = ☐

12 9 − 3 = ☐

13 10 − 10 = ☐

14 9 − 8 = ☐

15 10 − 4 = ☐

VOCABULARY
10-group

1 Ring **10-groups**. Count by tens and ones. Write the number.

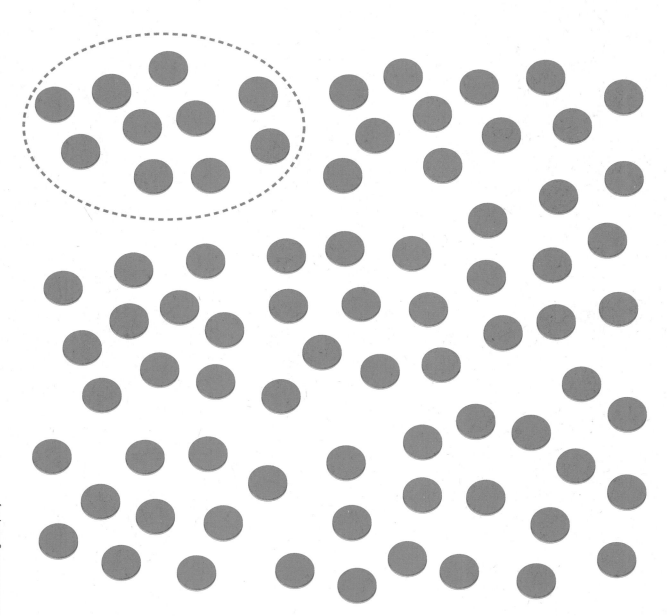

Count with Groups of 10 **247**

2 Color each 10-group a different color.
Count by tens and ones. Write the number.

✓ **Check Understanding**

Explain how to use tens and ones to
count 95 counters.

Count with Groups of 10

Dear Family:

The next several lessons of this unit build upon what the class learned previously about tens and ones. The Hundred Grid is a tool that allows children to see 10-based patterns in sequence. Seeing numbers in the ordered rows and columns of the Hundred Grid helps children better understand number relationships as they:

- continue to practice with 10-groups, adding tens to any 2-digit number, with totals to 100;
- explore 2-digit subtraction, subtracting tens from decade numbers;
- connect what they know about 10-partners to now find 100-partners.

1	11	21	31	41	51	61	71	81	91
2	12	22	32	42	52	62	72	82	92
3	13	23	33	43	53	63	73	83	93
4	14	24	34	44	54	64	74	84	94
5	15	25	35	45	55	65	75	85	95
6	16	26	36	46	56	66	76	86	96
7	17	27	37	47	57	67	77	87	97
8	18	28	38	48	58	68	78	88	98
9	19	29	39	49	59	69	79	89	99
10	20	30	40	50	60	70	80	90	100

3   ○○○
13 | ○○○
23 | | ○○○
33 | | | ○○○
43 | | | | ○○○
53 | | | | | ○○○
63 | | | | | | ○○○
73 | | | | | | | ○○○
83 | | | | | | | | ○○○
93 | | | | | | | | | ○○○

If you have any questions or problems, please contact me.

Sincerely,
Your child's teacher

Estimada familia:

Las siguientes lecciones en esta unidad amplían lo que la clase aprendió anteriormente acerca de decenas y unidades. La Cuadrícula de 100 es un instrumento que permite observar patrones de base 10 en secuencia. Observar los números ordenados en hileras y columnas en la Cuadrícula de 100 ayudará a los niños a comprender mejor la relación entre los números mientras:

- continúan practicando con grupos de 10, sumando decenas a números de 2 dígitos con totales hasta 100;
- exploran la resta de números de 2 dígitos, restando decenas de números que terminan en cero;
- relacionan lo que saben acerca de las partes de 10 para hallar partes de 100.

1	11	21	31	41	51	61	71	81	91
2	12	22	32	42	52	62	72	82	92
3	13	23	33	43	53	63	73	83	93
4	14	24	34	44	54	64	74	84	94
5	15	25	35	45	55	65	75	85	95
6	16	26	36	46	56	66	76	86	96
7	17	27	37	47	57	67	77	87	97
8	18	28	38	48	58	68	78	88	98
9	19	29	39	49	59	69	79	89	99
10	20	30	40	50	60	70	80	90	100

3   ○○○
13 | ○○○
23 | | ○○○
33 | | | ○○○
43 | | | | ○○○
53 | | | | | ○○○
63 | | | | | | ○○○
73 | | | | | | | ○○○
83 | | | | | | | | ○○○
93 | | | | | | | | | ○○○

Si tiene alguna pregunta o algún comentario comuníquese conmigo.

Atentamente,
El maestro de su niño

Name _____

VOCABULARY
column
grid

1 Write the numbers 1–120 in **columns**.

1	11										
2											
10									100		120

Use the **grid** to find 10 more. Write the number.

2 29 ☐   **3** 72 ☐   **4** 45 ☐   **5** 90 ☐

Use the grid to find 10 less. Write the number.

6 39 ☐   **7** 72 ☐   **8** 91 ☐   **9** 20 ☐

VOCABULARY
row

10 Write the numbers 1–120 in **rows**.

1	2								10
11									
									100
									120

Use the grid to find 10 less and 10 more.
Write the numbers.

11 51   **12** 36

Name _____

Use the **number line** to count forward
or backward. Write the numbers.

VOCABULARY
number line

(13) 2, 3, 4, _____, _____, _____

(14) 9, 8, 7, _____, _____, _____

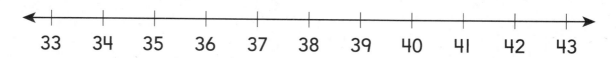

(15) 42, 41, 40, _____, _____, _____

(16) 33, _____, _____, _____, 37, 38

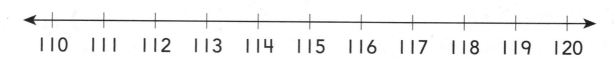

(17) 111, _____, 113, _____, 115 _____

(18) 120, _____, _____, 117, 116, _____

(19) Count backward from 115. Write the numbers.

115, _____, _____, _____, _____, _____

(20) Count forward from 115. Write the numbers.

115, _____, _____, _____, _____, _____

Write the number.

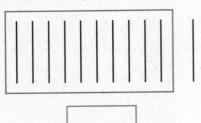

21

22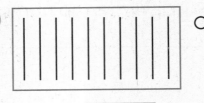

23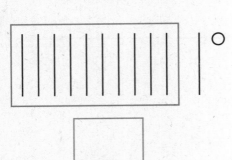

24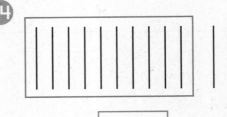

Draw 10-sticks and circles.
Draw a box around 10 tens.

25   102

26   112

27   117

28   109

 Check Understanding

How can you tell if 48 is 10 more or 10
less than 58?

Name _____

1 Listen to the directions.

1	11	21	31	41	51	61	71	81	91
2	12	22	32	42	52	62	72	82	92
3	13	23	33	43	53	63	73	83	93
4	14	24	34	44	54	64	74	84	94
5	15	25	35	45	55	65	75	85	95
6	16	26	36	46	56	66	76	86	96
7	17	27	37	47	57	67	77	87	97
8	18	28	38	48	58	68	78	88	98
9	19	29	39	49	59	69	79	89	99
10	20	30	40	50	60	70	80	90	100

Add tens.

2 $89 + 10 = $ ☐

3 $43 + 20 = $ ☐

4 $28 + 50 = $ ☐

5 $32 + 40 = $ ☐

6 $11 + 20 = $ ☐

7 $42 + 30 = $ ☐

8 $52 + 40 = $ ☐

9 $12 + 40 = $ ☐

10 $27 + 60 = $ ☐

11 $61 + 30 = $ ☐

Subtract tens.

12 $30 - 20 = $ ☐

13 $60 - 10 = $ ☐

14 $70 - 40 = $ ☐

15 $70 - 20 = $ ☐

16 $90 - 60 = $ ☐

17 $80 - 70 = $ ☐

18 $90 - 10 = $ ☐

19 $50 - 40 = $ ☐

20 $20 - 10 = $ ☐

21 $40 - 10 = $ ☐

Add and Subtract Tens and Number Patterns

Name _____

Write the number pattern rule.

22 5, 10, 15, 20, 25, 30   Rule: _____

23 10, 20, 30, 40, 50, 60   Rule: _____

24 33, 38, 43, 48, 53, 58   Rule: _____

25 22, 24, 26, 28, 30, 32   Rule: _____

Find the unknown numbers in the pattern.

26 46, 56, 66, _____, 86, _____

27 17, 19, 21, 23, _____, 27, 29, _____

Extend the number pattern.

28 62, 67, 72, 77, _____, _____, _____

29 34, 44, 54, 64, _____, _____, _____

30 47, 49, 51, 53, _____, _____, _____

31 12, 17, 22, 27, _____, _____, _____

32 Make a number pattern.
Use add 5 as the rule.

Look for the pattern. Write the rule and complete the table.

33 Maria runs every day for one week.   Rule: _____

Maria's Running Schedule

Day	Mon.	Tues.	Wed.	Thur.	Fri.	Sat.
Number of Minutes	12	17	22	27		

34 Choi reads every day for one week.   Rule: _____

Choi's Reading Schedule

Day	Mon.	Tues.	Wed.	Thur.	Fri.	Sat.
Number of Pages	11	13	15	17		

35 David practices every day for one week.   Rule: _____

David's Piano Practice Schedule

Day	Mon.	Tues.	Wed.	Thur.	Fri.	Sat.
Number of Minutes	16	21	26		36	

✔ Check Understanding

Write an equation to solve each problem.

Add 4 tens to 35.   Subtract 6 tens from 9 tens.

Add and Subtract Tens and Number Patterns

Name _____

Solve.

1. $80 + 20 = \boxed{}$

2. $30 + 70 = \boxed{}$

3. $10 + \boxed{} = 100$

4. $50 + \boxed{} = 100$

5. $100 = 20 + \boxed{}$

6. $100 = 40 + \boxed{}$

7. $20 + 50 = \boxed{}$

8. $10 + 80 = \boxed{}$

9. $0 + 60 = \boxed{}$

10. $20 + 20 = \boxed{}$

11. $40 - 40 = \boxed{}$

12. $80 - 0 = \boxed{}$

13. $70 - 60 = \boxed{}$

14. $60 - 30 = \boxed{}$

15. $60 - 10 = \boxed{}$

   $10 + \boxed{} = 60$

16. $70 - 40 = \boxed{}$

   $40 + \boxed{} = 70$

17. $50 - 20 = \boxed{}$

   $20 + \boxed{} = 50$

18. $90 - 50 = \boxed{}$

   $50 + \boxed{} = 90$

19 Look at what Puzzled Penguin wrote.

70 − 20 = | 5 |

Am I correct?

20 Help Puzzled Penguin.

70 − 20 =

PATH to FLUENCY **Add.**

1 1 + 8 =

2 5 + 4 =

3 4 + 6 =

PATH to FLUENCY **Subtract.**

4 9 − 3 =

5 6 − 1 =

6 7 − 6 =

✔ **Check Understanding**

Add and subtract tens.

60 + 40 =   60 − 40 =

Name _____

Use the picture.
Write the numbers to solve.

---

1 Casey helps gather fruit. How many pieces of fruit does Casey gather?

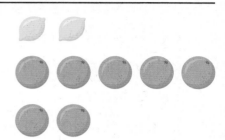

□ + □ = □ pieces of fruit

---

2 Casey helps gather vegetables. How many vegetables does Casey gather?

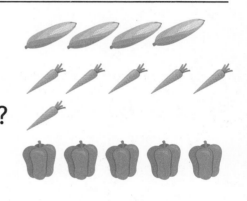

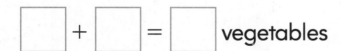

□ + □ = □ vegetables

---

3 Casey helps gather flowers. How many flowers does Casey gather?

□ + □ = □ flowers

© Houghton Mifflin Harcourt Publishing Company

Use the picture.
Write the numbers to solve.

4 Some carrots are in a garden.
Each bunny eats 1 carrot.
Now there are 9 carrots.
How many carrots were
in the garden to start?

☐ − ☐ = ☐

☐ carrots

---

5 Some bunnies are in a garden.
7 more bunnies hop in. Now
there are 13 bunnies in the
garden. How many bunnies
were in the garden before?

☐ + ☐ = ☐

☐ bunnies

Focus on Problem Solving

Name _____   Date _____

Use the grid.

51	52	53	54	55	56	57	58	59	60
61	62	63	64	65	66	67	68	69	70
71	72	73	74	75	76	77	78	79	80

1 10 more than 54 is ⬜ .

2 10 more than 68 is ⬜ .

Add or subtract tens.

3 $68 + 30 =$ ⬜

4 $52 + 20 =$ ⬜

5 Find the unknown numbers in the pattern.

33, 35, 37, _____, 41, _____

Name _____ Date _____

PATH to FLUENCY

Add.

1 3 + 3 = ▢

2 6 + 1 = ▢

3 4 + 2 = ▢

4 3 + 4 = ▢

5 6 + 2 = ▢

6 5 + 4 = ▢

Subtract.

7 6 − 4 = ▢

8 8 − 5 = ▢

9 7 − 3 = ▢

10 8 − 6 = ▢

11 9 − 2 = ▢

12 7 − 1 = ▢

13 10 − 10 = ▢

14 10 − 7 = ▢

15 9 − 8 = ▢

Match the box to the unknown partner.

1 $9 +$ ☐ $= 15$ **2** $8 +$ ☐ $= 15$ **3** $8 +$ ☐ $= 17$

•   •   •

•   •   •

9   6   7

Solve the story problem.

---

4 Beth has 16 bagels. She gives 8 to her
friends. How many bagels does Beth
have now?

bagel

☐ _____
        label

---

5 Meg has 6 books. Jen gives her some
more books. Now Meg has 11 books.
How many books does Jen give Meg?

book

☐ _____
        label

---

6 Luis has 7 blue pens, 4 red pens,
and 3 green pens. How many pens
does Luis have?

pen

☐ _____
        label

7   Is the sentence true? Choose Yes or No.

$14 - 8 = 5$	○ Yes	○ No
$16 - 7 = 9$	○ Yes	○ No
$17 - 9 = 8$	○ Yes	○ No

8   Start at 81. Count. Write the numbers through 110.

81	82	83							
91									

9   Draw a picture to solve the story problem.
Write a number sentence.
Answer the question.

There are 15 squirrels. Some are brown and
6 are gray. How many squirrels are brown?

☐ – ☐ = ☐

☐ _____
         label

Name _____   Date _____

Solve.

10 57 + 20 = ☐   **11** 13 + 60 = ☐

12 80 − 40 = ☐   **13** 70 − 50 = ☐

14 80 + ☐ = 100   **15** 90 − ☐ = 70

Ring the number that makes the sentence true.

16 There are 9 red crayons, 3 green crayons, and 7 blue crayons in the box. How many crayons are in the box?

crayon

| 10 |
| 16 | crayons are in the box.
| 19 |

---

17 Count backward from 118. Write the numbers.

118, _____, _____, _____, _____

---

18 Extend the number pattern.

53, 58, 63, 68, _____, _____, _____

19 There are 12 boys and girls on the bus.
How many boys and girls can there be?
Choose all possible answers.

- ○ 2 boys and 14 girls
- ○ 2 boys and 10 girls
- ○ 3 boys and 9 girls
- ○ 4 boys and 6 girls
- ○ 5 boys and 7 girls

20 Draw 20 to 30 more triangles.
Ring 10-groups. Count by tens and ones.
Write the numbers.

△ △ △ △ △ △ △ △ △ △

△ △ △ △ △ △ △ △ △ △

△ △ △ △ △ △ △ △ △ △

△ △ △ △ △ △ △ △ △ △

△ △ △ △ △ △

The number of triangles is ⬚.

10 less is ⬚. 10 more is ⬚.

Beach Day

Dan and Win look for shells at the beach.

1 Part A

Dan finds 32 shells. Draw to show 32 with tens and ones.

Dan finds 20 more shells. How many shells does he have in all?

[ ] shells

Part B

Draw or tell how you know.

---

2 Part A

Win finds 5 white shells, 3 brown shells, and 2 black shells. How many shells does she have in all?

[ ] shells

Part B

Draw or write to tell how you know.

3 **Part A**

Win finds 50 white shells, 30 brown shells, and 20 black shells. How many shells does she have in all?

☐ shells

Part B

Draw or tell how you know.

☐

Part C

Tell how adding 50, 30, and 20 is like adding 5, 3, and 2.

☐

4 **Part A**

At noon, Win had 50 white shells.
At 4 P.M., Win had 80 white shells.
How many shells did she find after noon?

☐ shells

Part B

Draw or tell how you know.

☐

Dear Family:

Children begin this unit by learning to organize, represent, and interpret data with two and three categories.

In the example below, children sort apples and bananas and represent the data using circles. They ask and answer questions about the data and learn to express comparative statements completely.

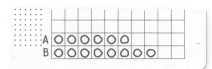

There are 2 more bananas than apples.

There are 2 fewer apples than bananas.

Later in the unit, children solve *Compare* story problems using comparison bars. Two examples are given below.

Jeremy has 10 crayons. Amanda has 3 crayons. How many more crayons does Jeremy have than Amanda?

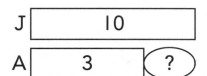

Abby has 8 erasers. Ramon has 6 more erasers than Abby has. How many erasers does Ramon have?

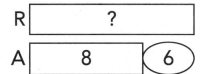

While working on homework, ask your child to explain to you how to use comparison bars to solve these types of story problems.
If you have any questions, please do not hesitate to contact me.

Sincerely,
Your child's teacher

Estimada familia:

Al comenzar esta unidad, los niños aprenderán a organizar, representar e interpretar datos de dos y tres categorías.

En el ejemplo de abajo, los niños clasifican manzanas y plátanos, y representan los datos usando círculos. Formulan y responden preguntas acerca de los datos y aprenden cómo expresar enunciados comparativos completos.

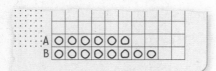

Hay 2 plátanos más que manzanas.

Hay 2 manzanas menos que plátanos.

Más adelante en la unidad, los niños resolverán problemas que requieran *comparar*, usando barras de comparación. Abajo se dan dos ejemplos.

Jeremy tiene 10 crayones.
Amanda tiene 3 crayones.
¿Cuántos crayones más que
Amanda tiene Jeremy?

J | 10

A | 3 | ?

Abby tiene 8 borradores.
Ramón tiene 6 borradores
más que Abby. ¿Cuántos
borradores tiene Ramón?

R | ?

A | 8 | 6

Mientras hace la tarea, pida a su niño que le explique cómo usar las barras de comparación para resolver este tipo de problemas.

Si tiene alguna pregunta, no dude en comunicarse conmigo.

Atentamente,
El maestro de su niño

Explore Representing Data

bar graph

fewest

data

more

fewer

most

Eggs Laid This Month

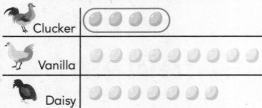

Clucker laid the **fewest** eggs.

Vegetables We Like						
Carrots						
Corn						
Peppers						

0 1 2 3 4 5 6

Eggs Laid This Month

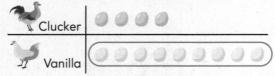

Vanilla laid **more** eggs than Clucker.

Colors in the Bag							
Red	○	○	○				
Yellow	○	○	○	○	○	○	○
Blue	○	○	○	○	○		

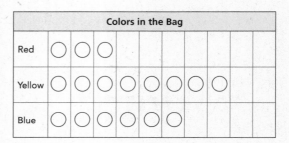

The **data** show how many of each color.

Eggs Laid This Month

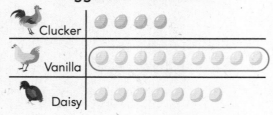

Vanilla laid the **most** eggs.

Eggs Laid This Month

Clucker laid **fewer** eggs than Vanilla.

sort

tally mark

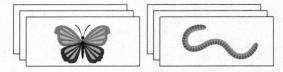

You can **sort** the animals into groups.

Vegetables	Tally Marks	Number
Carrots	IIII	5
Corn	IIII	4
Peppers	IIII II	7

Cut out the cards.
Which animals have legs?
Which animals do not have legs?
Sort the animals.

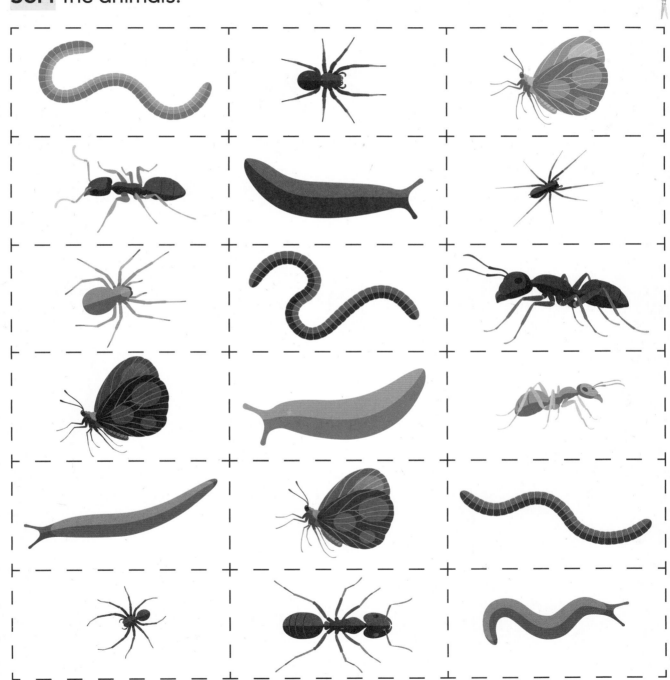

Explore Representing Data

Name _____

1 Use circles and 5-groups to record.
Write how many in each group.

VOCABULARY
data
more
fewer

Legs	No Legs

Use the **data** to complete.

2 How many animals in all? _____

3 Ring the group with **more** animals.

4 Cross out the group with **fewer** animals.

Explore Representing Data **275**

5 Use circles and 5-groups to record.
Write how many in each group.

VOCABULARY
most
fewest

Brown	**Red**	**Black**

Use the data to complete.

6 How many animals in all? _____

7 Ring the group with the **most** animals.

8 Cross out the group with the **fewest** animals.

✓ **Check Understanding**
Draw circles and 5-groups to show 9 black
animals and 8 green animals.

black animals:

green animals:

Explore Representing Data

1 Draw matching lines to compare.
Complete the sentences.
Ring the word **more** or **fewer**.

Mara

Todd

Mara has ☐ **more fewer** apples than Todd.

Todd has ☐ **more fewer** apples than Mara.

2 Each ant gets 1 crumb.
How many more crumbs are needed? ☐

3 Draw circles for the crumbs.

Crumbs	🍪 🍪 🍪 🍪
Ants	🐜 🐜 🐜 🐜 🐜 🐜 🐜 🐜 🐜 🐜

4 Each bee gets 1 flower.
How many extra flowers are there? ☐

5 Ring the extra flowers.

Flowers	🌹 🌹 🌹 🌹 🌹 🌹 🌹 🌹 🌹
Bees	🐝 🐝 🐝 🐝

© Houghton Mifflin Harcourt Publishing Company

6 Sort the fruit. Record with pictures.
Write how many in each group.

Bananas										
Oranges										

_____

_____

7 Complete the sentences. Ring the word **more** or **fewer**.

There are ☐ **more fewer** bananas than oranges.

There are ☐ **more fewer** oranges than bananas.

---

8 Sort the vegetables. Record with circles.
Write how many in each group.

Carrots										
Peppers										

_____

_____

9 Complete the sentence. Ring the word **more** or **fewer**.

There are ☐ **more fewer** peppers than carrots.

✓ **Check Understanding**

Represent 5 apples and 9 bananas. How many more
bananas are there? How many fewer apples are there?

Organize Categorical Data

Name _____

1 Look at what Puzzled Penguin wrote.

Am I correct?

Stripes	O	O	O	O	O	O	O	O	O
Spots	O	O	O	O	O				

There are 4 more fish with stripes than with spots.

There are 4 fewer fish with spots than with stripes.

2 Help Puzzled Penguin.

Stripes									
Spots									

There are ☐ more fish with stripes than with spots.

There are ☐ fewer fish with spots than with stripes.

3 Sort the animals. Record with circles.
Write how many in each group.

Dogs									___
Cats									___

4 Complete the sentence. Ring the word **more** or **fewer**.

There are ☐ **more fewer** dogs than cats.

  Add.

1 4
   $+3$

2 8
   $+1$

3 5
   $+5$

4 10
   $+0$

5 4
   $+6$

✓ **Check Understanding**
Draw Stair Steps to compare 9 and 5.

Use Stair Steps to Represent Data

Name ______________________________

1. Discuss the data.
2. Write how many in each category.

Eggs Laid This Month

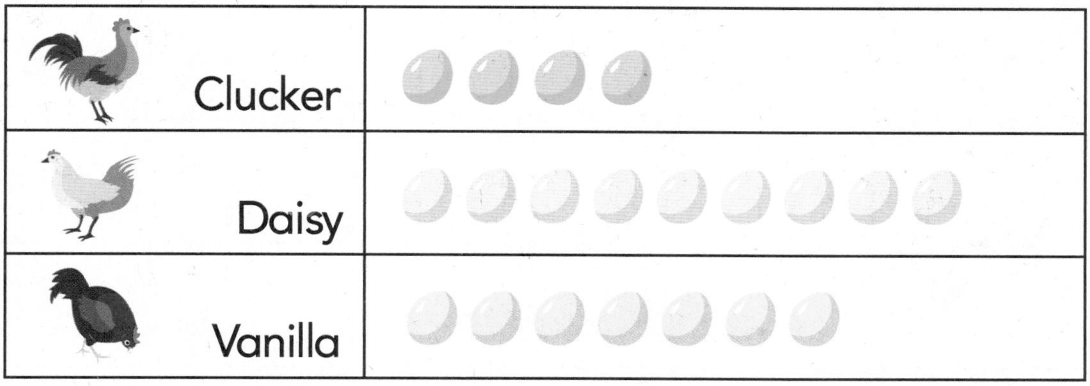
Clucker
Daisy
Vanilla

______

______

______

Animals in the Pond

Frogs
Fish
Ducks

______

______

______

Hot Dogs Sold at the Fair

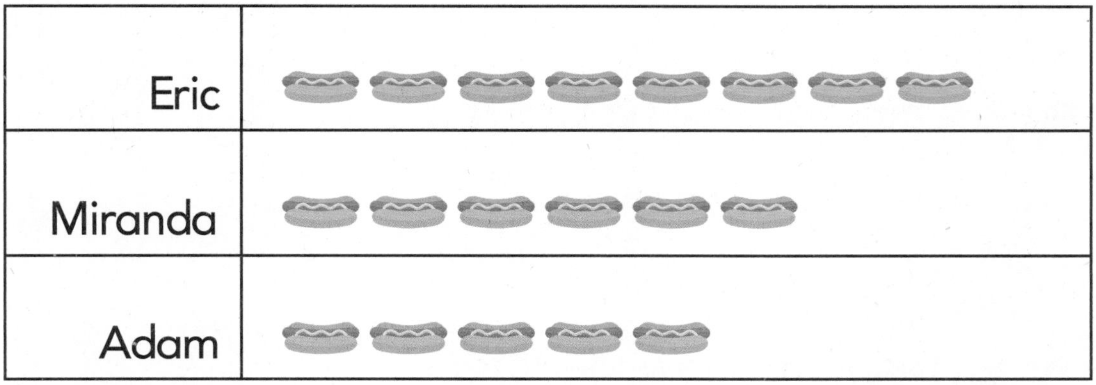
Eric
Miranda
Adam

______

______

______

Watch as each cube is taken from the bag.

3 Draw squares to show how many of each color.

Colors in the Bag										
Red										
Yellow										
Blue										

Use the data to answer the questions.

4 How many red cubes are in the bag? _____

5 How many yellow cubes are in the bag?

_____

6 How many blue cubes are in the bag? _____

7 How many more blue cubes are there than red cubes?

_____

8 How many fewer red cubes are there than yellow cubes?

_____

9 There are the most of which color? _____

10 There are the fewest of which color? _____

✓ **Check Understanding**

Write an equation to show the total number of cubes in the bag.

Data Sets with Three Categories

Name _____

Use the data to answer the questions.

Favorite Vegetable

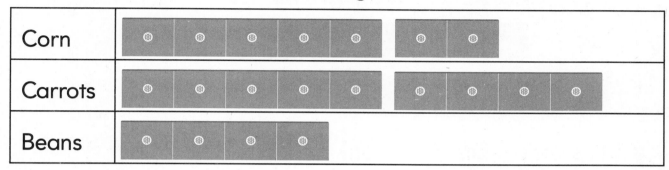

Corn	⊙	⊙	⊙	⊙	⊙	⊙	⊙		
Carrots	⊙	⊙	⊙	⊙	⊙	⊙	⊙	⊙	⊙
Beans	⊙	⊙	⊙	⊙					

1. Which vegetable do the fewest people like? _____

2. How many more people like carrots than corn? _____

3. How many people voted altogether? _____

Favorite Animal

Parrot	⊙	⊙	⊙							
Tiger	⊙	⊙	⊙	⊙	⊙	⊙	⊙	⊙	⊙	⊙
Monkey	⊙	⊙	⊙	⊙	⊙	⊙	⊙			

4. Which animal do the most people like? _____

5. How many fewer people like monkeys than tigers? _____

6. How many people like parrots best? _____

Solve.

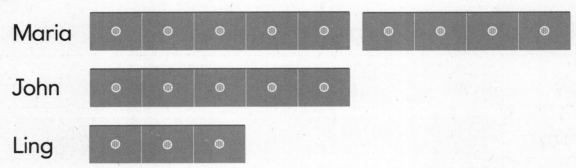

Maria

John

Ling

7 Maria has 9 dots. How many fewer dots does Ling have than Maria?   _____ dots

8 John has 5 dots. How many dots does he need to take away to have the same number as Ling?   _____ dots

9 John has 5 dots. How many dots does John need to add to have as many as Maria?   _____ dots

10 Teo has 5 more dots than Ling. Draw to show Teo's dots.

11 How many dots does Teo need to add to have the same number as Maria?   _____

Data Collecting

Name _____

12 Sort the vegetables. Record with **tally marks**. Make a **bar graph**.

Vegetables	Tally Marks	Number
Carrots		
Corn		
Peppers		

Number of Vegetables

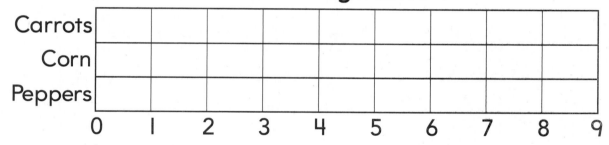

Carrots
Corn
Peppers

0   1   2   3   4   5   6   7   8   9

Use the data to answer the questions.

13 How many more carrots are there than ears of corn?

_____

14 How many more peppers are there than carrots?

_____

15 How many fewer ears of corn are there than peppers?

_____

16 Sort the balls. Record with tally marks.
Make a bar graph.

Balls	Tally Marks	Number
Baseballs		
Basketballs		
Soccer balls		

Number of Balls

Baseballs

Basketballs

Soccer balls

0 1 2 3 4 5 6 7 8 9

✓ **Check Understanding**

Draw 3 Stair Steps of different lengths.
Use the terms more, fewer, most,
and fewest to compare the dots.

Data Collecting

Name _____   Date _____

1 Write how many in each group.

Pencils	○	○	○	○	○	○			___
Crayons	○	○	○	○	○	○	○	○	___
Markers	○	○							___

Use the data to complete each sentence.

2 There are [ ] more pencils than markers.

3 There are [ ] more crayons than pencils.

4 There are [ ] fewer markers than crayons.

5 There are [ ] fewer pencils than crayons.

Name _____ Date _____

Add.

1. 1
   + 2
   ___

2. 3
   + 1
   ___

3. 2
   + 3
   ___

4. 2
   + 4
   ___

5. 4
   + 3
   ___

6. 6
   + 1
   ___

7. 4
   + 4
   ___

8. 5
   + 2
   ___

9. 4
   + 5
   ___

10. 6
    + 3
    ___

11. 5
    + 3
    ___

12. 8
    + 2
    ___

13. 6
    + 2
    ___

14. 5
    + 5
    ___

15. 2
    + 7
    ___

Name _____

Solve the story problem.
Use comparison bars.

Show your work.

1) Tessa has 15 pens.
Sam has 9 pens.
How many more pens
does Tessa have than Sam?

☐ _____
label

2) Tessa has 15 pens.
Sam has 9 pens.
How many fewer pens
does Sam have than Tessa?

☐ _____
label

3) Tessa has 15 pens. Sam has
6 fewer pens than Tessa. How
many pens does Sam have?

☐ _____
label

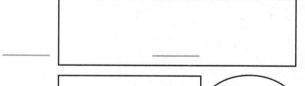

4) Sam has 9 pens. Tessa has
6 more than Sam. How many
pens does Tessa have?

☐ _____
label

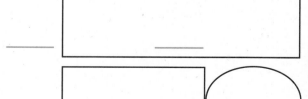

Solve the story problem. Use comparison bars.   **Show your work.**

5 Ed sees 9 cars. Al sees 11 cars.
How many fewer cars does
Ed see than Al?

[ ] _____
        label

6 Liz has 7 dolls. Em has 3 dolls.
How many more dolls does
Liz have than Em?

[ ] _____
        label

7 Noah has 10 more caps than Ben.
Ben has 10 caps. How many
caps does Noah have?

[ ] _____
        label

8 Jen eats 2 fewer peas than Dan.
Dan eats 9 peas. How many
peas does Jen eat?

[ ] _____
        label

✓ **Check Understanding**
Listen to the story problem, and solve it.

Introduce Comparison Bars

Name _____

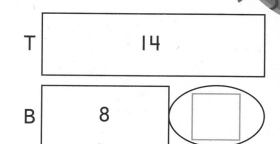

Solve and discuss.

 There are 14 tigers and 8 bears. How many more tigers than bears are there?

T | 14

B | 8 | ☐

[☐] _____
label

$14 = 8 + ☐$

$14 - 8 = ☐$

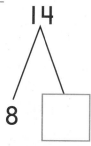

14
/\
8   ☐

② There are 12 lions. There are 5 fewer camels than lions. How many camels are there?

L | 12

C | ☐ | 5

[☐] _____
label

$5 + ☐ = 12$

$12 - 5 = ☐$

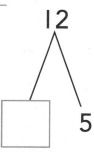

12
/\
☐   5

③ There are 7 elephants. There are 6 more zebras than elephants. How many zebras are there?

Z | ☐

E | 7 | 6

[☐] _____
label

$7 + 6 = ☐$

Comparison Bars and Comparing Language **291**

Solve the story problem. Use comparison bars.   **Show your work.**

4 Ty makes 5 goals and Jon makes 8. How many more goals does Jon make than Ty?

☐ _____
      label

5 There are 11 cars and 19 trucks on the road. How many fewer cars are there than trucks?

☐ _____
      label

6 I see 8 more lilacs than roses. I see 9 roses. How many lilacs do I see?

☐ _____
      label

7 Ken has 3 fewer balls than Meg. Meg has 10 balls. How many balls does Ken have?

☐ _____
      label

✓ **Check Understanding**
Listen and solve the story problem with comparison bars.

Name _____

Solve the story problem.
Use comparison bars.

Show your work.

---

1 Cory's cat has 11 kittens.
Eva's cat has 3 kittens.
How many fewer kittens does
Eva's cat have than Cory's?

☐ _____
label

---

2 There were 3 bicycles here
yesterday. There are 7 more
bicycles here today. How many
bicycles are here today?

☐ _____
label

---

3 Ms. Perez has 15 horses.
Mr. Drew has 9 horses.
How many more horses does
Ms. Perez have than Mr. Drew?

☐ _____
label

Solve *Compare* Problems **293**

Solve the story problem. Use comparison bars.   **Show your work.**

4 Jim pops 5 fewer balloons than Sadie. Jim pops 9 balloons. How many balloons does Sadie pop?

☐ _____
label

5 Nick hikes 12 miles in the forest. Nick hikes 4 more miles than Zia. How many miles does Zia hike?

☐ _____
label

PATH to FLUENCY Subtract.

1 $\begin{array}{r} 9 \\ -1 \\ \hline \end{array}$ **2** $\begin{array}{r} 6 \\ -3 \\ \hline \end{array}$ **3** $\begin{array}{r} 8 \\ -6 \\ \hline \end{array}$ **4** $\begin{array}{r} 5 \\ -5 \\ \hline \end{array}$ **5** $\begin{array}{r} 9 \\ -7 \\ \hline \end{array}$

6 $\begin{array}{r} 4 \\ -2 \\ \hline \end{array}$ **7** $\begin{array}{r} 10 \\ -6 \\ \hline \end{array}$ **8** $\begin{array}{r} 9 \\ -3 \\ \hline \end{array}$ **9** $\begin{array}{r} 7 \\ -5 \\ \hline \end{array}$ **10** $\begin{array}{r} 6 \\ -1 \\ \hline \end{array}$

 Check Understanding

Listen to the story problem, and use comparison bars and an equation to solve.

Solve *Compare* Problems

Name _____

Liam collects data at the park. He wants to know how many animals can fly and how many animals cannot fly.

1 Sort the animals.
Record with circles and 5-groups.

Animals That Can Fly	Animals That Cannot Fly

Use the data to complete.

2 How many animals can fly? _____

3 How many animals cannot fly? _____

4 How many animals does Liam see in all?

_____

5 How many more animals can fly than cannot fly?

_____

Solve.
Show your work.

6 There are 8 swings.
12 children want to swing.
How many children must
wait to swing?

◻ _____
label

_____

7 10 bikes are on the rack.
7 children start to ride. How
many bikes do not have a rider?

◻ _____
label

Focus on Problem Solving

Name _____   Date _____

Solve the story problem.   **Show your work.**
Use comparison bars.

1 Keith scores 10 points. Eric
scores 7 points. How many
fewer points does Eric score
than Keith?

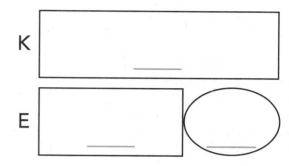

[   ] _____
            label

2 There are 2 more white rabbits
than brown rabbits. There are
9 brown rabbits. How many
white rabbits are there?

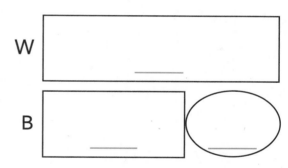

[   ] _____
            label

3 Don eats 6 more grapes than
Meg. Meg eats 12 grapes.
How many grapes does
Don eat?

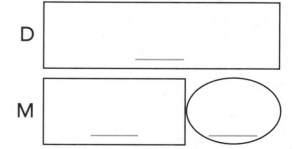

[   ] _____
            label

Name _____ Date _____

Subtract.

1　4
　　− 2

2　5
　　− 1

3　3
　　− 3

4　6
　　− 5

5　7
　　− 4

6　6
　　− 3

7　8
　　− 3

8　8
　　− 8

9　7
　　− 2

10　9
　　− 6

11　8
　　− 5

12　9
　　− 4

13　10
　　− 3

14　10
　　− 8

15　9
　　− 3

1 Sort the animals. Record with circles.

2 Write how many in each group.

Stripes									
Spots									
Solid									

Use the data. Choose the answer.

3 How many fewer solid-color animals
   are there than animals with stripes?

   ○ 4   ○ 6   ○ 7

4 How many animals are there in all?
   ○ 9   ○ 16   ○ 19

5 Sort the fruit. Record with circles.
Write how many in each group.

Apples								
Bananas								
Oranges								

_____

_____

_____

6 Is the sentence true? Choose Yes or No.

There are more oranges than bananas.   ○ Yes   ○ No
There are more apples than oranges.   ○ Yes   ○ No
There are fewer bananas than apples.   ○ Yes   ○ No

7 How many fewer oranges are there than apples? ☐

8 How many more bananas are there than oranges? ☐

9 How many pieces of fruit are there in all?

☐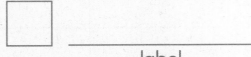

label

Solve the story problem.
Use comparison bars.

10 Rico sees 5 more cats than dogs.
He sees 7 dogs.
How many cats does he see?

□ _____
        label

11 Nori has 15 coins.
Maria has 6 coins.
How many more coins does
Nori have than Maria?

□ _____
        label

Ring the answer. Use comparison bars.

12 Kim picks 13 tulips.
Emily picks 8 tulips.
How many fewer tulips does
Emily pick than Kim?

Emily picks | 5 |
            | 8 | fewer tulips than Kim.
            | 13 |

Name _____   Date _____

13 A class is going on a field trip. They collect data about places to go. Each child votes. The teacher draws one circle for each vote.

Field Trip Ideas

Park	Zoo	Museum
OOOOO	OOOOO OOOOO	OOOO

Write two questions about the data.
Answer each question.

_____

- -

_____

- -

_____

- -

_____

- -

_____

- -

_____

Sort and Compare

Use all 20 strips of paper for this activity.

1 **Part A** Sort the strips. Draw 5-groups
and circles in the table to show how
many strips you have of each color.

My Color Strips		
Red	**Blue**	**Yellow**

Part B How many strips are **not** blue?

[ ] not blue

Draw or tell how you know.

2 **Part A** How many more strips are
there of the color with the most
strips than the color with the

fewest strips? [ ]

Part B Draw or tell how you know.

Compare Animals

Use the data to answer the questions.

Frogs	○	○	○	○					
Bunnies	○	○	○	○	○	○	○	○	○
Deer	○	○	○	○	○	○	○		

3 **Part A** There are ⬜ frogs.

There are ⬜ fewer frogs than deer.

How many frogs and bunnies are there?

⬜ frogs and bunnies

Part B How many more bunnies are there than deer?

⬜ more bunnies

Draw or tell how you know.

⬜

4 **Part A** How many animals are there in all?

⬜ animals

Part B Draw or tell how you know.

⬜

Dear Family:

Your child has begun a unit that focuses on measurement and geometry. Children will begin the unit by learning to tell and write time in hours and half-hours on an analog and digital clock.

2:00

hour : minute

Later in the unit, children will work with both 2-dimensional and 3-dimensional shapes.

They will learn to distinguish between defining and non-defining attributes of shapes. For example, rectangles have four sides and four square corners. A square is a special kind of rectangle with all sides the same length. The shapes below are different sizes, colors, and orientations, but they are all rectangles.

   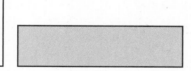

Later in the unit, children will compose shapes to create new shapes.

 A cone and a rectangular prism were used to make this new shape.

Children will also learn to partition circles and rectangles into two and four equal shares. They describe the shares using the words *halves*, *fourths*, and *quarters*.

 This circle is partitioned into halves.

 This circle is partitioned into fourths or quarters.

Children generalize that partitioning a shape into more equal shares creates smaller shares: one fourth of the circle above is smaller than one half of the circle.

Another concept in this unit is length measurement. Children order three objects by length.

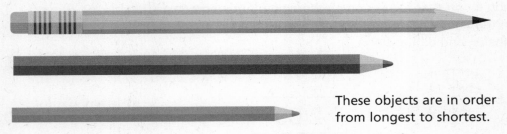

These objects are in order from longest to shortest.

They also use same-size length units such as paper clips to measure the length of an object.

This ribbon is 4 paper clips long.

You can help your child practice these new skills at home. If you have any questions, please contact me.

Sincerely,
Your child's teacher

Estimada familia:

Su niño ha comenzado una unidad sobre medidas y geometría. Comenzará esta unidad aprendiendo a leer y escribir la hora en punto y la media hora en un reloj analógico y en uno digital.

2:00

hora : minuto

Después, trabajará con figuras bidimensionales y tridimensionales.

Aprenderá a distinguir entre atributos que definen a una figura y los que no la definen. Por ejemplo, los rectángulos tienen cuatro lados y cuatro esquinas. Un cuadrado es un tipo especial de rectángulo que tiene lados de igual longitud. Las figuras de abajo tienen diferente tamaño, color y orientación, pero todas son rectángulos.

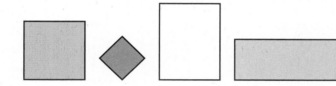

Más adelante en la unidad, los niños acomodarán figuras de diferentes maneras para formar nuevas figuras.

Para formar esta nueva figura se usaron un cono y un prisma rectangular.

También aprenderán a dividir círculos y rectángulos en dos y cuatro partes iguales. Describirán esas partes usando *mitades* y *cuartos*.

Este círculo está dividido en mitades.

Este círculo está dividido en cuartos.

Deducirán que si dividen un figura en más partes iguales, obtendrán partes más pequeñas: un cuarto del círculo es más pequeño que una mitad.

Otro concepto que se enseña en esta unidad es la medición de longitudes. Los niños ordenan tres objetos según su longitud.

Estos objetos están en orden del más largo al más corto.

También usan unidades de la misma longitud, tales como clips, para medir la longitud de un objeto.

Esta cinta mide 4 clips de longitud.

Usted puede ayudar a su niño a practicar estas nuevas destrezas en casa. Si tiene alguna pregunta, comuníquese conmigo.

Atentamente,
El maestro de su niño

circle

cube

clock

cylinder

cone

equal shares

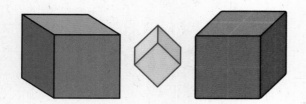

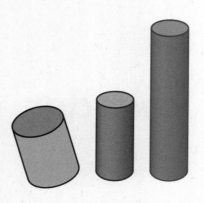

analog
clock

digital
clock

  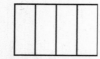

2 equal shares   4 equal shares

These show **equal shares**.

fourth of	half of
fourths	halves
half-hour	hour hand

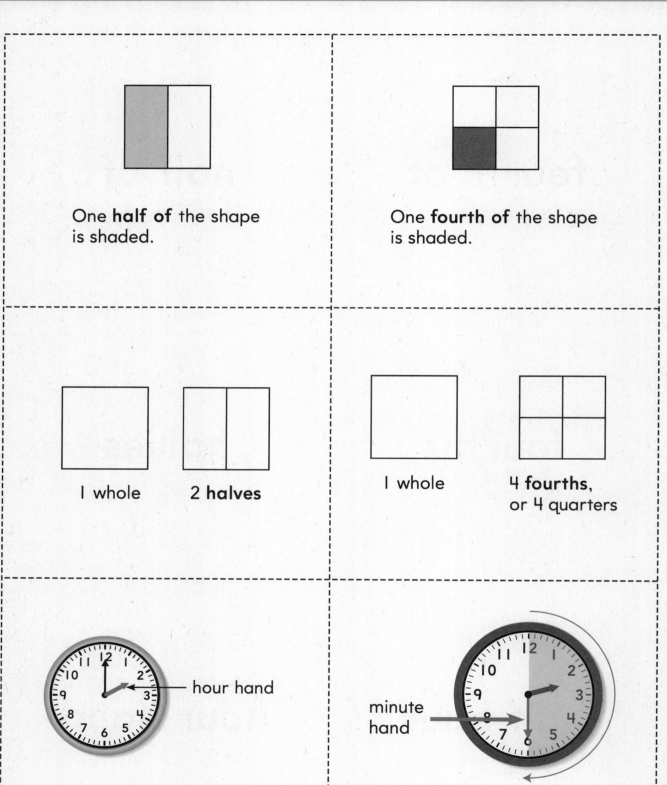

One **half of** the shape is shaded.

One **fourth of** the shape is shaded.

I whole   **2 halves**

I whole   **4 fourths,** or 4 quarters

hour hand

minute hand

A **half-hour** is 30 minutes.

rectangle

sphere

rectangular prism

square corner

side

square

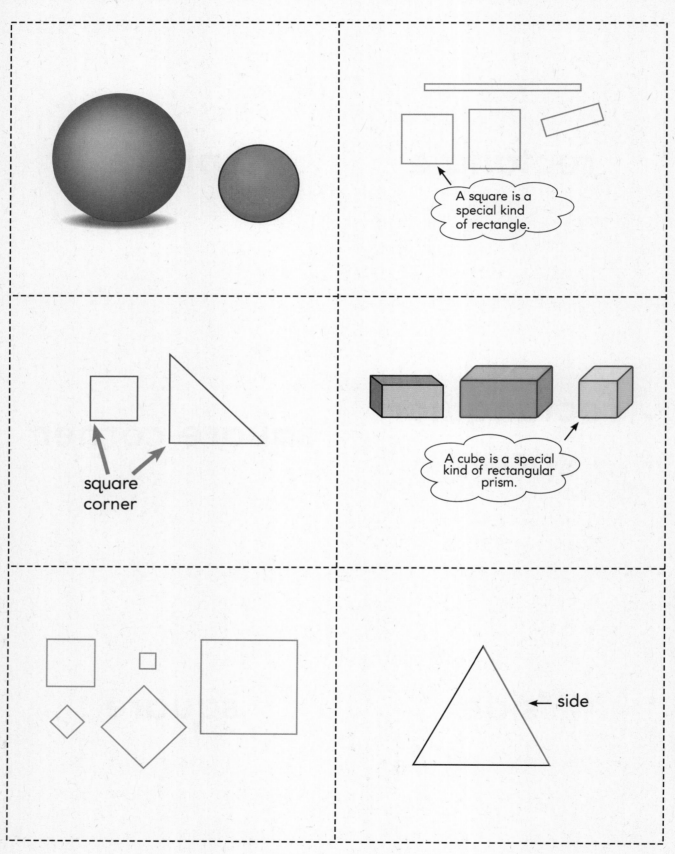

A square is a
special kind
of rectangle.

square
corner

A cube is a special
kind of rectangular
prism.

side

triangle

Name _____

Write the number to show the time.

1

_____ o'clock

2

_____ o'clock

3

_____ o'clock

4

_____ o'clock

5

_____ o'clock

6

_____ o'clock

Draw lines to match the time.

7  •

• 12:00

8  •

• 2:00

9  •

• 10:00

10  •

• 8:00

11  •

• 5:00

© Houghton Mifflin Harcourt Publishing Company

✓ Check Understanding

Write the digital time for 9 o'clock.

Introduction to Time

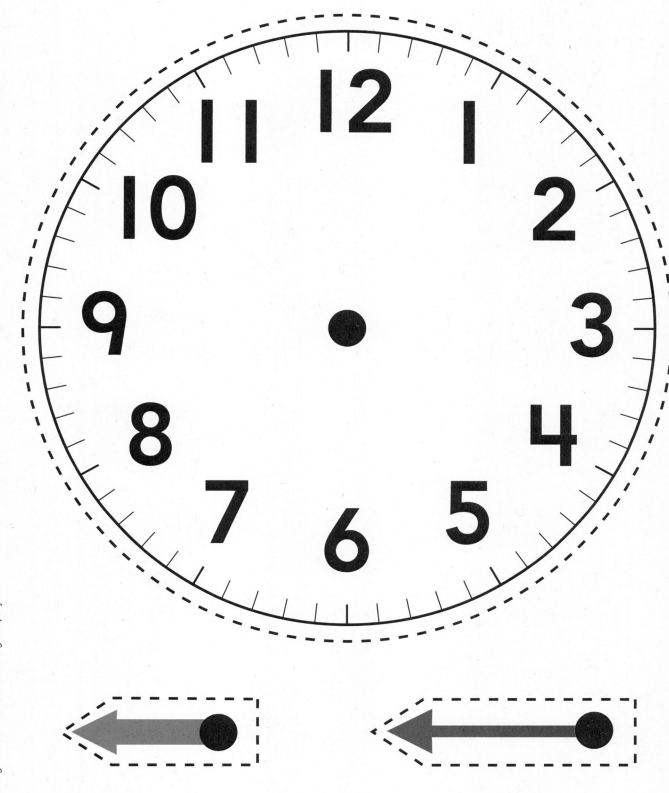

Student Clock (with hands) **311**

Student Clock (with hands)

Name _____

Read the **clock**.
Write the time on the digital clock.

VOCABULARY
clock

1   **2:00**

hour : minute

2   **:**

hour : minute

 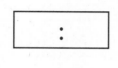

3   **:**

4   **:**

 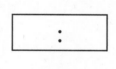

5   **:**

6   **:**

 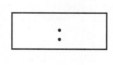

7   **:**

8   **:**

 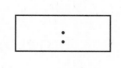

9   **:**

10   **:**

Draw the **hour hand** on the clock
to show the time.

11 4:00

12 10:00

13 5:00

14 8:00

15 Look at the hour hand Puzzled Penguin drew.

3:00

Am I correct?

16 Help Puzzled Penguin.

3:00

✔ **Check Understanding**

Show 7 o'clock on
your Student Clock.
Write the digital
time below.

Tell and Write Time in Hours

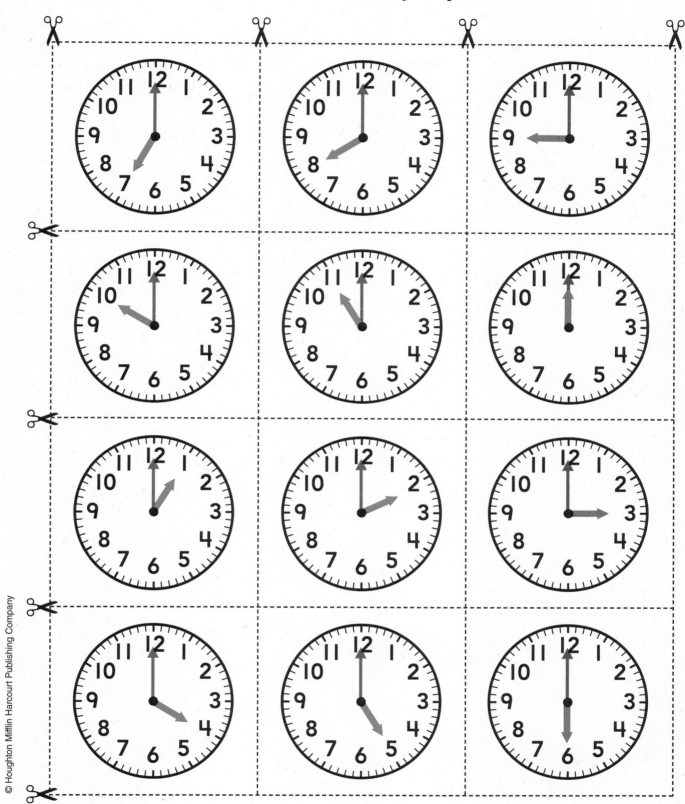

Clocks for "Our Busy Day" Book

Name _____

Read the clock.
Write the time on the digital clock.

①
┌─────────┐
│   :   │
└─────────┘
hour : minute

②
┌─────────┐
│   :   │
└─────────┘
hour : minute

③
┌─────────┐
│   :   │
└─────────┘

④
┌─────────┐
│   :   │
└─────────┘

Draw the hour hand on the clock to show the time.

⑤  6:00

⑥  9:00

⑦  8:00

⑧  7:00

⑨  4:00

⑩  3:00

Fill in the numbers on the clock.
Choose an hour time.
Draw the hands to show the time. Write the time.

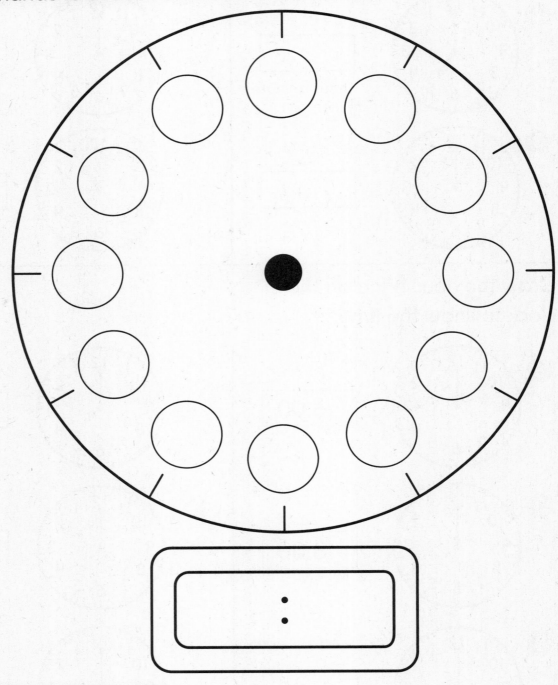

✓ Check Understanding

Choose another hour time and show the
time on both an analog and digital clock.

Time in Our Day

Name _____

VOCABULARY
half-hour

Read the clock.
Write the **half-hour** time on the digital clock.

:
hour : minute

:
hour : minute

| : |

 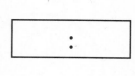

| : |

| : |

 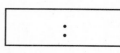

| : |

| : |

 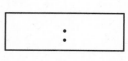

| : |

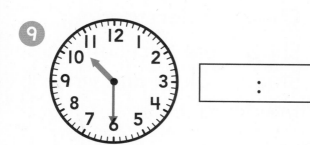

| : |

| : |

Ring the clock that shows the correct time.
Cross out the clock that shows the wrong time.

11   7:30

12   4:30

13   12:30

14   9:30

15   Look at the hour hand Puzzled Penguin drew.

1:30   Am I correct?

16   Help Puzzled Penguin.

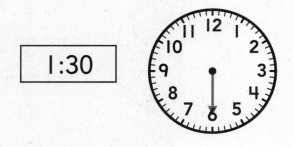

1:30

Check Understanding

Show three thirty on your
Student Clock and write
the digital time.

Name _____

Show the same half-hour time on both clocks.

1

:

2

:

3

:

4

:

5

:

6

:

7

:

8

:

9

:

　　　　　　　　Practice Telling and Writing Time **321**

Show the same time on both clocks.
Pick hour and half-hour times.

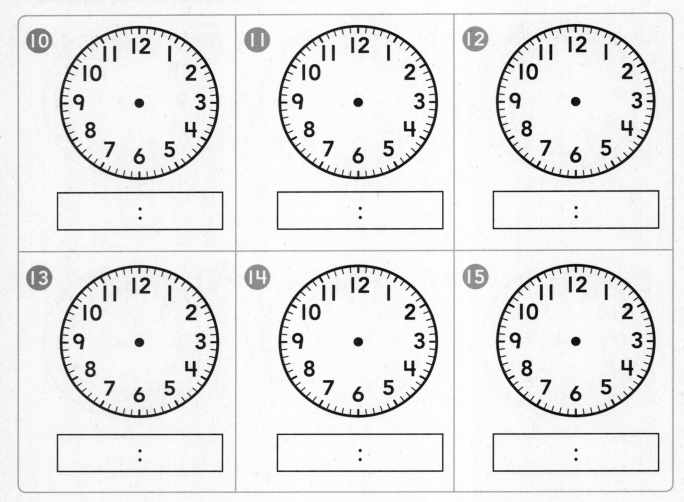

© Houghton Mifflin Harcourt Publishing Company

(PATH to FLUENCY) **Find the unknown partner.**

1 4 + ☐ = 8   **2** 4 + ☐ = 10   **3** 8 + ☐ = 9

✔ **Check Understanding**

Show eight thirty and eight o'clock on
your Student Clock and write the times.

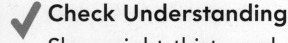

Practice Telling and Writing Time

Read the clock.

Write the time on the digital clock.

Name _____ Date _____

Add.

1 1 + 1 = ☐   **2** 5 + 3 = ☐   **3** 3 + 1 = ☐

4 5 + 5 = ☐   **5** 4 + 4 = ☐   **6** 5 + 1 = ☐

7 4 + 3 = ☐   **8** 4 + 5 = ☐   **9** 5 + 2 = ☐

Find the unknown partner.

10 1 + ☐ = 8   **11** 3 + ☐ = 6   **12** 5 + ☐ = 8

13 ☐ + 3 = 9   **14** ☐ + 5 = 10   **15** ☐ + 2 = 10

2-Dimensional Shape Set

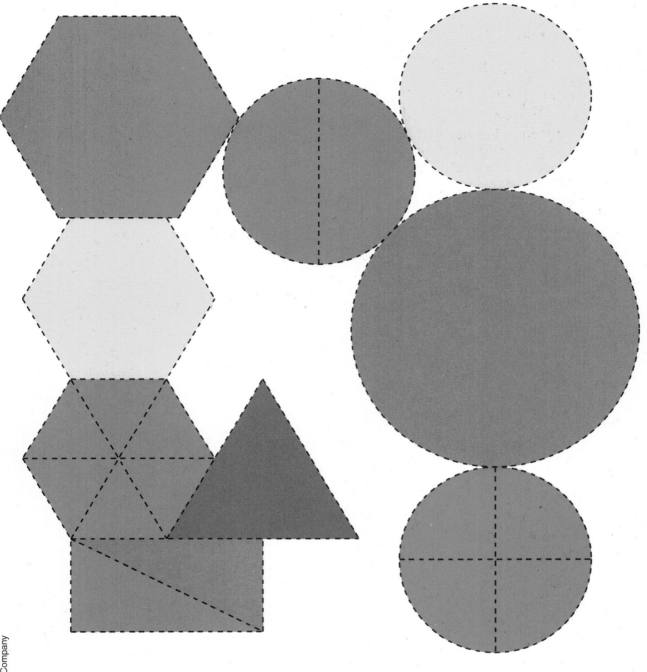

2-Dimensional Shape Set **327**

2-Dimensional Shape Set

① **Which shapes are NOT rectangles or squares?**
Draw an X on each one.

VOCABULARY
rectangle
square
side
square corner

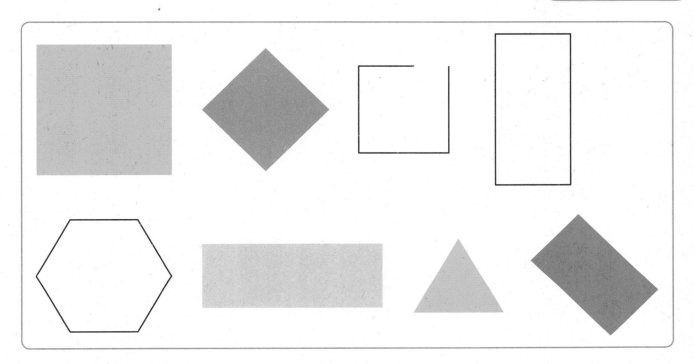

Draw the shape.

② 4 **sides**, 4 **square corners**	③ 4 sides the same length, 4 square corners

Squares and Other Rectangles **329**

4 Sort the shapes into three groups:

- Squares
- Rectangles That Are Not Squares
- Not Squares or Rectangles

Draw each shape in the correct place
on the sorting mat.

Squares	Rectangles That Are Not Squares	Not Squares or Rectangles

✓ Check Understanding

Draw a rectangle. Explain how you know
that it is a rectangle.

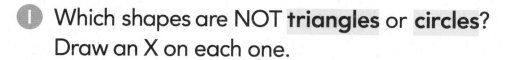

VOCABULARY
triangle
circle

1 Which shapes are NOT **triangles** or **circles**?
Draw an X on each one.

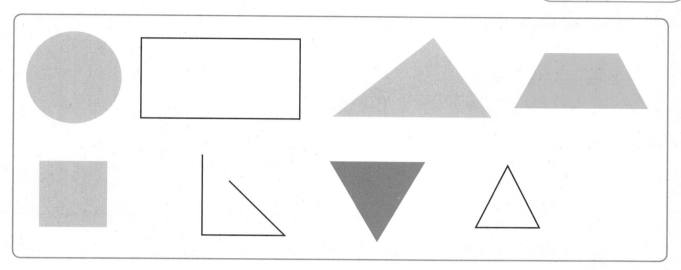

Draw the shape.

2 closed, 3 sides, 3 corners

3 closed, no corners

Ring the shapes that follow the sorting rule.
Draw a shape that fits the rule.

4 Shapes that are closed

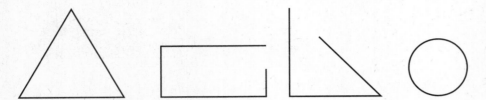

5 Shapes with three sides and three corners

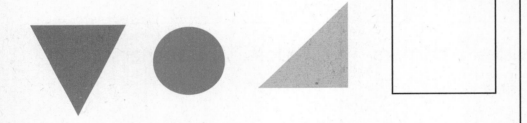

6 Shapes with a square corner

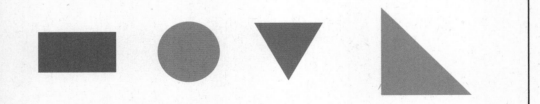

✔ **Check Understanding**
Draw and describe a triangle and circle.

Triangles and Circles

Name _____

Cut out the shapes below.
How many ways can you fold them into **halves**?

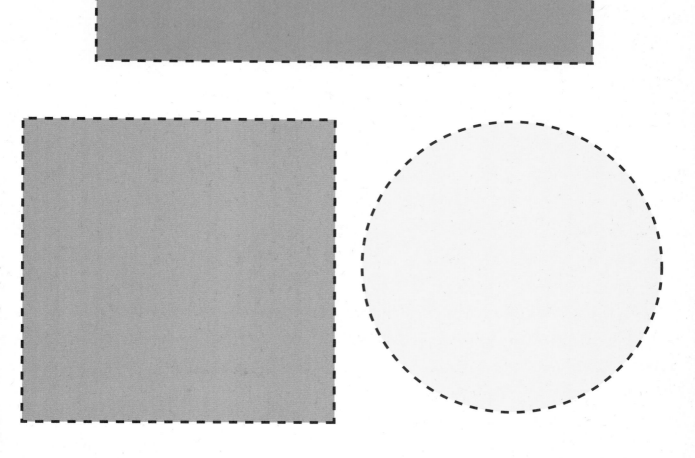

Equal Shares

Name _____

Draw a line to show halves.
Color one **half of** the shape.

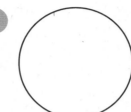

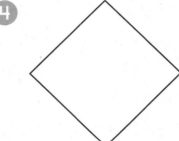

Draw lines to show **fourths**.
Color one **fourth of** the shape.

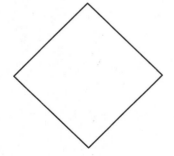 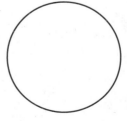

Solve the story problem.

VOCABULARY
equal shares

9 Four friends want to share a sandwich. How can they cut the sandwich into four **equal shares**? Draw lines. Color each share a different color.

10 The four friends want to share a pie for dessert. How can they cut the pie into four equal shares? Draw lines. Color each share a different color.

11 One friend only wants one half of her granola bar. How can she cut her granola bar into halves? Draw a line to show two equal shares. Color each share a different color.

PATH to FLUENCY **Subtract.**

1 $10 - 3 = \boxed{}$ **2** $8 - 8 = \boxed{}$ **3** $9 - 1 = \boxed{}$

 Check Understanding

Show two equal shares of a circle.
Show four equal shares of a circle.

Equal Shares

Build and draw the shape.

1 Build a square. Use rectangles.

---

2 Build a rectangle with all sides the same length.
Use triangles with a square corner.

---

3 Build a rectangle with two short sides and two
long sides. Use triangles and rectangles.

Compose 2-Dimensional Shapes

Name _____

Use to make the new shape.

4

5

6

7 Use 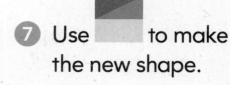 to make the new shape.

✓ Check Understanding

Explain how to use shapes to make a new rectangle and triangle.

Compose 2-Dimensional Shapes

Name _____

Draw a line to match like shapes.
Write the name of the shape.

Shape Names
cone
cube
cylinder
rectangular prism
sphere

1 • •

_____

2 • •

_____

3  • •

_____

4  • •

_____

5  • •

_____

6 Which shapes are NOT **rectangular prisms**?
Draw an X on each one.

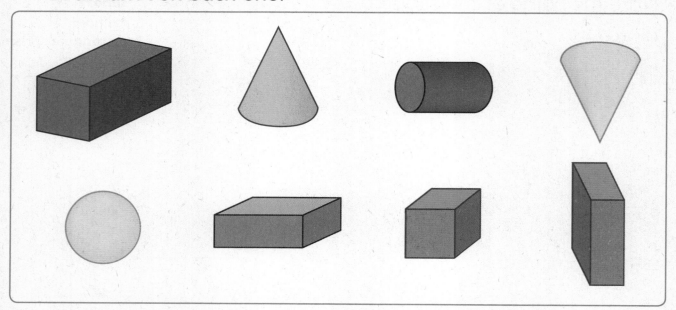

7 Ring the shapes that are **cubes**.

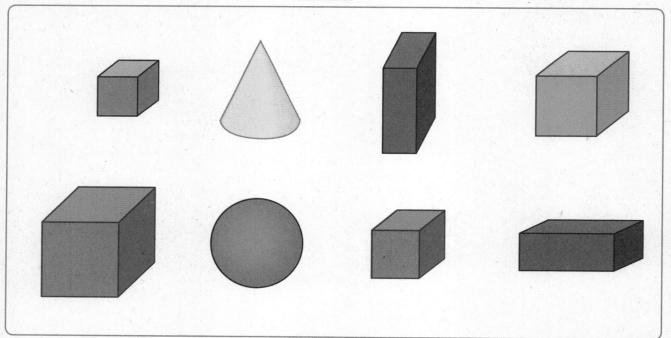

✓ **Check Understanding**
Compare a **cylinder**, a **cone**, and a
sphere. Explain what is the same and
different about the shapes.

3-Dimensional Shapes

Ring the shapes used to make the new shape.

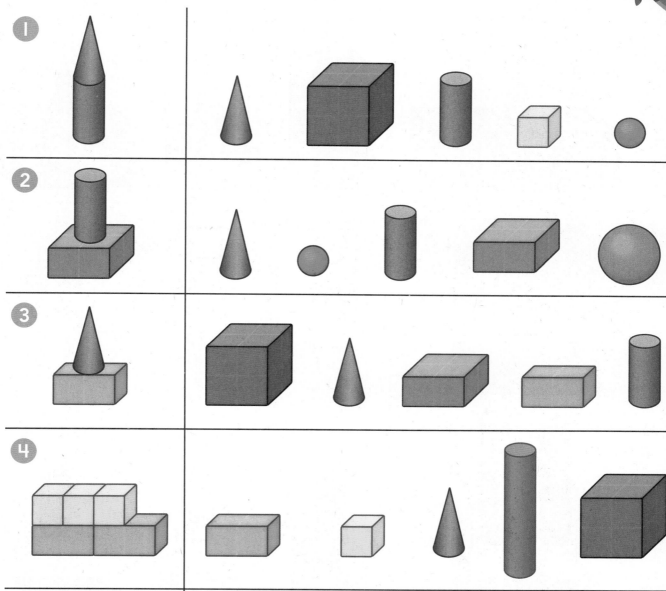

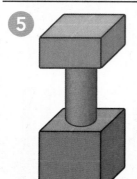
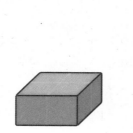

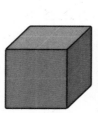

Ring the shape used to make the larger shape.

6

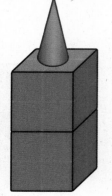  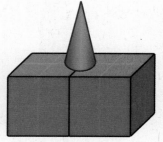

7

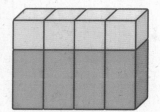 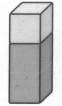 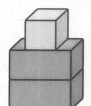 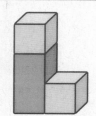

8

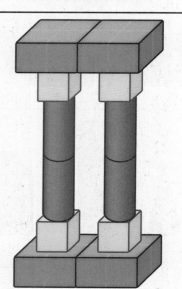 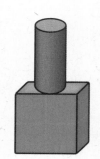 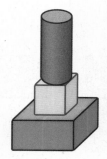 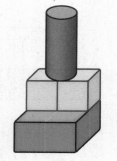

✓ Check Understanding

Ring the new shape that could be made from the shape shown.

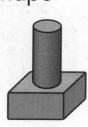 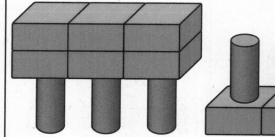

Compose 3-Dimensional Shapes

1 Draw an X on the shape that is NOT a square.

2 Ring the shapes used to make the new shape.

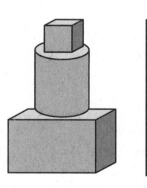   

3 Draw a line to show halves. Color one half of the shape.

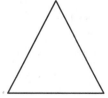

4 Draw lines to show fourths. Color one fourth of the shape.

Name _____ Date _____

PATH to
FLUENCY

Subtract.

1 2 − 1 = ☐   **2** 4 − 2 = ☐   **3** 3 − 0 = ☐

4 5 − 4 = ☐   **5** 6 − 3 = ☐   **6** 7 − 5 = ☐

7 6 − 4 = ☐   **8** 8 − 8 = ☐   **9** 7 − 3 = ☐

10 8 − 6 = ☐   **11** 9 − 2 = ☐   **12** 9 − 5 = ☐

13 10 − 8 = ☐ **14** 8 − 3 = ☐   **15** 10 − 4 = ☐

VOCABULARY
shortest
longest

Write 1, 2, 3 to order from **shortest** to **longest**.

1

2

Draw three lines of different lengths.
Write 1, 2, 3 to order from longest to shortest.

3

4

Order by Length

Use a strip of paper to measure the blue box.
Then measure the objects with the paper strip.

5 Ring the objects that will fit in the length of the box.

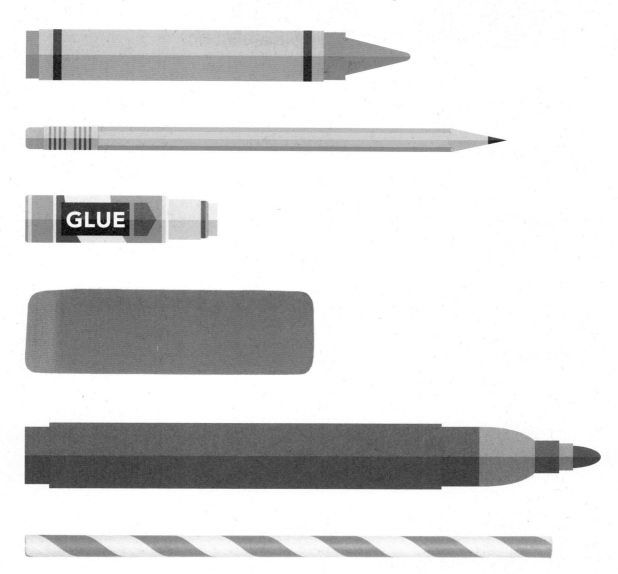

Draw to show the possible length of each object.

6 The blue box is the same length as the string.
The string is longer than the pencil.
The string is shorter than the drinking straw
and the spoon.

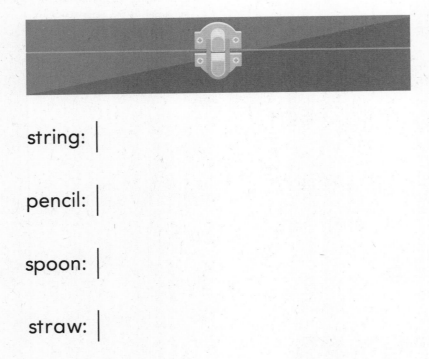

string:

pencil:

spoon:

straw:

Write the correct object.

7 The _____ will fit inside the box because
it is shorter than the box.

8 The _____ and _____ will not fit
inside the box. They are longer than the box.

✓ **Check Understanding**
Explain how to put 3 lengths of ribbon in
order from shortest to longest.

Order by Length

Name _____

Use paper clips. Measure the object.

1 Red ribbon   How long? ☐ paper clips

2 Blue ribbon   How long? ☐ paper clips

3 Green pencil   How long? ☐ paper clips

4 Purple pencil   How long? ☐ paper clips

Use paper clips. Measure the object.

5 Orange crayon   How long? ☐ paper clips

6 Blue paintbrush   How long? ☐ paper clips

PATH to FLUENCY Add.

1	2	3	4	5
7	2	4	1	0
+3	+6	+5	+7	+9

 Check Understanding

Use paper clips.
Measure the yellow chalk.

How long? ☐ paper clips

Measure with Length Units

Jay and his family are going on a picnic.
Draw lines to show equal shares.

1 Jay wants to share his burger
with his mom. How can he cut
his burger into two equal shares?

2 Jay and his three sisters want
to share a pan of corn bread.
How can he cut the bread into
four equal shares?

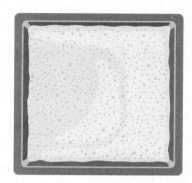

3 Jay's mom and his three
sisters want to share a block of
cheese. How can they cut the
block of cheese into four
equal shares?

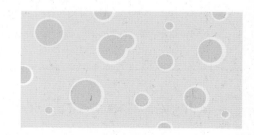

There will be lots of food at the picnic.
Measure the food in small paper clips.

4 Orange slice   How long? ☐ paper clips

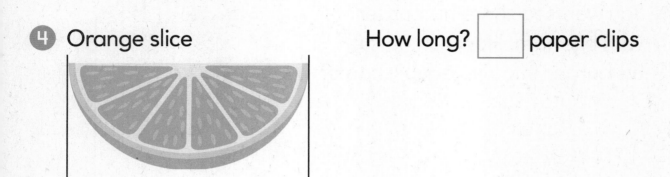

5 Celery   How long? ☐ paper clips

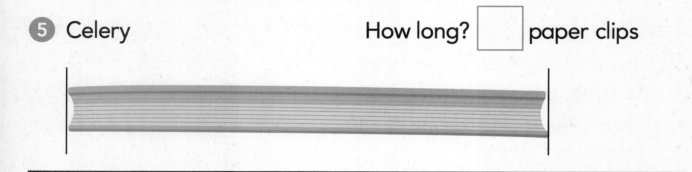

6 Cracker   How long? ☐ paper clips

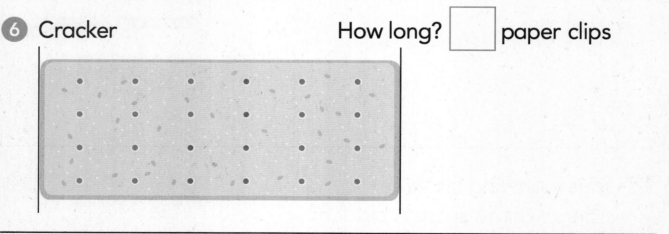

7 Order the picnic food from longest
to shortest. Write the names.

      Focus on Problem Solving

Write 1, 2, 3 to order from longest to shortest.

Measure in paper clips. How long?

paper clips

 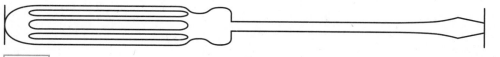

paper clips

paper clips

Name _____ Date _____

Add.

1. 0
 + 1
 —

2. 3
 + 0
 —

3. 1
 + 1
 —

4. 2
 + 2
 —

5. 1
 + 5
 —

6. 3
 + 4
 —

7. 4
 + 2
 —

8. 8
 + 0
 —

9. 2
 + 5
 —

10. 6
 + 1
 —

11. 3
 + 5
 —

12. 7
 + 2
 —

13. 2
 + 8
 —

14. 3
 + 6
 —

15. 6
 + 4
 —

Read the clock.

Write the time on the digital clock.

1  ☐ : ☐

2  ☐ : ☐

Draw the hands to show the time.

3 8:30

4 3:00

5 Which shapes are NOT triangles?
Draw an X on each one.

6 Is the shape a square? Choose Yes or No.

    ○ Yes   ○ No

    ○ Yes   ○ No

Draw a line to show halves.

Color one half of the shape.

  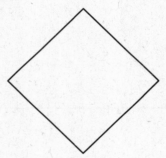   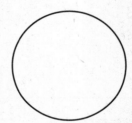

Draw lines to show fourths.

Color one fourth of the shape.

11 Draw a line from the shape to its name.

•

•

•

• rectangular prism

• sphere

• cylinder

12 Choose the shapes used to make the new shape.

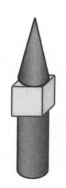

○   ○   ○   ○

13 Choose the shape used to make the larger shape.

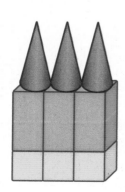

○ 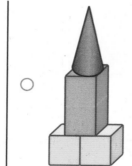   ○ 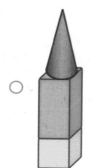   ○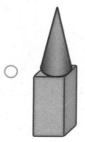

14 Measure in paper clips.

How long? ☐ paper clips

---

15 Eli has this crayon and this pencil.

Sam gives him an eraser that is shorter than the crayon.
Is the eraser shorter than the pencil? Explain.

_____

_____

_____

_____

_____

_____

_____

_____

Busy Bug's Day

1 **Part A**
The clock hands show Busy Bug's bedtime.

Write the same time on the digital clock.

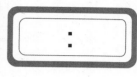

Part B Tell how you know what time it is.

2 **Part A** This is the shape of Busy Bug's snack.

He wants to share his snack with three friends.

Draw lines to show fourths.

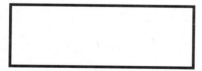

Part B Tell how you know the parts are fourths.

Busy Bug's Day (continued)

3 **Part A** Busy Bug likes only squares. Help him find the squares. Draw an X on each shape that is NOT a square.

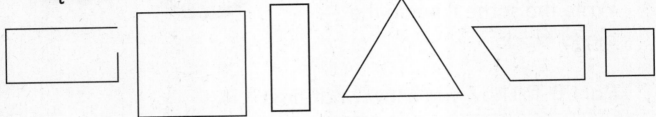

Part B Tell how you know a shape is a square.

4 **Part A**

This is Busy Bug's walking stick.

This is Busy Bug's bed.

How many paper clips long is the bed?

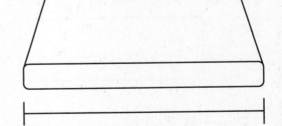

 _____

Part B

Busy Bug's table is longer than his walking stick. It is shorter than his bed. Draw Busy Bug's table.

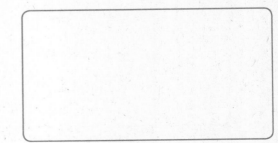

Dear Family:

Your child will be using special drawings of 10-sticks and circles to add greater numbers. The sticks show the number of tens, and the circles show the number of ones. When a new group of ten is made, a ring is drawn around it.

There are several ways for children to show the new group of ten when they add 2-digit numbers.

- Children can do the addition with a single total. The 1 for the new ten can be written either below the tens column or above it. Writing it below makes addition easier because the 1 new ten is added after children have added the two numbers that are already there. Also, children can see the 16 they made from 7 and 9 because the 1 and 6 are closer together than they were when the new ten was written above.

```
  27          new ten
+ 49          below
 ₁
  76
```

```
 ₁
  27          new ten
+ 49          above
  76
```

- Children can make separate totals for tens and ones. Many first-graders prefer to work from left to right because that is how they read. They add the tens (20 + 40 = 60) and then the ones (7 + 9 = 16). The last step is to add the two totals together (60 + 16 = 76).

```
  27
+ 49
  60
  16
  76
```
left to right

```
  27
+ 49
  16
  60
  76
```
right to left

You may notice your child using one of these methods as he or she completes homework.

Sincerely,
Your child's teacher

Estimada familia:

Su niño usará dibujos especiales de palitos de decenas y círculos para sumar números más grandes. Los palitos muestran el número de decenas y los círculos muestran el número de unidades. Cuando se forma un nuevo grupo de diez, se encierra.

Hay varias maneras en las que los niños pueden mostrar el nuevo grupo de diez al sumar números de 2 dígitos.

- Pueden hacer la suma con un total único. El 1 que indica la nueva decena se puede escribir abajo o arriba de la columna de las decenas. Escribirlo abajo hace que la suma sea más fácil porque la nueva decena se suma después de sumar los dos números que ya estaban allí. Además, los niños pueden ver el 16 que obtuvieron de 7 y 9 porque el 1 y el 6 están más juntos que cuando la nueva decena estaba escrita arriba.

nueva decena abajo

nueva decena arriba

- Pueden hacer totales separados para decenas y para unidades. Muchos estudiantes de primer grado prefieren trabajar de izquierda a derecha porque así leen. Suman las decenas (20 + 40 = 60) y luego las unidades (7 + 9 = 16). El último paso es sumar ambos totales (60 + 16 = 76).

de izquierda a derecha

de derecha a izquierda

Es posible que su niño use uno de estos métodos al hacer la tarea.

Atentamente,
El maestro de su niño

Explore 2-Digit Addition

Name _____

Draw circles to show the apples.

Uncle David
28 Apples

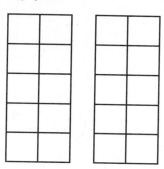

28 apples   16 apples

Put extra apples here.

Aunt Sarah
16 Apples

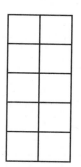

Put extra apples here.

Total Apples

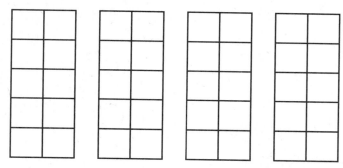

Put extra apples here.

Draw circles to show the apples.

Uncle David
26 Apples

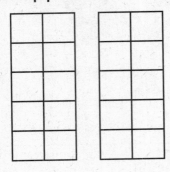

Aunt Sarah
20 Apples

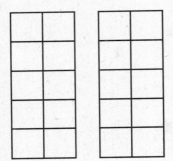

Put extra apples here.

Total Apples

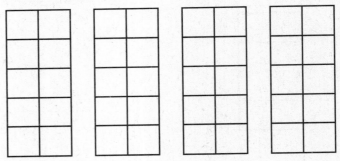

Put extra apples here.

✔ **Check Understanding**
Make a stick-and-circle
drawing to solve 65 + 29.

Explore 2-Digit Addition

Name _____

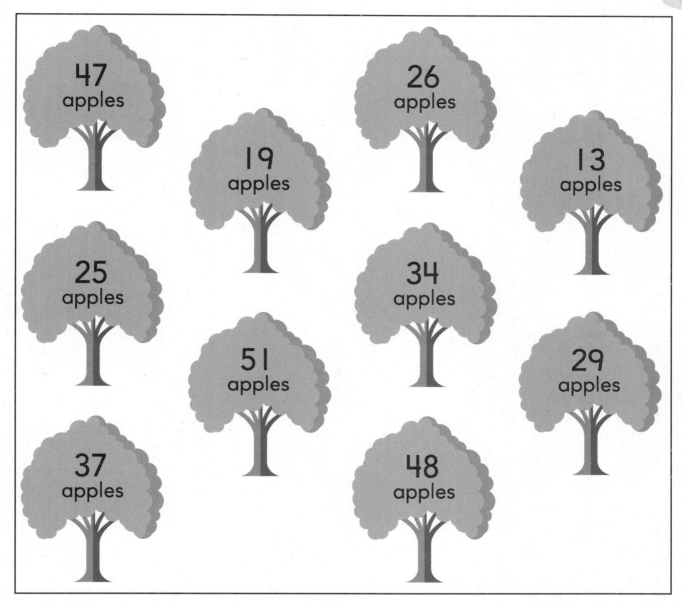

1. Work in pairs. Each child chooses one apple tree.

2. On your MathBoard or paper, add the number of apples in the two trees.

3. Check to see if you both got the same answer.

4. Repeat with other trees.

24 apples

36 apples

9 apples

30 apples

5 apples

20 apples

40 apples

2 apples

19 apples

53 apples

5. Work in pairs. One child chooses one apple tree with a 2-digit number. The other child chooses another tree.

6. On your MathBoard or paper, add the apples in the two trees.

7. Check to see if you both got the same answer.

✓ **Check Understanding**

Use the New Group Below method to solve 55 + 36.

Methods of 2-Digit Addition

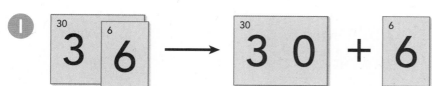

Write the numbers to show addition.

1.   3 6 ⟶ 3 0 + 6

   5 5 ⟶ 5 0 + 5

$$36 = 30 + 6$$
$$+\ 55 = 50 + 5$$

⬚ + ⬚ = ⬚

2.   5 4 ⟶ 5 0 + 4

   3 8 ⟶ 3 0 + 8

$$54 = 50 + 4$$
$$+\ 38 = 30 + 8$$

⬚ + ⬚ = ⬚

Addition of Tens and Ones **369**

Write the numbers to show addition.

3 Mark built a tower using 67 blocks. Elizabeth built a tower using 18 blocks. How many blocks did they use together?

Step 1: Add the tens.

$$
\begin{array}{r}
67 \\
+ \ 18 \\
\hline
\end{array}
$$

Step 2: Add the ones.

$$
\begin{array}{r}
67 \\
+ \ 18 \\
\hline
70 \\
\end{array}
$$

Step 3: Add the totals together.

$$
\begin{array}{r}
67 \\
+ \ 18 \\
\hline
70 \\
15 \\
\hline
\end{array}
$$

✔ **Check Understanding**

Use the Show All Totals method and make a Proof Drawing to solve 63 + 28.

Addition of Tens and Ones

Name _____

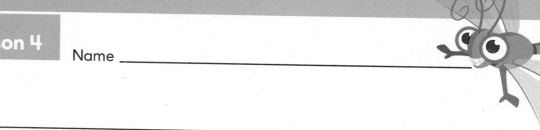

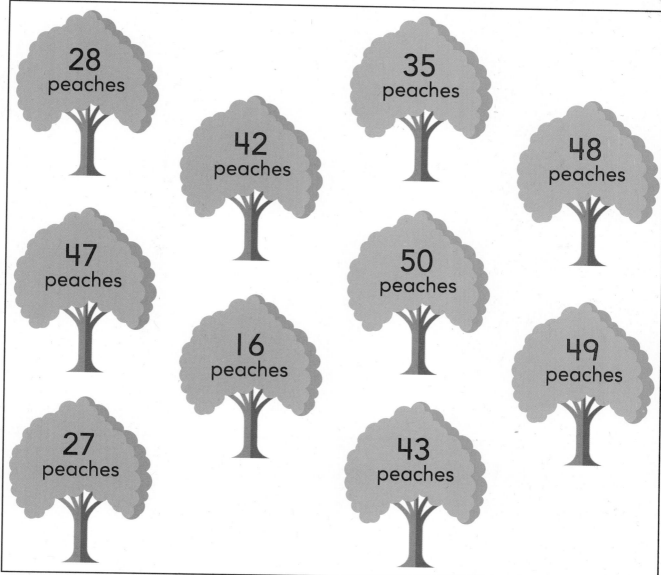

1. Work in pairs. Each child chooses one peach tree.

2. On your MathBoard or paper, add the number of peaches in the two trees.

3. Check to see if you both got the same answer.

4. Repeat with other trees.

5. For which problems did you make a new ten?

Add.

6   53
     + 38

7   16
     + 6

8   67
     + 15

9   72
     + 20

10   56
      + 13

11   47
      + 30

12   48
      + 5

13   82
      + 14

14   17
      + 2

Write the vertical form. Then add.

15 65 + 8

16 56 + 28

17 6 + 73

✔ **Check Understanding**

Use two different methods to solve 15 + 18.

Discuss Solution Methods

Name _____

Add.

1. 93
    + 6

2. 28
    + 18

3. 66
    + 7

4. 49
    + 30

5. 56
    + 25

6. 15
    + 4

Write the vertical form. Then add.

7. 71 + 19

8. 54 + 20

9. 33 + 29

10. 44 + 4

11. 8 + 74

12. 19 + 67

Practice 2-Digit Addition **373**

13 Look at the total Puzzled Penguin wrote.

$$\begin{array}{r} 43 \\ +\ 39 \\ \hline 712 \end{array}$$

Am I correct?

14 Help Puzzled Penguin.

$$\begin{array}{r} 43 \\ +\ 39 \\ \hline \end{array}$$

PATH to FLUENCY Add.

1 $5 + 2 = \boxed{}$

2 $7 + 1 = \boxed{}$

3 $3 + 2 = \boxed{}$

4 $\boxed{} = 8 + 2$

5 $\boxed{} = 3 + 6$

6 $\boxed{} = 4 + 3$

7 $5 + 1 = \boxed{}$

8 $6 + 2 = \boxed{}$

9 $5 + 3 = \boxed{}$

10 $\boxed{} = 7 + 2$

11 $\boxed{} = 4 + 2$

12 $\boxed{} = 2 + 1$

✓ **Check Understanding**

Write $26 + 18$ as a vertical form and solve.

© Houghton Mifflin Harcourt Publishing Company

Practice 2-Digit Addition

Name _____

Use the pictures to solve. Show your work.

1 How many potatoes are there?

49 potatoes   47 potatoes

[ ] potatoes

2 How many cartons of milk are there?

37 cartons of milk   23 cartons of milk

[ ] cartons of milk

3 20 cartons of milk spill.
How many cartons of milk are there now?

[ ] cartons of milk

Use the pictures to solve. Show your work.

4 How many jars of honey are there?

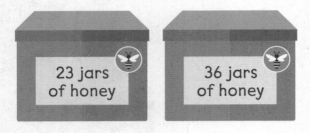

23 jars of honey   36 jars of honey

☐ jars of honey

5 How many jars of jam are there?

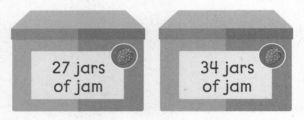

27 jars of jam   34 jars of jam

☐ jars of jam

6 Compare the number of jars of honey to the number of jars of jam. Write the comparison 2 ways.

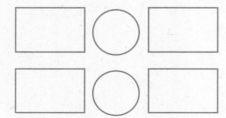

Add.

1   27
    + 5

2   43
    + 30

3   58
    + 26

Write the vertical form. Then add.

4 29 + 34

5 38 + 6

Name _____   Date _____

Add.

1 $2 + 2 = \boxed{}$ **2** $3 + 3 = \boxed{}$ **3** $1 + 3 = \boxed{}$

4 $3 + 2 = \boxed{}$ **5** $4 + 3 = \boxed{}$ **6** $1 + 7 = \boxed{}$

7 $2 + 4 = \boxed{}$ **8** $4 + 6 = \boxed{}$ **9** $6 + 2 = \boxed{}$

10 $7 + 2 = \boxed{}$ **11** $5 + 4 = \boxed{}$ **12** $7 + 3 = \boxed{}$

13 $\boxed{} = 3 + 5$ **14** $\boxed{} = 2 + 8$ **15** $\boxed{} = 5 + 4$

Solve. Group ones to make tens.

1 Grace has 18 apples.   Jake has 24 apples.

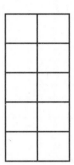   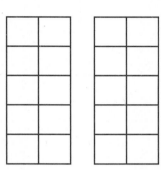

_____ extra apples   _____ extra apples

How many apples do they have?

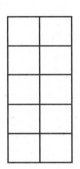 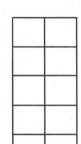 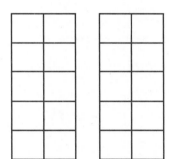

_____ extra apples

_____
label

2 Is the total correct? Choose Yes or No.

$45 + 20 = 47$	○ Yes	○ No
$30 + 25 = 55$	○ Yes	○ No
$79 + 10 = 89$	○ Yes	○ No
$14 + 50 = 74$	○ Yes	○ No

Add.

3
$$63$$
$$+\ 29$$

4
$$52$$
$$+\ 20$$

5
$$78$$
$$+\ \ 5$$

6
$$26$$
$$+\ 15$$

Write the vertical form. Then add.

7 $28 + 9$

8 $45 + 18$

9 Choose the totals that equal 55.

    ○ $51 + 4$ ○ $46 + 9$ ○ $34 + 22$ ○ $35 + 20$

10 Choose the totals that equal 84.

    ○ $35 + 49$ ○ $34 + 44$ ○ $42 + 42$ ○ $50 + 34$

Name _____   Date _____

11 How many apples are there?
Show your work.

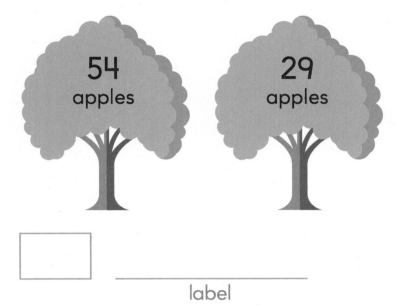

54
apples

29
apples

┌──────┐
│   │   _____
└──────┘
         label

_____

Choose the correct answer.

12 57 + 15

  ○ 62

  ○ 68

  ○ 72

  ○ 82

_____

13 51 + 40

  ○ 55

  ○ 71

  ○ 91

  ○ 95

14 How many peaches are there?
Show your work.

[   ]   _____
        label

15 Write an addition exercise that you must
make a new ten to solve. Use two 2-digit
numbers. Make a Proof Drawing.

How Many Pears?

Some friends pick pears.

Choose one of the numbers below for each ◯.
Use each number only one time.

9   16   27   35

1 Lisa picks more pears than Rena.
Together they pick 36 pears.
How many does each girl pick?

Lisa picks ◯ pears.

Rena picks ◯ pears.

Show how you know.

2 Luis and Tran pick ◯ pears.
Then they pick 20 more pears.
What is the total number of
pears they pick?

☐ pears

Show how you know.

3 Maya picks ◯ pears. Vinny
picks 15 pears. How many
pears do they pick in all?

☐ pears

Show how you know.

How Many Pears? (continued)

4 Jamal picks 38 pears.
His grandma picks 24 pears.
How many pears do they pick
altogether?

Show and tell how you know.

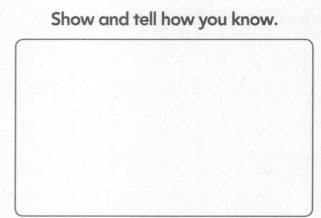

[ ] pears

5 Kat picks 25 pears. Alex picks
19 pears. They want to find how
many pears they pick altogether.
Look at the total.

$$
\begin{array}{r}
25 \\
+\ 19 \\
\hline
3\!\!\!/14 \\
\end{array}
$$

Tell why the total is not correct.
Find the correct total.

Addition and Subtraction Problem Types

	Result Unknown	Change Unknown	Start Unknown
Add To	Six children are playing tag in the yard. Three more children come to play. How many children are playing in the yard now? *Situation and Solution Equation*[1]: $6 + 3 = \square$	Six children are playing tag in the yard. Some more children come to play. Now there are 9 children in the yard. How many children came to play? *Situation Equation:* $6 + \square = 9$ *Solution Equation:* $9 - 6 = \square$	Some children are playing tag in the yard. Three more children come to play. Now there are 9 children in the yard. How many children were in the yard at first? *Situation Equation:* $\square + 3 = 9$ *Solution Equation:* $9 - 3 = \square$
Take From	Jake has 10 trading cards. He gives 3 to his brother. How many trading cards does he have left? *Situation and Solution Equation:* $10 - 3 = \square$	Jake has 10 trading cards. He gives some to his brother. Now Jake has 7 trading cards left. How many cards does he give to his brother? *Situation Equation:* $10 - \square = 7$ *Solution Equation:* $10 - 7 = \square$	Jake has some trading cards. He gives 3 to his brother. Now Jake has 7 trading cards left. How many cards does he start with? *Situation Equation:* $\square - 3 = 7$ *Solution Equation:* $7 + 3 = \square$

[1]A situation equation represents the structure (action) in the problem situation. A solution equation shows the operation used to find the answer.

Problem Types

Addition and Subtraction Problem Types (continued)

	Total Unknown	Addend Unknown	Other Addend Unknown
Put Together/ Take Apart	There are 9 red roses and 4 yellow roses in a vase. How many roses are in the vase? *Math Drawing²:*  *Situation and Solution Equation:* $9 + 4 = \square$	Thirteen roses are in the vase. 9 are red and the rest are yellow. How many roses are yellow? *Math Drawing:* 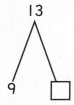 *Situation Equation:* $13 = 9 + \square$ *Solution Equation:* $13 - 9 = \square$	Thirteen roses are in the vase. Some are red and 4 are yellow. How many are red? *Math Drawing:* 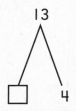 *Situation Equation:* $13 = \square + 4$ *Solution Equation:* $13 - 4 = \square$

Both Addends Unknown is a productive extension of this basic situation, especially for small numbers less than or equal to 10. Such take apart situations can be used to show all the decompositions of a given number. The associated equations, which have the total on the left of the equal sign, help children understand that the = sign does not always mean makes or results in but always does mean is the same number as.

Both Addends Unknown

Ana has 13 roses. How many can she put in her red vase and how many in her blue vase?

Math Drawing:

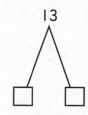

Situation Equation:
$13 = \square + \square$

²These math drawings are called Math Mountains in Grades 1–3 and break-apart drawings in Grades 4 and 5.

Addition and Subtraction Problem Types (continued)

	Difference Unknown	Bigger Unknown	Smaller Unknown
Compare[3]	Aki has 8 apples. Sofia has 14 apples. How many more apples does Sofia have than Aki? Aki has 8 apples. Sofia has 14 apples. How many fewer apples does Aki have than Sofia? *Math Drawing:* S [14] A [8] (?) *Situation Equation:* $8 + \square = 14$ *Solution Equation:* $14 - 8 = \square$	**Leading Language** Aki has 8 apples. Sofia has 6 more apples than Aki. How many apples does Sofia have? **Misleading Language** Aki has 8 apples. Aki has 6 fewer apples than Sofia. How many apples does Sofia have? *Math Drawing:* S [?] A [8] (6) *Situation and Solution Equation:* $8 + 6 = \square$	**Leading Language** Sofia has 14 apples. Aki has 6 fewer apples than Sofia. How many apples does Aki have? **Misleading Language** Sofia has 14 apples. Sofia has 6 more apples than Aki. How many apples does Aki have? *Math Drawing:* S [14] A [?] (6) *Situation Equation:* $\square + 6 = 14$ *Solution Equation:* $14 - 6 = \square$

[3]A comparison sentence can always be said in two ways. One way uses *more*, and the other uses *fewer* or *less*. Misleading language suggests the wrong operation. For example, it says *Aki has 6 fewer apples than Sofia*, but you have to add 6 to Aki's 8 apples to get 14 apples.

5-group*

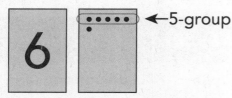

← 5-group

10-group

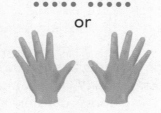

or

10-stick*

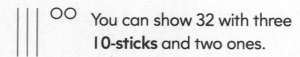

You can show 32 with three **10-sticks** and two ones.

A

add

$$3 + 2 = 5$$

addend

$$5 + 4 = 9 \qquad 5 + 4 + 8 = 17$$

addends
(partners)

addends

addition story problem

There are 5 ducks.
Then 3 more come.
How many ducks are there now?

B

bar graph

Vegetables We Like						
Carrots						
Corn						
Peppers						

0 1 2 3 4 5 6

break-apart*

You can **break apart** the number 4.

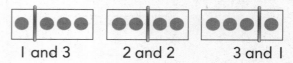

1 and 3   2 and 2   3 and 1

1 and 3, 2 and 2, and 3 and 1 are
break-aparts of 4.

C

cents (¢)

The number of cents is the value of
a coin or a set of coins.

7 cents

circle

*A classroom research-based term developed for *Math Expressions*

circle drawing*

3 + 4

9 − 5

clock

analog
clock

digital
clock

column

1	11	21	31	41	51	61	71	81	91
2	12	22	32	42	52	62	72	82	92
3	13	23	33	43	53	63	73	83	93
4	14	24	34	44	54	64	74	84	94
5	15	25	35	45	55	65	75	85	95
6	16	26	36	46	56	66	76	86	96
7	17	27	37	47	57	67	77	87	97
8	18	28	38	48	58	68	78	88	98
9	19	29	39	49	59	69	79	89	99
10	20	30	40	50	60	70	80	90	100

compare

You can **compare** numbers.

11 is less than 12.

$$11 < 12$$

12 is greater than 11.

$$12 > 11$$

You can **compare** objects by length.

The crayon is shorter than the pencil.

The pencil is longer than the crayon.

comparison bars*

Joe has 6 roses. Sasha has 9 roses.
How many more roses does Sasha have
than Joe?

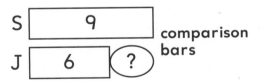

comparison
bars

cone

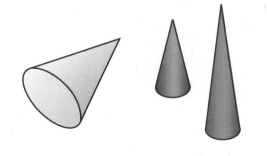

*A classroom research-based term developed for *Math Expressions*

Glossary

corner

count

count all

$5 + 4 = \boxed{9}$

1 2 3 4 5   6 7 8 9

count on

$5 + 4 = \boxed{9}$

$5 + \boxed{4} = 9$

$9 - 5 = \boxed{4}$

5 . . . .
6 7 8 9

Count on from 5 to get the answer.

cube

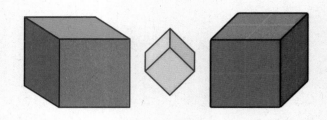

cylinder

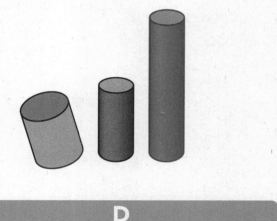

D

data

Colors in the Bag								
Red	◯	◯	◯					
Yellow	◯	◯	◯	◯	◯	◯	◯	◯
Blue	◯	◯	◯	◯	◯	◯		

The **data** show how many of each color.

decade numbers

10, 20, 30, 40, 50, 60, 70, 80, 90

© Houghton Mifflin Harcourt Publishing Company

*A classroom research-based term developed for *Math Expressions*

difference

$$11 - 3 = 8$$

$$\begin{array}{r} 11 \\ -\ 3 \\ \hline 8 \end{array}$$

difference → 8

digit

15 is a 2-**digit** number.

The 1 in 15 means 1 ten.

The 5 in 15 means 5 ones.

dime

front   back

10 cents or 10¢

dot array

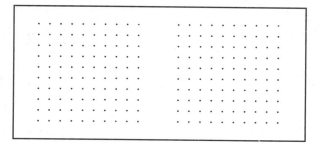

doubles

$$4 + 4 = 8$$

Both partners are the same.
They are doubles.

doubles minus 1

$7 + 7 = 14$, so

$7 + 6 = 13$, 1 less than 14.

doubles minus 2

$7 + 7 = 14$, so

$7 + 5 = 12$, 2 less than 14.

doubles plus 1

$6 + 6 = 12$, so

$6 + 7 = 13$, 1 more than 12.

doubles plus 2

$6 + 6 = 12$, so

$6 + 8 = 14$, 2 more than 12.

E

edge

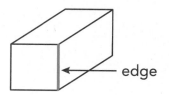

edge

equal shares

2 equal shares   4 equal shares

These show **equal shares**.

Glossary

equal to (=)

$$4 + 4 = 8$$

4 plus 4 is **equal to** 8.

equation

$$4 + 3 = 7 \qquad 7 = 4 + 3$$

$$9 - 5 = 4 \qquad 4 = 9 - 5$$

F

face

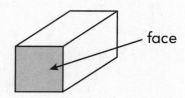

fewer

Eggs Laid This Month

Clucker laid **fewer** eggs than Vanilla.

fewest

Eggs Laid This Month

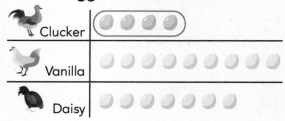

Clucker laid the **fewest** eggs.

fourth of

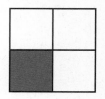

One **fourth of** the shape is shaded.

fourths

1 whole

4 **fourths**, or
4 quarters

G

greater than (>)

34 > 25

34 is **greater than** 25.

grid

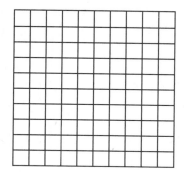

halves

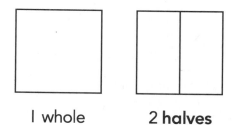

I whole   2 **halves**

growing pattern

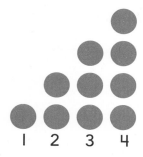

1 2 3 4

hexagon

H

half-hour

minute
hand

A **half-hour** is 30 minutes.

hour

hour
hand

An **hour** is 60 minutes.

hour hand

hour hand

half of

One **half of** the shape is shaded.

hundred

1	11	21	31	41	51	61	71	81	91
2	12	22	32	42	52	62	72	82	92
3	13	23	33	43	53	63	73	83	93
4	14	24	34	44	54	64	74	84	94
5	15	25	35	45	55	65	75	85	95
6	16	26	36	46	56	66	76	86	96
7	17	27	37	47	57	67	77	87	97
8	18	28	38	48	58	68	78	88	98
9	19	29	39	49	59	69	79	89	99
10	20	30	40	50	60	70	80	90	100

or

K

known partner*

$5 + \boxed{} = 7$

5 is the **known partner**.

L

length

The **length** of this pencil is 6 paper clips.

---

less than (<)

45   <   46

45 is **less than** 46.

---

longer

The pencil is **longer** than the crayon.

---

longest

The pencil is the **longest**.

M

make a ten

$8 + 6 = \boxed{}$

⑧ ○○ ○○○○

$10 + 4 = 14$,
so $8 + 6 = 14$.

---

*A classroom research-based term developed for *Math Expressions*

Math Mountain*

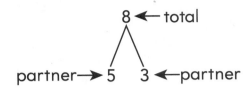

partner→ 5   3 ←partner

8 ← total

measure

You can use paper clips to **measure** the length of the pencil.

minus (−)

$$8 - 3 = 5 \qquad \begin{array}{r} 8 \\ -3 \\ \hline 5 \end{array}$$

8 **minus** 3 equals 5.

minute

I minute

minute hand

There are 60 **minutes** in an hour.

more

Eggs Laid This Month

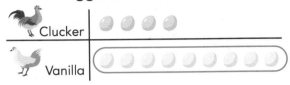

Clucker

Vanilla

Vanilla laid **more** eggs than Clucker.

most

Eggs Laid This Month

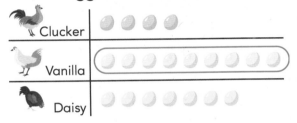

Clucker

Vanilla

Daisy

Vanilla laid the **most** eggs.

N

New Group Above Method*

$$\begin{array}{r} \overset{1}{5}6 \\ +\ 28 \\ \hline 84 \end{array}$$

6 + 8 = 14
The I new ten in 14 goes up to the tens place.

New Group Below Method*

$$\begin{array}{r} 56 \\ +\ 28 \\ \hline 8\underset{1}{4} \end{array}$$

6 + 8 = 14
The I new ten in 14 goes below in the tens place.

*A classroom research-based term developed for *Math Expressions*

nickel

front

back

5 cents or 5¢

not equal to (≠)

6 ≠ 8

6 is **not equal to** 8.

number line

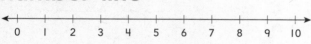

number word

12

twelve ◄—— number word

O

ones

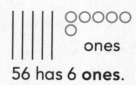
ones

56 has 6 **ones**.

order

You can change the **order** of the partners.

7 + 2 = 9

2 + 7 = 9

You can **order** objects by length.

P

partner*

5 = 2 + 3

2 and 3 are **partners** of 5.
2 and 3 are 5-**partners**.

partner house*

9

5 + 4
6 + 3
3 + 6
4 + 5
7 + 2
8 + 1
2 + 7
1 + 8

*A classroom research-based term developed for *Math Expressions*

partner train*

4-train

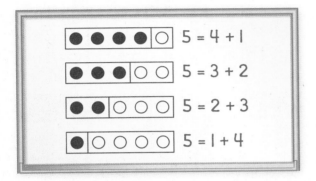

3 + 1   2 + 2   1 + 3

pattern

●●●●○	5 = 4 + 1
●●●○○	5 = 3 + 2
●●○○○	5 = 2 + 3
●○○○○	5 = 1 + 4

The partners of a number show a **pattern**.

penny

front   back

1 cent or 1¢

plus (+)

$3 + 2 = 5$ $\begin{array}{r} 3 \\ + 2 \\ \hline 5 \end{array}$

3 **plus** 2 equals 5.

Proof Drawing*

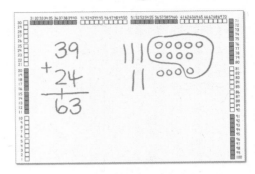

$$\begin{array}{r} 39 \\ + 24 \\ \hline 63 \end{array}$$

Q

quarter

front   back

25 cents or 25¢

quarter of

One **quarter of** the shape is shaded.

quarters

1 whole   4 **quarters**, or 4 fourths

*A classroom research-based term developed for *Math Expressions*

Glossary

R

rectangle

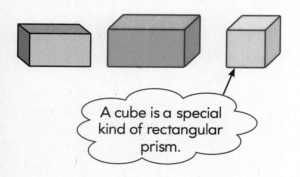

A square is a special kind of rectangle.

rectangular prism

A cube is a special kind of rectangular prism.

repeating pattern

▲ ■ ▲ ■ ▲ ■ ▲ ■ ▲ ■

row

1	11	21	31	41	51	61	71	81	91
2	12	22	32	42	52	62	72	82	92
3	13	23	33	43	53	63	73	83	93
4	14	24	34	44	54	64	74	84	94
5	15	25	35	45	55	65	75	85	95
6	16	26	36	46	56	66	76	86	96
7	17	27	37	47	57	67	77	87	97
8	18	28	38	48	58	68	78	88	98
9	19	29	39	49	59	69	79	89	99
10	20	30	40	50	60	70	80	90	100

S

shapes

2-dimensional

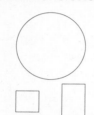

3-dimensional

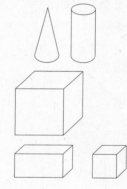

shorter

The crayon is **shorter** than the pencil.

*A classroom research-based term developed for *Math Expressions*

shortest

The paper clip is the **shortest**.

Show All Totals Method*

$$\begin{array}{r} 25 \\ + 48 \\ \hline 60 \\ 13 \\ \hline 73 \end{array}$$

shrinking pattern

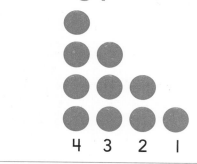

4 3 2 1

side

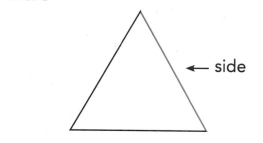
← side

sort

You can **sort** the animals into groups.

sphere

square

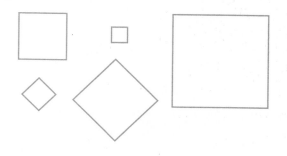

square corner

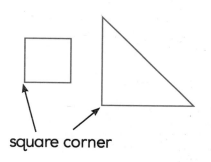

square corner

sticks and circles*

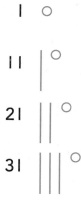

1

11

21

31

*A classroom research-based term developed for *Math Expressions*

Glossary

subtract

$8 - 3 = 5$

subtraction story problem

8 flies are on a log.
6 are eaten by a frog.
How many flies are left?

switch the partners*

 7 + 2

 2 + 7

T

tally mark

Vegetables	Tally Marks	Number
Carrots	ⅢⅠ	5
Corn	ⅢⅠ	4
Peppers	Ⅲ Ⅱ	7

teen number

11 12 13 14 15 16 17 18 19

teen numbers

teen total*

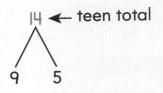

14 ← teen total

9   5

tens

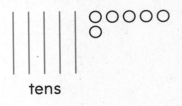

tens

56 has 5 **tens**.

total

$4 + 3 = 7$

total

$\begin{array}{r} 4 \\ + 3 \\ \hline 7 \end{array}$

trapezoid

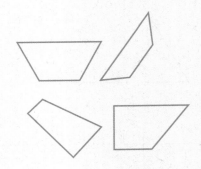

*A classroom research-based term developed for *Math Expressions*

S16 Glossary

triangle

U

unknown partner*

$$4 + \square = 7$$

unknown total*

$$5 \quad 3 \quad 5 + 3 = \square$$

V

vertex

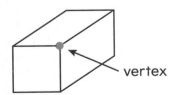

vertex

vertical form

$$\begin{array}{r} 6 \\ + 3 \\ \hline 9 \end{array} \qquad \begin{array}{r} 9 \\ - 3 \\ \hline 6 \end{array}$$

Z

zero

There are **zero** apples on the plate.

*A classroom research-based term developed for *Math Expressions*

1.ARO Algebraic Reasoning and Operations

1.ARO.1	Solve addition and subtraction word problems that involve adding to, putting together, taking from, taking apart, and comparing and have unknown quantities in all positions; represent problems using words, objects, drawings, length-based models (connecting cubes), numerals, number lines, as well as equations with a symbol for the unknown quantity.	Unit 1 Lessons 2, 3, 4, 5, 6, 7, 8; Unit 2 Lessons 1, 2, 3, 4, 6, 8, 10, 11, 12, 13, 14, 15, 16; Unit 3 Lessons 2, 3, 4, 5, 6, 7, 8, 9, 10, 11, 12; Unit 4 Lesson 5; Unit 5 Lessons 1, 2, 3, 4, 5, 11; Unit 6 Lessons 1, 2, 3, 4, 5, 6, 7, 8, 9
1.ARO.2	Solve addition word problems that involve three addends with a sum less than or equal to 20; represent a problem using objects or pictures or other methods, and equations that have a symbol for the unknown quantity.	Unit 5 Lessons 6, 11; Unit 6 Lessons 1, 4, 5, 9
1.ARO.3	Add and subtract applying the properties of operations.	Unit 1 Lessons 3, 4, 5, 6, 7, 8, 9; Unit 2 Lessons 7, 8, 9, 13; Unit 3 Lesson 5; Unit 4 Lessons 5, 10; Unit 5 Lessons 4, 6
1.ARO.4	Understand that a subtraction problem can be thought of as an unknown addend situation.	Unit 3 Lessons 6, 7, 8, 9, 10, 12; Unit 5 Lessons 2, 5, 10
1.ARO.5	Recognize the relationship between addition/subtraction and counting and understand that counting strategies can be used to add and subtract.	Unit 1 Lessons 1, 2, 3, 4, 9; Unit 2 Lessons 5, 6, 7, 8, 9; Unit 3 Lessons 1, 3, 4, 6, 7, 11; Unit 4 Lessons 1, 4, 5, 7, 15, 16, 17; Unit 5 Lessons 1, 2, 4

1.ARO.6	Fluently add and subtract through 10. Know how to add and subtract through 20 using strategies such as: for addition, *count on; make a ten* (example: 7 + 5 = 7 + 3 + 2, so 7 + 3 + 2 = 10 + 2, and 10 + 2 = 12); *make an easier equal sum* (example: 9 + 6 = ?, think 9 + 1 + 5 = 10 + 5, so 10 + 5 = 15; for subtraction, *decompose a number to get ten* (example: 17 − 8 = 17 − 7 − 1, think 17 − 7 = 10 and 10 − 1 = 9); *use a related addition to subtract* (example: if you know 5 + 6 = 11, then you can find 11 − 5 = 6).	Unit 1 Lessons 3, 4, 5, 6, 7, 8, 9; Unit 2 Lessons 1, 2, 3, 5, 6, 7, 8, 9, 10, 11, 12, 13, 14, 15, 16; Unit 3 Lessons 1, 3, 4, 5, 6, 7, 10, 12; Unit 4 Lessons 4, 5, 6, 10, 15; Unit 5 Lessons 1, 2, 3, 4, 5, 10, 11; Unit 6 Lessons 3, 8; Unit 7 Lessons 5, 8, 13; Unit 8 Lesson 5
1.ARO.7	Know the meaning of the equal sign; decide whether or not an equation that involves addition or subtraction is true or false.	Unit 2 Lessons 3, 4, 11, 12, 13, 16; Unit 3 Lesson 12; Unit 5 Lesson 11
1.ARO.8	Find the unknown number in an addition or subtraction equation (examples: 9 + ? = 12; 8 = ? − 5; 7 + 2 = ?).	Unit 1 Lessons 3, 4, 5, 6, 7, 8; Unit 2 Lessons 5, 6, 7, 8, 9, 10, 12, 13, 14, 16; Unit 3 Lessons 3, 4, 5, 6, 7, 8, 9, 11, 12; Unit 4 Lessons 4, 5, 6, 10, 13, 14, 15, 16; Unit 5 Lessons 1, 2, 3, 4, 5, 10; Unit 6 Lessons 6, 7
1.ARO.9	Create simple patterns using objects, pictures, numbers and rules. Identify possible rules to complete or extend patterns. Patterns may be repeating, growing or shrinking. Calculators can be used to create and explore patterns.	Unit 1 Lessons 10, 11; Unit 5 Lesson 9

1.PVO Place Value and Operations

1.PVO.1	Count, with or without objects, forward and backward to 120, starting at any number less than 120. For the number sequence to 120, read and write the corresponding numerals; represent a group of objects with a written numeral, addition and subtraction, pictures, tally marks, number lines and manipulatives, such as bundles of sticks and base 10 blocks. Skip count by 2s, 5s, and 10s.	Unit 4 Lessons 1, 2, 7, 8, 9, 10, 11, 15, 16, 18; Unit 5 Lessons 7, 8, 9; Unit 6 Lessons 4, 5

Mathematical Standards

1.PVO.2	For a two-digit number, understand that the digit to the right represents ones and the digit to the left represents tens.	Unit 4 Lessons 1, 2, 3, 4, 7, 8, 9, 10, 11, 12, 13, 14, 16, 17, 18; Unit 5 Lessons 7, 8, 9; Unit 8 Lesson 1
1.PVO.2.a	Understand that 10 can be thought of as a group of ten ones named *ten*.	Unit 4 Lessons 1, 2, 3, 4, 9, 10, 16, 18; Unit 5 Lessons 8, 10; Unit 8 Lesson 1
1.PVO.2.b	Understand that the numbers 11 through 19 are made up of one ten and one through nine ones.	Unit 4 Lessons 2, 3, 4, 5, 8, 10; Unit 5 Lesson 8
1.PVO.2.c	Know that the decade numbers 10 through 90 represent one through nine tens and zero ones.	Unit 4 Lessons 1, 7, 8, 9, 13, 14, 18; Unit 5 Lesson 10; Unit 8 Lesson 1
1.PVO.3	Apply place value concepts to compare two 2-digit numbers using the symbols >, <, and =.	Unit 4 Lessons 3, 12, 16, 18; Unit 8 Lesson 6
1.PVO.4	Add numbers through 100, such as a two-digit number and a one-digit number or a two-digit number and a multiple of ten. Understand that groups of objects or drawings and strategies can be used to find sums (examples of strategies: *relationship between addition and subtraction, place value, properties of operations*) and explain how the strategy and recorded result are related. Know that to add two-digit numbers, ones are added to ones and tens are added to tens and in some instances, ten ones will result in making one ten.	Unit 4 Lessons 9, 10, 11, 13, 14, 15, 16, 17, 18; Unit 5 Lessons 9, 10, 11; Unit 8 Lessons 1, 2, 3, 4, 5, 6
1.PVO.5	Use mental math to find a number that is 10 more or 10 less than any given two-digit number (without using counting) and explain the reasoning used to find the result.	Unit 5 Lessons 8, 9
1.PVO.6	For numbers 10 through 90, subtract multiples of 10 resulting in differences of 0 through 80. Use groups of objects or pictures and strategies to subtract. Strategies can include place value concepts, the relationship between addition and subtraction, and properties of operations. Explain how the strategy and recorded result are related.	Unit 5 Lessons 9, 10, 11; Unit 8 Lesson 6

1.MDA Measurement and Data Analysis

1.MDA.1	Compare to order three items by length. Compare the lengths of two items using a third item (indirect comparison).	Unit 7 Lessons 12, 14
1.MDA.2	Determine the length of an object by placing as many same-size smaller units end-to-end as needed along the span of the object ensuring no gaps or overlaps. Understand that length of the object is the number of same-size units that were used. (Note: The number of "length-units" should not extend beyond the end of the object being measured.)	Unit 7 Lessons 13, 14
1.MDA.3	Use analog and digital clocks to express time orally and in written form in hours and half-hours.	Unit 7 Lessons 1, 2, 3, 4, 5, 14
1.MDA.4	Organize, represent, and interpret data with up to three categories using picture graphs, bar graphs, and tally charts. Ask questions and provide answers about how many in all comprise the data and how many are in each category. Compare the number in one category to that in another category.	Unit 6 Lessons 1, 2, 3, 4, 5, 9
1.MDA.5	Recognize and identify coins (penny, nickel, dime, and quarter) and their value and use the ¢ (cent) symbol appropriately.	Unit 2 Lesson 7; Unit 4, Lessons 8, 19, 20
1.MDA.6	Know the comparative values of all U.S. coins (e.g. a dime is of greater value than a nickel). Find equivalent values (e.g., a nickel is equivalent to 5 pennies.) Solve problems and use the values of the coins in the solutions of the problems.	Unit 2 Lesson 7; Unit 4 Lessons 8, 19, 20
1.MDA.7	Explore dimes and pennies as they relate to place value concepts.	Unit 4 Lessons 8, 19, 20

1.GSR Geometry and Spatial Reasoning

1.GSR.1	Understand the difference between defining attributes of a figure (examples: a square has 4 sides of equal length and 4 vertices) and non-defining attributes (examples: size, color, position). Using concrete materials and paper and pencil, build and draw geometric figures according to their defining attributes.	Unit 7 Lessons 6, 7, 8, 9, 10
1.GSR.2	Create composite geometric figures by putting together two-dimensional figures (triangles, squares, rectangles, trapezoids, half-circles, and quarter-circles) or three-dimensional figures (cubes, rectangular prisms, cylinders, and cones), then form a new figure from the composite figure.	Unit 7 Lessons 9, 10, 11
1.GSR.3	Separate rectangles and circles into two or four equal shares, and use the words *halves, fourths,* and *quarters,* and the phrases *half of, fourth of,* and *quarter of* to identify the equal-size shares. Use the terms "two of" or "four of" to describe the number of equal shares in the whole. Understand that when a figure is separated into more equal shares, the size of the shares is smaller.	Unit 7 Lessons 8, 9, 14

Mathematical Processes and Practices

MPP1

Problem Solving

Unit 1 Lessons 2, 3, 4, 6, 8, 9, 10, 11
Unit 2 Lessons 1, 2, 3, 4, 6, 7, 8, 9, 10, 13, 14, 16
Unit 3 Lessons 1, 2, 3, 4, 6, 7, 8, 9, 10, 11, 12
Unit 4 Lessons 2, 3, 5, 10, 18, 19, 20
Unit 5 Lessons 1, 2, 3, 4, 5, 6, 9, 11
Unit 6 Lessons 1, 2, 4, 5, 6, 7, 8, 9
Unit 7 Lessons 8, 12, 14
Unit 8 Lessons 1, 3, 4, 6

MPP2

Abstract and Quantitative Reasoning

Unit 1 Lessons 3, 4, 5, 6, 7, 8, 9
Unit 2 Lessons 1, 2, 3, 4, 6, 10, 11, 12, 13, 15, 16
Unit 3 Lessons 3, 5, 6, 12
Unit 4 Lessons 1, 3, 4, 6, 7, 8, 9, 10, 11, 12, 14, 15, 16, 17, 18, 19
Unit 5 Lessons 1, 2, 3, 4, 5, 9, 10, 11
Unit 6 Lessons 1, 2, 3, 5, 6, 8, 9
Unit 7 Lessons 8, 9, 14
Unit 8 Lessons 1, 2, 3, 4, 5, 6

MPP3

Use and Evaluate Logical Reasoning

Unit 1 Lessons 1, 2, 3, 4, 5, 6, 7, 8, 9, 10
Unit 2 Lessons 1, 2, 3, 4, 6, 7, 8, 9, 10, 11, 12, 13, 14, 16
Unit 3 Lessons 2, 3, 4, 6, 7, 8, 9, 10, 11, 12
Unit 4 Lessons 1, 2, 3, 4, 5, 6, 7, 8, 9, 10, 11, 12, 13, 14, 15, 16, 17, 18, 19, 20
Unit 5 Lessons 1, 2, 3, 4, 5, 6, 7, 8, 9, 10, 11
Unit 6 Lessons 1, 2, 3, 4, 5, 6, 7, 8, 9
Unit 7 Lessons 1, 2, 3, 4, 5, 6, 7, 8, 9, 10, 11, 12, 13, 14
Unit 8 Lessons 1, 2, 3, 4, 5, 6

MPP4

Mathematical Modeling

Unit 1 Lessons 2, 3, 9
Unit 2 Lessons 1, 2, 6, 10, 13, 16
Unit 3 Lessons 1, 2, 5, 6, 7, 8, 9, 10, 11, 12
Unit 4 Lessons 2, 3, 4, 5, 10, 18, 19, 20
Unit 5 Lessons 1, 2, 3, 4, 6, 8, 9, 11
Unit 6 Lessons 2, 3, 4, 5, 6, 7, 8, 9
Unit 7 Lessons 3, 8, 12, 14
Unit 8 Lessons 1, 2, 3, 6

MPP5

Use Mathematical Tools

Unit 1 Lessons 1, 2, 3, 4, 5, 6, 7, 8, 9
Unit 2 Lessons 5, 6, 7, 8, 16
Unit 3 Lessons 1, 2, 3, 4, 7, 11
Unit 4 Lessons 1, 2, 3, 4, 5, 6, 7, 8, 9, 10, 11, 12, 13, 14, 16, 17, 18, 19
Unit 5 Lessons 1, 2, 6, 7, 8, 9, 10, 11
Unit 6 Lessons 3, 4, 5, 8, 9
Unit 7 Lessons 1, 2, 5, 6, 7, 8, 9, 10, 11, 12, 13, 14
Unit 8 Lessons 2, 3, 6

MPP6

Use Precise Mathematical Language

Unit 1 Lessons 1, 2, 3, 4, 5, 6, 7, 8, 9, 10
Unit 2 Lessons 1, 3, 4, 5, 6, 7, 8, 9, 10, 11, 12, 13, 14, 16
Unit 3 Lessons 1, 2, 3, 4, 5, 6, 7, 8, 9, 10, 11, 12
Unit 4 Lessons 1, 2, 3, 4, 5, 6, 7, 8, 9, 10, 11, 12, 13, 14, 15, 16, 17, 18, 19, 20
Unit 5 Lessons 1, 2, 3, 4, 5, 6, 7, 8, 9, 10, 11
Unit 6 Lessons 1, 2, 3, 4, 5, 6, 7, 8, 9
Unit 7 Lessons 1, 2, 3, 4, 5, 6, 7, 8, 9, 10, 11, 12, 13, 14
Unit 8 Lessons 1, 2, 3, 4, 5, 6

MPP7

See Structure

Unit 1 Lessons 1, 2, 3, 4, 5, 6, 7, 8, 9, 10, 11
Unit 2 Lessons 13, 14, 16
Unit 3 Lessons 1, 3, 9, 12
Unit 4 Lessons 1, 2, 3, 5, 6, 7, 8, 9, 10,13, 17, 18, 19
Unit 5 Lessons 1, 2, 3, 5, 6, 7, 8, 9, 10, 11
Unit 6 Lessons 6, 8, 9
Unit 7 Lessons 1, 2, 3, 4, 5, 6, 7, 9, 10, 11, 14
Unit 8 Lessons 2, 6

MPP8

Generalize

Unit 1 Lessons 1, 2, 3, 4, 5, 6, 7, 8, 9
Unit 2 Lessons 6, 7, 8, 11, 14, 16
Unit 3 Lessons 8, 9, 12
Unit 4 Lessons 1, 2, 5, 6, 7, 9, 10, 12, 13, 14, 15, 17, 18
Unit 5 Lessons 1, 2, 4, 5, 6, 7, 8, 9, 10, 11
Unit 6 Lessons 1, 6, 7, 9
Unit 7 Lessons 3, 6, 7, 8, 9, 10, 12, 14
Unit 8 Lessons 1, 2, 4, 6

Index

B

C

D

Less than, 191–192, 202, 376

Longest, 347–348

M

Make-a-Ten strategy, 229, 235–236, 239

Manipulatives
clock for "busy day" book, 315
count-on cards, 71–72, 113–114, 125–126
Make-a-Ten cards
    addition, 165–168, 225–228
    subtraction, 231–234
number cards, 9–10
Number Quilt, 73, 115, 139
Secret Code cards, 187–188
Stair Steps, 5–6, 8
student clock, 311
triangle grid, 339
two-dimensional shape set, 325–328

Math Mountains, 19, 21, 23, 25, 26–27, 50, 108, 119–120, 138, 142

Measurement. *See also* **Time.**
length, 349–352
with length units, 351–352

Money
coin stories, 213–214
dimes, 179, 181–182, 209, 211–213
nickels, 67, 69–70, 209, 211–213
pennies, 67, 69–70, 179, 181–182, 209, 211–213
quarters, 209, 211–213
story problems, 214

More, 275

Most, 276

N

Nickel, 67, 69–70, 209, 211–223

Number line, 253

Number partners
of 2 through 5, 19–20
of 6, 21–22
of 7, 23–24
of 8, 25–26
of 9, 27–28
of 10, 29–30
unknowns, 107–108, 115, 117–120, 229–230

Number patterns
of addition, 20, 23–24, 26, 28, 30, 195–198
with doubles, 30
growing, 37
with numbers, 36
in partners, 22, 23
repeating, 35–36
shrinking, 38
of tens, 255–260
with zero, 30

Numbers. *See also* **Teen numbers.**
comparing using place value, 191–192
five-groups, 11–12, 275–276
greater, 65–66, 76
on a number line, 253
one through ten, 7–8
representations of, 175–176, 183–185, 189–190, 254
teens, 157–158, 161–162
ten more or ten less, 254
through 120, 251–252
two-digit, 199–204

Number words, 177–178

Index

Repeating pattern, 35–36

Rows, 31, 252

S

Shapes
  2-dimensional, 325–328, 338, 340
    circles, 331–332
    rectangles, 329–330, 337, 340
    squares, 329–330, 337
    triangles, 331–332, 337, 340
  3-dimensional, 341–344
    cones, 341–342
    cubes, 341–342
    cylinders, 341–342
    rectangular prisms, 341–342
    spheres, 341–342
  building and drawing, 337, 343–344
  composing, 338, 340, 343–344
  equal shares of, 336
  fourths of, 335
  halves of, 333, 335
  names of, 341–342
  sorting, 330

Shortest, 347–348

Shrinking pattern, 37–38

Sides, 329

Skip-counting
  by tens, 155–156, 247, 248
  by twos, 38

Solution Methods, 61–62

Sort, 273, 278, 280, 285
  shapes, 330

Spheres, 341–342

Squares, 329–330, 337

Stair Steps, 5–6, 8

Story problems, 95–96, 129–130, 133–138, 141, 237–238, 262, 289
  addition, 109–110, 230
  equations for, 87
  more and fewer, 289–294
  subtraction, 87, 109, 123–124, 127–130
  using pictures, 94
  with various unknowns, 241
  writing, 94
  writing equations for, 143–144

Subtraction. *See also* **Story problems.**
  within 10, 20, 22, 24, 25, 27, 29, 81–86, 124, 127–128
  circle drawings for, 85–86
  with drawings and equations, 83–84
  games, 127–128
  generating problems, 87–88
  multiples of ten, 255–256, 259–260
  partners of, 128
  practice, 85–86, 141–142
  practice with equations, 93–94
  problem solving, 137–138
  relating to addition, 91–92, 133–136
  representation of, 81–82
  strategies
    crossing out, 81–82
    Make-a-Ten, 236
  with teen numbers, 235–238
  tens, 255–256
  true or false equations, 87–88
  vertical forms, 92–93

T

Tally mark, 285–286

Teen numbers
  addition of, 163–164
  exploring, 157–158
  modeling, 161–162
  representation of, 158, 161–162

© Houghton Mifflin Harcourt Publishing Company

Index

Illustrator: Josh Brill

Did you ever try to use shapes to draw animals like the frog on the cover?

Over the last 10 years Josh has been using geometric shapes to design his animals. His aim is to keep the animal drawings simple and use color to make them appealing.

Add some color to the frog Josh drew. Then try drawing a cat or dog or some other animal using the shapes below.

Shape Toolbox

math
expressions

Dr. Karen C. Fuson

HMH

Watch the frog come alive in its pond as you discover and solve math challenges.

Download the *Math Worlds AR* app available on Android or iOS devices.

Grade 1

Volume 1

This material is based upon work supported by the
National Science Foundation
under Grant Numbers
ESI-9816320, REC-9806020, and RED-935373.

Any opinions, findings, and conclusions, or recommendations expressed in this material
are those of the author and do not necessarily reflect the views of the National Science Foundation.

BIG IDEA 3 - Find and Create Patterns

© Houghton Mifflin Harcourt Publishing Company

BIG IDEA 3 - Mixed Story Problems

Dear Family:

Your child is learning math in an innovative program that interweaves abstract mathematical concepts with the everyday experiences of children. This helps children to understand math better.

In this program, your child will learn math and have fun by

- working with objects and making drawings of math situations
- working with other children and sharing problem-solving strategies with them
- writing and solving problems and connecting math to daily life
- helping classmates learn

Your child will have homework almost every day. He or she needs a **Homework Helper.** The helper may be anyone—you, an older brother or sister (or other family member), a neighbor, or a friend. Make a specific time for homework and provide your child with a quiet place to work (for example, no TV). Encourage your child to talk about what is happening in math class.

In Lessons 1 and 2, your child will learn to see numbers as a group of 5 and extra ones. Making mental pictures by grouping units in this way will later help your child add and subtract quickly. Children benefit greatly from learning to "see" numbers without counting every unit.

- -

Please fill out the following and return it to the teacher.

My child _____ will have _____ as his or her
　　　　　　　(child's name)　　　　　　　　　　　　　　(Homework Helper's name)

Homework Helper. This person is my child's _____.
　　　　　　　　　　　　　　　　　　　　　(relationship to child)

Children start exploring these 5-groups by looking at dots arranged in a row of 5 plus some extra ones. Below are samples that show the numbers from 6 through 10.

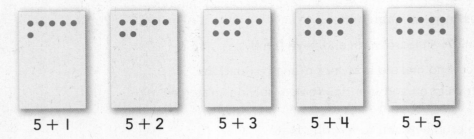

5 + 1   5 + 2   5 + 3   5 + 4   5 + 5

The teacher gives the children a number and asks them to say it as a 5 plus extra ones. Children say the numbers in order at first. Later they can "see" the quantities even when the numbers are shown randomly.

On some homework pages, you will find instructions that ask children to "see the 5." Your child is being encouraged to make a mental picture of a number that contains a 5-group. Later, the children will be asked to see groups of 10 by combining two 5-groups. This will help them learn place value.

It takes repeated exposure to such groups for children to see the numbers quickly. Many of the visual aids in your child's classroom include 5-groups. Children tend to absorb these visual patterns without realizing it.

If you have any questions or if your child is having problems with math, please contact me.

Sincerely,
Your child's teacher

Estimada familia:

Su niño está aprendiendo matemáticas con un programa innovador que relaciona conceptos matemáticos abstractos con la experiencia diaria de los niños. Esto ayuda a los niños a entender mejor las matemáticas.

Con este programa, su niño aprenderá matemáticas y se divertirá mientras:

- trabaja con objetos y hace dibujos de problemas matemáticos;
- trabaja con otros niños y comparte estrategias para resolver problemas;
- escribe y resuelve problemas y relaciona las matemáticas con la vida diaria;
- ayuda a sus compañeros a aprender.

Su niño tendrá tarea casi todos los días y necesita a una persona que lo ayude con la tarea. Esa persona puede ser usted, un hermano mayor (u otro familiar), un vecino o un amigo. Establezca una hora para la tarea y ofrezca a su niño un lugar tranquilo donde trabajar (por ejemplo un lugar sin TV). Anime a su niño a comentar lo que está aprendiendo en la clase de matemáticas.

En las Lecciones 1 y 2, su niño aprenderá a ver los números como un grupo de 5 más otras unidades. El hecho de agrupar mentalmente unidades de esa manera ayudará a su niño a sumar y restar rápidamente en el futuro. Los niños se benefician muchísimo de aprender a "ver" los números sin contar cada unidad.

- -

Por favor complete la siguiente información y devuelva este formulario al maestro.

La persona que ayudará a mi niño _____ es
(nombre del niño)

_____ . Esta persona es _____ de mi niño.
(nombre de la persona)   (relación con el niño)

Los niños comienzan a practicar con estos grupos de 5 observando puntos distribuidos en una fila de 5 más otras unidades. Estos ejemplos muestran los números del 6 al 10.

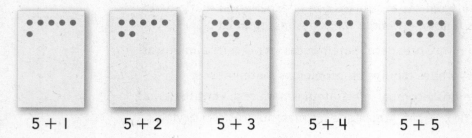

El maestro les da un número a los niños y les pide que lo digan como 5 más otras unidades. Al principio, los niños dicen los números en orden. Más adelante pueden "ver" las cantidades incluso cuando los números se muestran sin un orden específico.

En algunas páginas de tarea hallará instrucciones que piden a los niños "ver el número 5". A su niño se le está animando a que visualice un número que contenga un grupo de 5. Más adelante, se les pedirá que vean grupos de 10, combinando dos grupos de 5. Esto les ayudará a aprender el valor posicional.

Es necesario que los niños practiquen muchas veces los grupos de este tipo para que puedan llegar a ver los números rápidamente. Muchas de las ayudas visuales que hay en el salón de clase incluyen grupos de 5. Los niños tienden a absorber estos patrones visuales sin darse cuenta.

Si tiene alguna pregunta o algún comentario, por favor comuníquese conmigo.

Atentamente,
El maestro de su niño

doubles

repeating
pattern

growing
pattern

shrinking
pattern

pattern

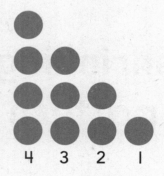

$4 + 4 = 8$

Both partners are the same. They are **doubles**.

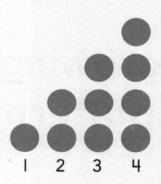

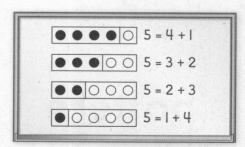

The partners of a number show a **pattern**.

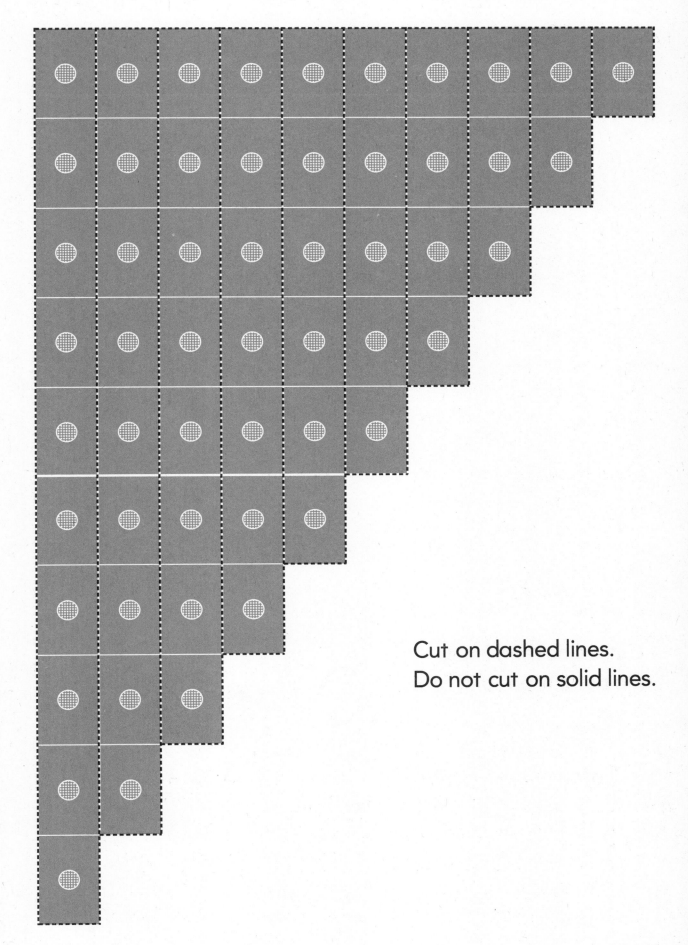

Cut on dashed lines.
Do not cut on solid lines.

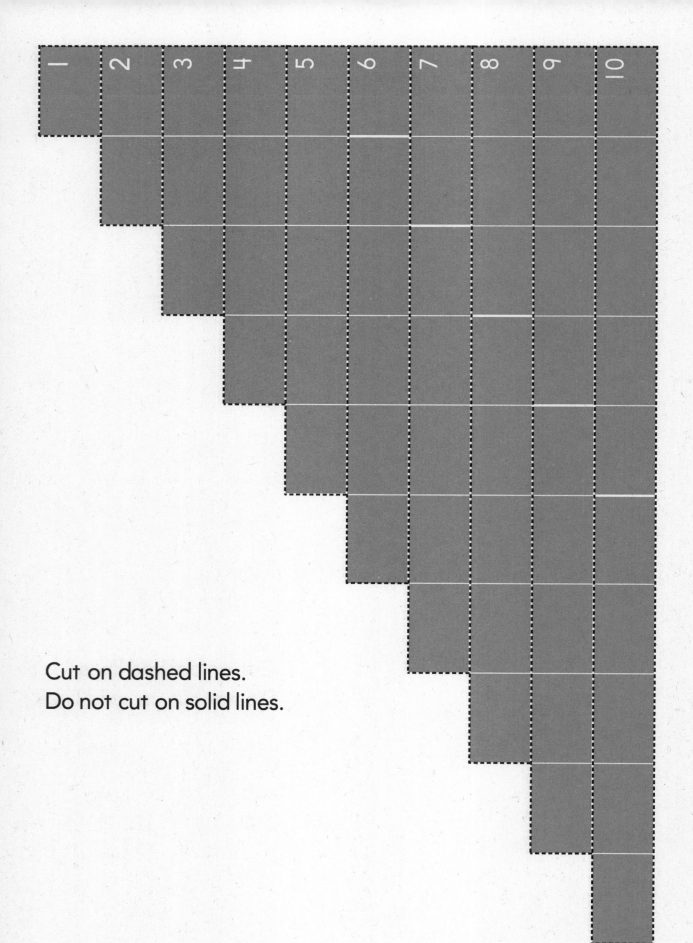

Cut on dashed lines.
Do not cut on solid lines.

Stair Steps

Write how many dots.

1 and 1 more is _____.

3 and 1 more is _____.

5 and 1 more is _____.

 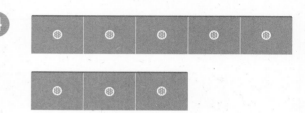

5 and 3 more is _____.

5 and 4 more is _____.

6

5 and 5 more is _____.

 7 5 crows in a row
and 4 below.
How many crows?

_____ crows

 5 in a row ⟵

4 below ⟶

Solve.

8 Chen says 5 and 4 more is 7.
Help Chen find the error.

Draw to explain.

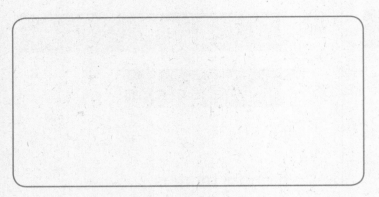

5 and 4 more is ☐.

9 Use a 5-group to find how many.
Write the numbers.

_____ and 3 more is _____.

Draw to explain.

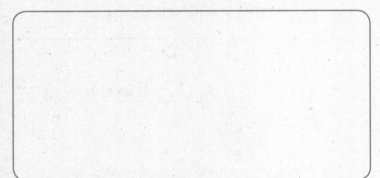

✓ **Check Understanding**
Explain how to use Stair Steps to show 6 as a
5-group and extra ones.

6	1
7	2
8	3
9	4
10	5

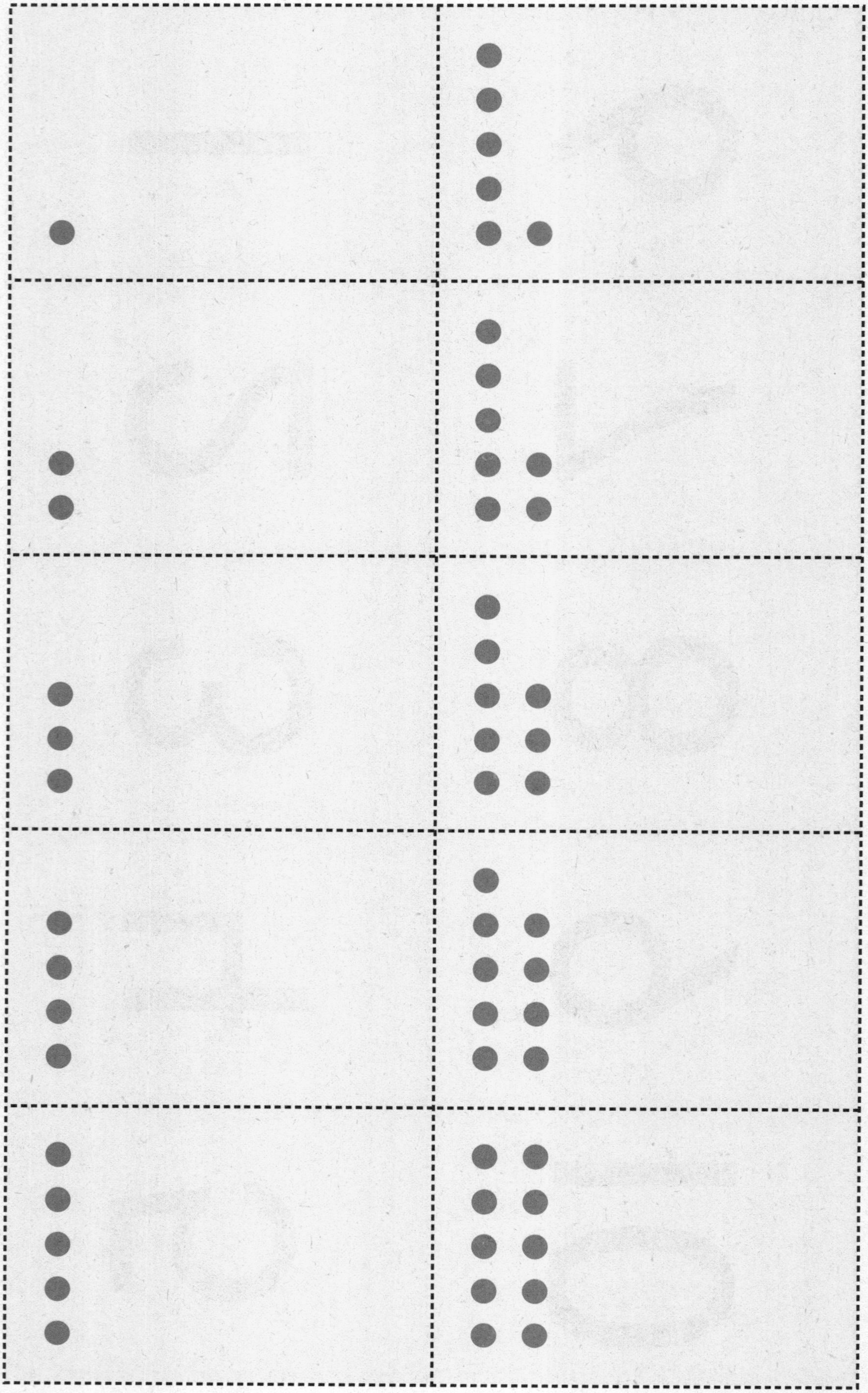

Circle the 5-group. Write how many dots.

1

☐

2

☐

3 ● ● ● ● ●
● ● ● ● ●

☐

4

☐

5 ● ● ● ● ●
● ● ● ● ●

☐

6

☐

7 Match the dots to 5 plus extra ones.

● ● ● ● ●
● ● ● ● •   • **5 + 1**

● ● ● ● ●
● ● ● •   • **5 + 3**

● ● ● ● ●
● ● ● ● ● •   • **5 + 4**

● ● ● ● ●
● •   • **5 + 2**

● ● ● ● ●
● ● •   • **5 + 5**

8 Draw a 5-group and extra ones to show 6.

9 Draw a 5-group and extra ones to show 9.

10 Create a story for 7. Draw a 5-group and extra ones to show your story.

_____

_____

_____

_____

✓ **Check Understanding**

Show numbers 6 through 10 as 5-groups and extra ones.

Visualize Numbers as a 5-Group and Ones

See the 5-group.
Draw extra dots to show the number.

1 8

2 10

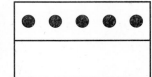

See the 5 in each group.
Write how many dots.

3

4

5

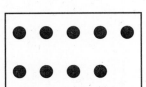

1 Show 9 with a 5-group and extra ones.

2 Use words or pictures to tell a story for 9.

Dear Family:

Your child is learning to find the smaller numbers that are "hiding" inside a larger number. He or she will be participating in activities that will help him or her master addition, subtraction, and equation building.

To make the concepts clear, this program uses some special vocabulary and materials that we would like to share. Below are two important terms that your child is learning:

- **Partners:** Partners are two numbers that can be put together to make a larger number. For example, 2 and 5 are partners that go together to make the number 7.
- **Break Apart:** Children can "break apart" a larger number to form two smaller numbers. Your child is using objects and drawings to explore ways of "breaking apart" numbers of ten or less.

Partners of 7

Children can discover the break-aparts of a number with circle drawings. They first draw the "Break-Apart Stick" and then color the circles to show the different partners, as shown below. Sometimes they also write the partners on a special partner train, which is also shown below.

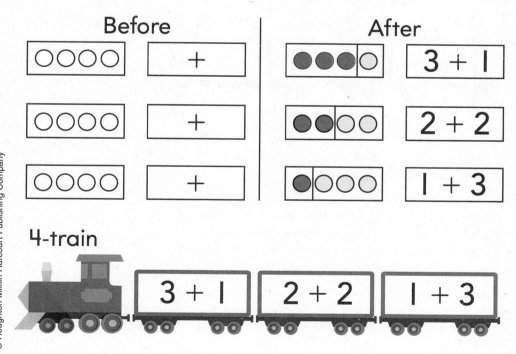

Later, children will discover that partners can change places without changing the total. This concept is called "switch the partners." Once children understand switching partners, they can find the break-aparts of a number more quickly. They simply switch each pair of partners as they discover them.

Shown below are the break-aparts and switched partners of the number 7. Sometimes children also write this information on a double-decker train.

Break-Aparts of 7

 | 6 + 1 | or | 1 + 6 |

 | 5 + 2 | or | 2 + 5 |

 | 4 + 3 | or | 3 + 4 |

Double-Decker Train

7-train

| 6 + 1 | 5 + 2 | 4 + 3 |
| 1 + 6 | 2 + 5 | 3 + 4 |

You will see the circle drawings and the partner trains on your child's math homework. Be ready to offer help if it is needed. Children are doing these activities in class, but they may still need help at home.

Children are introduced to patterns later in the unit. Working with patterns helps children develop an understanding of mathematical relationships. They learn to identify, extend, and complete repeating, growing, and shrinking patterns. Ask your child to look for different patterns around them. For example, they may find patterns on clothing, furniture, or rugs.

If you have any questions or problems, please contact me.

Sincerely,
Your child's teacher

Estimada familia:

Su niño está aprendiendo a hallar los números más pequeños que están "escondidos" dentro de un número más grande. Va a participar en actividades que le ayudarán a dominar la suma, la resta y la formación de ecuaciones.

Para clarificar los conceptos, este programa usa un vocabulario especial y algunos materiales que nos gustaría mostrarle. A continuación hay dos términos importantes que su niño está aprendiendo:

- **Partes:** Partes son dos números que se pueden unir para formar un número más grande. Por ejemplo, 2 y 5 son partes que se unen para formar el número 7.

- **Separar:** Los niños pueden "separar" un número más grande para formar dos números más pequeños. Su niño está usando objetos y dibujos para explorar maneras de "separar" números iguales o menores que diez.

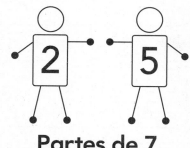

Partes de 7

Los niños pueden separar un número usando dibujos de círculos. Primero dibujan un "palito de separación" y luego colorean los círculos para indicar las partes, como se muestra a continuación. A veces los niños anotan las partes en un tren de partes especial, que también se muestra a continuación.

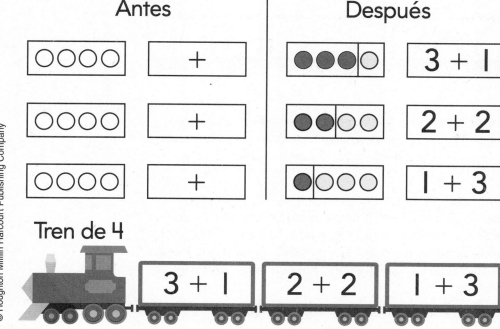

Luego, los niños van a aprender que las partes pueden intercambiar su posición sin que varíe el total. Este concepto se llama "cambiar el orden de las partes". Una vez que los niños entienden el cambio del orden de las partes, pueden encontrar las partes de un número con más rapidez. Sencillamente cambian cada par de partes a medida que las encuentran.

A continuación están las partes, y las partes en otro orden, del número 7. A veces los niños escriben esta información en un tren de dos pisos.

Partes de 7

●●●●●●●○	6 + 1 y	1 + 6
●●●●●○○	5 + 2 y	2 + 5
●●●●○○○	4 + 3 y	3 + 4

Tren de dos pisos

Tren de 7

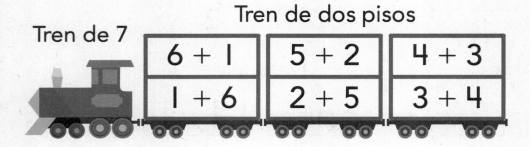

6 + 1	5 + 2	4 + 3
1 + 6	2 + 5	3 + 4

Usted verá los dibujos de los círculos y los trenes de partes en la tarea de matemáticas de su niño. Ayúdelo, si es necesario. Los niños están haciendo estas actividades en clase, pero es posible que aún así necesiten ayuda en casa.

Más adelante en la unidad se les presentarán a los niños los patrones. Trabajar con patrones ayuda a los niños a desarrollar la comprensión de la relación matemática. Aprenden a identificar, ampliar y completar los patrones que se repiten, aumentan y disminuyen. Pida a su niño que busque patrones diferentes a su alrededor. Por ejemplo, pueden hallar patrones en ropa, muebles o alfombras.

Si tiene preguntas o dudas, por favor comuníquese conmigo.

Atentamente,
El maestro de su niño

Name _____

Write the partners.

 5 = 4 + 1

5 =

5 =

5 =

 4 = 3 + 1

4 =

4 =

 3 = 2 + 1

3 =

 2 =

5

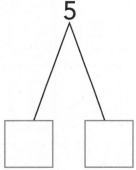

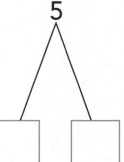

6

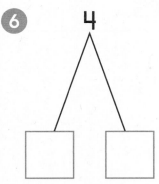

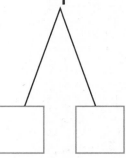

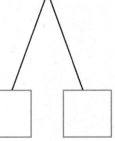

Use **patterns** to solve.

VOCABULARY
patterns

7 2 + 0 = ☐   5 + 0 = ☐   3 + 0 = ☐

   4 + 0 = ☐   1 + 0 = ☐   0 + 3 = ☐

   0 + 5 = ☐   0 + 2 = ☐   0 + 4 = ☐

8 4 + 1 = ☐   2 + 1 = ☐   3 + 1 = ☐

   1 + 1 = ☐   1 + 4 = ☐   1 + 3 = ☐

9 2 + 2 = ☐   3 + 2 = ☐   1 + 2 = ☐

10 2 − 0 = ☐   4 − 1 = ☐   3 − 2 = ☐

✔ Check Understanding
Make circle drawings for all the partners of 5.

© Houghton Mifflin Harcourt Publishing Company

Name _____

1 Show and write the 6-partners.

⬭〇〇〇〇〇〇 ___ + ___   6 = _____

⬭〇〇〇〇〇〇 ___ + ___   6 = _____

⬭〇〇〇〇〇〇 ___ + ___   6 = _____

⬭〇〇〇〇〇〇 ___ + ___   6 = _____

⬭〇〇〇〇〇〇 ___ + ___   6 = _____

2 Write the 6-partners.

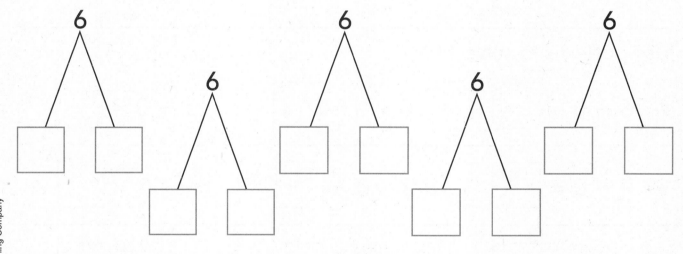

3 Write the 6-partners as a train.

6-train

▢ + ▢ + ▢ + ▢ + ▢ +

4 Discuss patterns in the partners.

2	**3**	**4**	**5**	**6**
1 + 1	2 + 1	3 + 1	4 + 1	5 + 1
		2 + 2	3 + 2	4 + 2
				3 + 3

Use **doubles** to solve.

5 3 + 3 = ☐   1 + 1 = ☐   2 + 2 = ☐

6 – 3 = ☐   2 – 1 = ☐   4 – 2 = ☐

Use patterns to solve.

6 6 + 0 = ☐   0 + 4 = ☐   1 + 0 = ☐

7 4 – 0 = ☐   2 – 0 = ☐   6 – 0 = ☐

8 3 – 3 = ☐   5 – 5 = ☐   1 – 1 = ☐

4 – 4 = ☐   2 – 2 = ☐   6 – 6 = ☐

 Check Understanding

Write all the partners of 6.

___ + ___ , ___ + ___ , ___ + ___ , ___ + ___ , ___ + ___

Name _____

Show the 7-partners and switch the partners.

1 ⬜ ○○○○○○○   ___ + ___   and   ___ + ___

2 ⬜ ○○○○○○○   ___ + ___   and   ___ + ___

3 ⬜ ○○○○○○○   ___ + ___   and   ___ + ___

Write the partners and the switched partners.

4   7-train

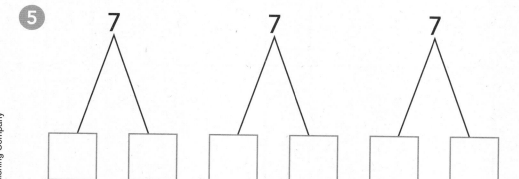

| + | + | + |
| + | + | + |

5

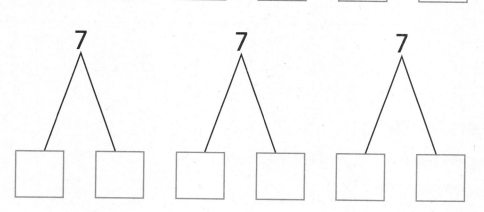

7 ╱╲ ⬜ ⬜   7 ╱╲ ⬜ ⬜   7 ╱╲ ⬜ ⬜

7 ╱╲ ⬜ ⬜   7 ╱╲ ⬜ ⬜   7 ╱╲ ⬜ ⬜

6 Discuss patterns in the partners.

2	**3**	**4**	**5**	**6**	**7**
1 + 1	2 + 1	3 + 1	4 + 1	5 + 1	6 + 1
		2 + 2	3 + 2	4 + 2	5 + 2
				3 + 3	4 + 3

Use patterns to solve.

7 $3 + 1 =$ ☐ $6 + 1 =$ ☐ $4 + 1 =$ ☐

  $5 + 1 =$ ☐ $2 + 1 =$ ☐ $1 + 1 =$ ☐

8 $1 + 2 =$ ☐ $1 + 5 =$ ☐ $1 + 4 =$ ☐

  $1 + 3 =$ ☐ $1 + 6 =$ ☐ $1 + 1 =$ ☐

9 $7 - 1 =$ ☐ $3 - 1 =$ ☐ $5 - 1 =$ ☐

  $4 - 1 =$ ☐ $6 - 1 =$ ☐ $2 - 1 =$ ☐

10 $5 - 4 =$ ☐ $7 - 6 =$ ☐ $3 - 2 =$ ☐

✓ **Check Understanding**

Explain the pattern you see when you switch the partners for 7.

Name _____

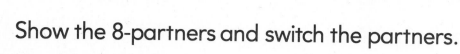

Show the 8-partners and switch the partners.

1  ____ + ____ and ____ + ____

2 ⬭⬭⬭⬭⬭⬭⬭⬭ ____ + ____ and ____ + ____

3 ⬭⬭⬭⬭⬭⬭⬭⬭ ____ + ____ and ____ + ____

4 ⬭⬭⬭⬭⬭⬭⬭⬭ ____ + ____ and ____ + ____

Write the partners and the switched partners.

5 8-train

 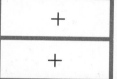  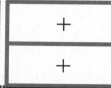

6

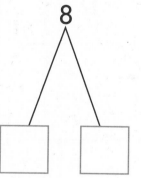 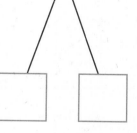 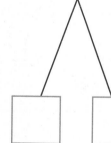 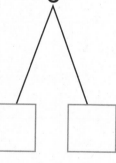

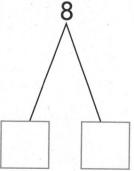 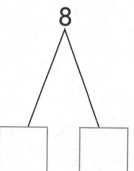 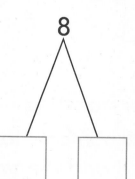 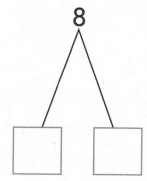

7 Discuss patterns in the partners.

2	**3**	**4**	**5**	**6**	**7**	**8**
1 + 1	2 + 1	3 + 1	4 + 1	5 + 1	6 + 1	7 + 1
		2 + 2	3 + 2	4 + 2	5 + 2	6 + 2
				3 + 3	4 + 3	5 + 3
						4 + 4

Use doubles to solve.

8 $4 + 4 = \square$ $3 + 3 = \square$ $2 + 2 = \square$

$8 - 4 = \square$ $6 - 3 = \square$ $4 - 2 = \square$

Use patterns to solve.

9 $8 + 0 = \square$ $6 + 0 = \square$ $7 + 0 = \square$

10 $7 - 0 = \square$ $2 - 0 = \square$ $8 - 0 = \square$

11 $4 - 4 = \square$ $6 - 6 = \square$ $2 - 2 = \square$

✓ **Check Understanding**

Draw Math Mountains to show the partners for 8 and the switched partners.

Name _____

Show the 9-partners and switch the partners.

1 ⬜ ○○○○○○○○○   ___ + ___   and   ___ + ___

2 ⬜ ○○○○○○○○○   ___ + ___   and   ___ + ___

3 ⬜ ○○○○○○○○○   ___ + ___   and   ___ + ___

4 ⬜ ○○○○○○○○○   ___ + ___   and   ___ + ___

Write the partners and the switched partners.

5   9-train

6

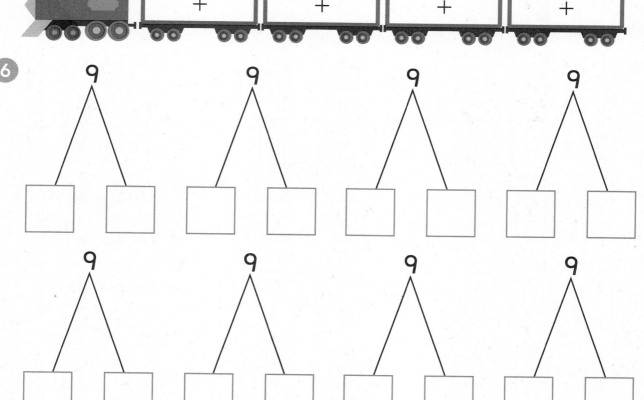

7 Discuss patterns in the partners.

2	**3**	**4**	**5**	**6**	**7**	**8**	**9**
1 + 1	2 + 1	3 + 1	4 + 1	5 + 1	6 + 1	7 + 1	8 + 1
	2 + 2	3 + 2	4 + 2	5 + 2	6 + 2	7 + 2
		3 + 3	4 + 3	5 + 3	6 + 3	7 + 2
			4 + 4	5 + 4	6 + 3
					5 + 4

© Houghton Mifflin Harcourt Publishing Company

Use patterns to solve.

8 6 + 1 = ☐   8 + 1 = ☐

4 + 1 = ☐   3 + 1 = ☐

9 1 + 7 = ☐   1 + 2 = ☐

1 + 8 = ☐   1 + 4 = ☐

10 9 − 1 = ☐   3 − 1 = ☐

7 − 1 = ☐   6 − 1 = ☐

11 9 − 8 = ☐   3 − 2 = ☐

7 − 6 = ☐   6 − 5 = ☐

✓ **Check Understanding**

Write all the partners of 9 and the switched partners. ___ + ___ , ___ + ___ , ___ + ___ ,

___ + ___ , ___ + ___ , ___ + ___ , ___ + ___ , ___ + ___ ,

Name _____

1 Discuss patterns.

Partners of 10

9 + 1   8 + 2   7 + 3   6 + 4   5 + 5

1 + 9   2 + 8   3 + 7   4 + 6

Write the 10-partners.

2

10 = 9 + 1

10 = 8 + 2

10 = _____

10 = _____

10 = _____

10 = _____

10 = _____

10 = _____

10 = _____

3

10

9 + 1

_____

_____

_____

_____

4 Discuss patterns.

Patterns with Partners

2	3	4	5	6	7	8	9	10
1+1	2+1	3+1	4+1	5+1	6+1	7+1	8+1	9+1
	2+2	3+2	4+2	5+2	6+2	7+2	8+2	
		3+3	4+3	5+3	6+3	7+3		
			4+4	5+4	6+4			
				5+5				

Patterns with Zero

1 + 0 = 1	1 − 0 = 1	1 − 1 = 0
2 + 0 = 2	2 − 0 = 2	2 − 2 = 0
3 + 0 = 3	3 − 0 = 3	3 − 3 = 0
4 + 0 = 4	4 − 0 = 4	4 − 4 = 0
5 + 0 = 5	5 − 0 = 5	5 − 5 = 0
6 + 0 = 6	6 − 0 = 6	6 − 6 = 0
7 + 0 = 7	7 − 0 = 7	7 − 7 = 0
8 + 0 = 8	8 − 0 = 8	8 − 8 = 0
9 + 0 = 9	9 − 0 = 9	9 − 9 = 0
10 + 0 = 10	10 − 0 = 10	10 − 10 = 0

Patterns with Doubles

1 + 1 = 2
2 + 2 = 4
3 + 3 = 6
4 + 4 = 8
5 + 5 = 10

Check Understanding

Write the partners of 10 and the switched partners of 10.

Partners of 10

Name _____

Write the number of band members in each column or row.

1

____ ____ ____ ____ ____ ____ ____ ____ ____ ____

2

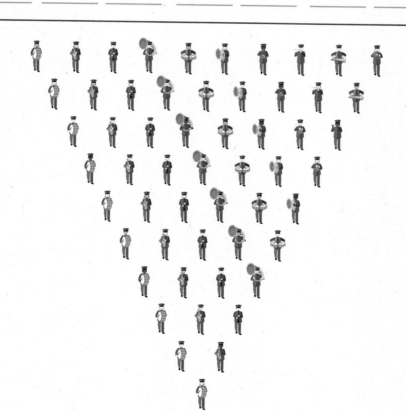

____
____
____
____
____
____
____
____
____
____
____

3 Show and write the partners of 10.

10 = _____ + _____

10 = _____ + _____

10 = _____ + _____

10 = _____ + _____

10 = _____ + _____

10 = _____ + _____

10 = _____ + _____

10 = _____ + _____

10 = _____ + _____

Focus on Problem Solving

Write two more partners for
the number.

1 6 ⬜⭕⭕⭕⭕⭕⭕⬜

6 = 5 + 1

6 = _____

6 = _____

2 8 ⬜⭕⭕⭕⭕⭕⭕⭕⬜

8 = 7 + 1

8 = _____

8 = _____

Use doubles or patterns to solve.

3 $0 + 4 =$ ☐

4 $4 + 4 =$ ☐

5 $7 - 0 =$ ☐

Name _____ Date _____

1 Write the partners.

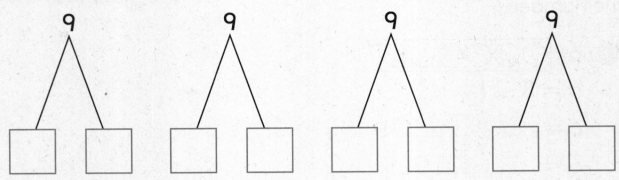

2 Choose a set of 9-partners. Write or draw a story about the 9-partners.

Ring the part of the pattern that repeats.
Label the pattern AB, ABCD, or AAB.

①    label: _____

②    label: _____

③ T B Y K T B Y K T B Y K   label: _____

④    label: _____

Extend the **repeating pattern**.
Draw the fruit.

⑤   _____ _____

⑥    _____ _____

⑦    _____ _____

⑧   _____ _____

Complete the pattern.

9  ____ ____

10 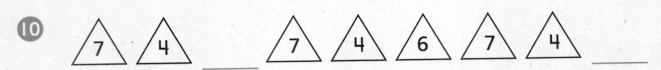 ____

11

12

13 Use numbers to create the same type of repeating pattern as problem 9.

14 Draw shapes to create an AB repeating pattern.

✓ **Check Understanding**
Draw a repeating pattern using this group of shapes.

Repeating Patterns

Name _____

Continue each growing pattern two more times.

VOCABULARY
growing pattern

1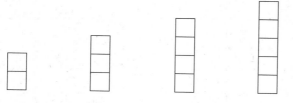

_____ _____

2 _____ _____

3 AB   ABB   ABBB   _____ _____

Complete the pattern. Write the pattern rule.

4
$$454$$
$$44544$$
$$4445444$$
$$444454444$$
$$\underline{\hspace{4cm}}$$
$$44444454444444$$

rule: _____

5 Create a growing pattern with shapes.

Count by 2s to complete the pattern.

VOCABULARY
shrinking pattern

 1, 3, 5, _____ , _____

_____

 4, 6, 8, _____

Continue each **shrinking pattern** two more times.

8 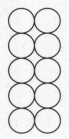    _____ _____

_____

9 ACCCCC   ACCCC   ACCC   _____ _____

_____

Complete the pattern. Write the pattern rule.

 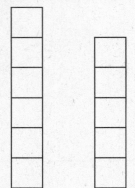

rule: _____

✓ **Check Understanding**

What is the pattern rule for Problem 8?

rule: _____

Growing and Shrinking Patterns

1 Ring the part of the pattern that repeats.

2 Draw a shape to complete the pattern.

3 Count by 2s to complete the pattern.

2, 4, 6, _____

4 Complete the pattern. Write the pattern rule.

XXXXXX
XXXXX
XXXX
XXX
_____

rule: _____

5 Continue the pattern two times.

Name _____ Date _____

Add.

1 1 + 0 = ☐ **2** 0 + 3 = ☐ **3** 9 + 0 = ☐

4 0 + 2 = ☐ **5** 4 + 0 = ☐ **6** 5 + 0 = ☐

7 7 + 0 = ☐ **8** 0 + 9 = ☐ **9** 8 + 0 = ☐

10 0 + 6 = ☐ **11** 2 + 0 = ☐ **12** 10 + 0 = ☐

13 0 + 1 = ☐ **14** 3 + 0 = ☐ **15** 0 + 7 = ☐

See the 5-group.
Draw extra dots to show the number.

1   7

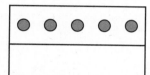

2   8

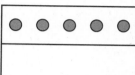

3 Does the picture match the number?
Choose Yes or No.

7

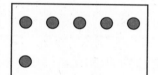

○ Yes   ○ No

4 Continue the pattern two more times.

5 Extend the pattern.

H   H   Y   H   H   Y   H   H   Y   ____

6 Choose all the 10-partners.

- ○ 2 + 8
- ○ 3 + 5
- ○ 8 + 3
- ○ 8 + 2

---

7 Complete the 6-partners.

$6 = 5 +$ | 1
2
3 |

$6 = 4 +$ | 0
1
2 |

$6 =$ | 0
1
2 | $+ 6$

---

8 Write the numbers in the boxes to show the partners.

| 1 | 2 | 3 | 4 | 5 | 6 | 7 | 8 |

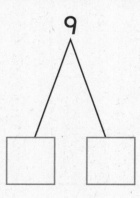   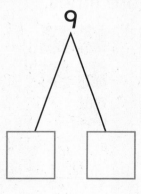   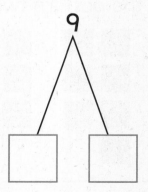

---

9 Use patterns to solve.

$6 + 1 = \boxed{}$ $5 + 1 = \boxed{}$ $4 + 1 = \boxed{}$

Write the partners.

10    5 = _____ + _____

_____

11    7 = _____ + _____

_____

12    6 = _____ + _____

_____

13 Write facts that match each total.

| 8 + 1 | 9 + 0 | 6 + 1 | 4 + 4 | 7 + 0 | 1 + 7 |

7	8	9

Write the partners and the switched partners.

14 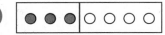   [____ + ____] and [____ + ____]

_____

15    [____ + ____] and [____ + ____]

_____

16   [____ + ____] and [____ + ____]

17 Use patterns to solve.

3 − 1 = ☐

4 − 1 = ☐

5 − 1 = ☐

---

18 Draw a story about a set of 8-partners.
Write the partners.

Plant Flowers

1 Draw 5 flowers growing in the pot.
Make some red. Make some yellow.

2 Write the 5-partners the flowers show.
Then switch the partners.

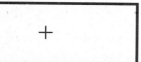   

3 Draw 10 flowers growing in the pot.
Make some blue. Make some yellow.

4 Write the 10-partners the flowers show.
Then switch the partners.

5 Can you show 10 with blue and yellow flowers
in other ways? Tell why or why not.

_____

_____

Color Plates

6 Draw 9 plates. Make some red. Make some blue.

7 Write the 9-partners that the plates show.
Then switch the partners.

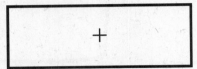   

---

8 Color the plates below yellow. Then draw blue
plates to make 10 plates in all.

9 Write the 10-partners the plates show.
Then switch the partners.

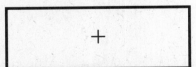   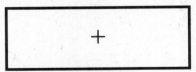

10 Can you show another number of blue plates to
add to the yellow plates to make 10 in all?
Tell why or why not.

_____

_____

Dear Family:

Your child has started a new unit on addition, subtraction, and equations. These concepts are introduced with stories that capture children's interest and help them to see adding and subtracting as real-life processes.

At the beginning of the unit, children show a story problem by drawing a picture of the objects. If they are adding 4 balloons and 2 balloons, for example, their pictures might look like the top one shown here. If they are subtracting, their pictures might look like the bottom one.

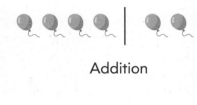

Addition

Subtraction

In a short time, children will show objects quickly with circles rather than pictures. This is a major conceptual advance because it requires the use of symbols. Children are asked to show the partners (4 + 2) as well as give the total (6). From here, children are just a small step away from writing standard equations, such as $4 + 2 = 6$ and $6 - 4 = 2$.

$$4 + 2$$

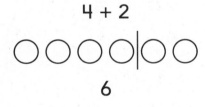

6

Addition Problem

$$6 - 4$$

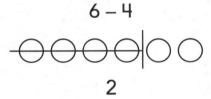

2

Subtraction Problem

To keep them focused on the actual problem, children are often asked to give a "complete answer" in class. This means that they should name the objects as well as give the number. Right now, complete answers are not required for homework. Even so, it would be helpful for you to ask your child to say the complete answer when working with you at home. Example: "You said the answer is 6. Is it 6 dinosaurs? No? Then 6 what? . . . Oh! 6 balloons!"

Sincerely,
Your child's teacher

Estimada familia:

Su niño ha empezado una nueva unidad sobre la suma, la resta y las ecuaciones. Estos conceptos se presentan con cuentos que captan el interés de los niños y les ayudan a ver la suma y la resta como procesos de la vida diaria.

Al comienzo de la unidad, los niños muestran un problema en forma de cuento haciendo un dibujo de los objetos. Por ejemplo, si están sumando 4 globos y 2 globos, sus dibujos pueden parecerse al dibujo de arriba. Si están restando, es posible que sus dibujos se parezcan al dibujo de abajo.

Suma

Al poco tiempo, los niños mostrarán objetos rápidamente con círculos en vez de dibujos. Esto es un gran paso conceptual, ya que requiere el uso de signos. A los niños se les pide que muestren las partes (4 + 2) y la respuesta (6). Una vez que hacen esto, están casi listos para escribir ecuaciones normales, tales como 4 + 2 = 6 y 6 − 4 = 2.

Resta

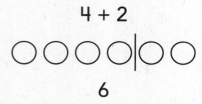

4 + 2

6

Problema de suma

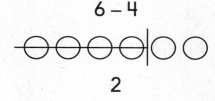

6 − 4

2

Problema de resta

Para que sigan concentrándose en el problema mismo, a los niños se les pide una "respuesta completa" en la clase. Esto significa que deben nombrar los objetos y dar el número. Actualmente, no se requieren respuestas completas en la tarea. Sin embargo, sería de ayuda si le pidiera a su niño que le dé la respuesta completa cuando trabaja con Ud. en casa. Por ejemplo: "Dijiste que la respuesta es 6. ¿Son 6 dinosaurios? ¿No? Entonces, ¿6 de qué?. . . ¡Ajá! ¡6 globos!"

Atentamente,
El maestro de su niño

Represent Addition

cent

nickel

count on

penny

equation

subtract

front   back

5 cents or 5¢

The number of **cents** is the value of a set of coins.

7 cents

front   back

1 cent or 1¢

$5 + 4 = \boxed{9}$

$5 + \boxed{4} = 9$

$9 - 5 = \boxed{4}$

5 . . . .
  6 7 8 9

Count on from 5 to get the answer.

$8 - 3 = 5$

$4 + 3 = 7$ $7 = 4 + 3$

$9 - 5 = 4$ $4 = 9 - 5$

total

vertical form

$$4 + 3 = 7 \qquad \begin{array}{r} 4 \\ +\ 3 \\ \hline 7 \end{array}$$

total →

$$\begin{array}{r} 6 \\ +\ 3 \\ \hline 9 \end{array} \qquad \begin{array}{r} 9 \\ -\ 3 \\ \hline 6 \end{array}$$

Name _____

VOCABULARY
total

Write the partners and the **total**.

1 ☐ + ☐

Total ☐

2 ☐ + ☐

Total ☐

3 ☐ + ☐

Total ☐

4 ☐ + ☐

Total ☐

5 ☐ + ☐

Total ☐

6 ☐ + ☐

Total ☐

7 Draw a picture of flowers to show 4 + 2. Write the total.

Write the partners and the total.

8

Total ☐

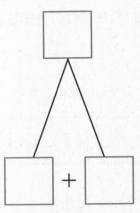

---

9 ☐ + ☐

Total ☐

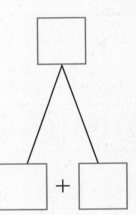

---

10 ☐ + ☐

Total ☐

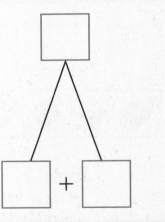

✔ Check Understanding

Listen to the math story. Then draw it and write the partners and the total.

Represent Addition

Name _____

Write the partners and total for each circle drawing.

1

Total

2

Total

3

Total

4

Total

5

Total

6

Total

7 Make a circle drawing to show 5 + 5.

Match the pictures to the circle drawings.

8  •

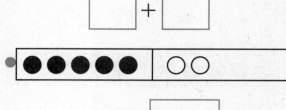

Total ☐

9  •

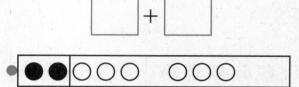

Total ☐

10  •

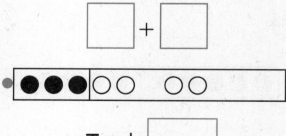

Total ☐

✓ **Check Understanding**

Use the circle drawing to tell a math story. Explain how to use the circles to represent the story.

Addition with Circle Drawings

Name _____

VOCABULARY
equation

Write the partners and the total. Then write the **equation**.

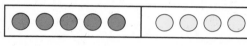

Total ☐

_____
Equation

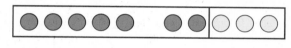

Total ☐

_____
Equation

Total ☐

_____
Equation

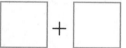

Total ☐

_____
Equation

5 Write an equation of your own. _____

Write the partners and the total. Then write the equation.

6

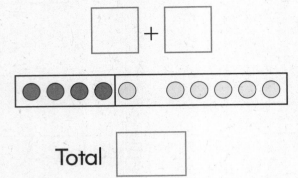

Total ☐

Equation _____

_____

7

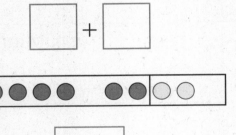

Total ☐

Equation _____

_____

 PATH to FLUENCY Add.

1 $1 + 0 = $ ☐   **2** $0 + 8 = $ ☐   **3** $6 + 0 = $ ☐

_____

✓ Check Understanding

Write an equation with numbers on each
side of an equal sign. ____ + ____ = ____

Addition Equations

Name _____

Make a circle drawing for the story problem.
Write the equation.

1 There are 4 elephants drinking from the
river. Then 2 more elephants join them.
How many elephants are there in all?

_____
Equation

2 Teresa plants 5 roses in the garden. Hugo
plants 4 roses. How many roses did they
plant in all?

_____
Equation

3 Henry played 6 outside games last week.
Then he played 3 computer games. How
many games did he play altogether?

_____
Equation

Addition Equations and Stories **55**

Circle if the equation is true or false.
Draw a line to change $=$ to $\neq$ if it is false.
Draw to explain.

4 $2 + 3 = 3 + 2$

true   false

5 $6 + 1 = 5 + 1$

true   false

6 $4 + 4 = 7 + 2$

true   false

7 $3 + 2 = 1 + 4$

true   false

✓ **Check Understanding**

Complete the equation to make it true.

$3 + 4 = 5 +$ ☐

Addition Equations and Stories

Write the partners and the total.

Total

Total

Write the partners and total.

Total

Total

Write a true equation for the story.

5 There are 7 plates on the table.
   Anna puts 3 more plates on the table.
   How many plates are on the table now?

_____

Name _____   Date _____

Add.

1 $2 + 0 = \boxed{}$ **2** $0 + 4 = \boxed{}$ **3** $7 + 0 = \boxed{}$

4 $0 + 1 = \boxed{}$ **5** $3 + 0 = \boxed{}$ **6** $0 + 5 = \boxed{}$

7 $9 + 0 = \boxed{}$ **8** $0 + 8 = \boxed{}$ **9** $6 + 0 = \boxed{}$

10 $0 + 10 = \boxed{}$ **11** $5 + 0 = \boxed{}$ **12** $0 + 7 = \boxed{}$

13 $8 + 0 = \boxed{}$ **14** $0 + 9 = \boxed{}$ **15** $10 + 0 = \boxed{}$

Dear Family:

Earlier in the unit, your child solved addition problems by making math drawings and counting every object. This is called *counting all*. Now your child is learning a faster strategy that allows them to work directly with numbers. The method they are learning is called *counting on*. It is explained below.

In an addition problem such as 5 + 4, children say (or "think") the first number as if they had already counted it. Then they count on from there. The last number they say is the total. Children can keep track by raising a finger or making a dot for each number as they count on. The diagram below shows both the finger method and the dot method.

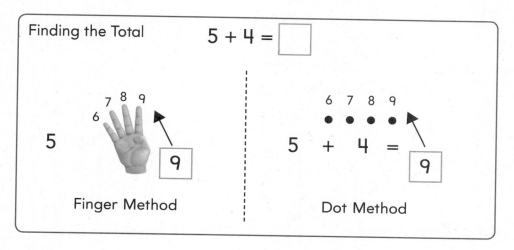

Finding the Total   5 + 4 = ☐

5   9

Finger Method

5 + 4 = 9

Dot Method

In this unit children are introduced to pennies and nickels. They apply the Counting On strategy as they count coins to find the total amount of cents.

Counting on requires repeated practice. This is provided in class activities and homework assignments. Right now, your child is learning how to find unknown totals. In the next unit, he or she will learn to use the Counting On strategy to subtract.

Counting on is a temporary method to help children build fluency with addition and subtraction within 10. The goal by the end of the grade is for children to automatically know the answer when the total is 10 or less.

Sincerely,
Your child's teacher

Estimada familia:

Un poco antes en la unidad su niño resolvió problemas de suma haciendo dibujos matemáticos y contando todos los objetos. A esto se le llama *contar todo*. Ahora su niño está aprendiendo una estrategia más rápida que le permite trabajar directamente con los números. El método que está aprendiendo se llama *contar hacia adelante*. Se explica a continuación.

En un problema de suma, como 5 + 4, los niños dicen (o "piensan") el primer número como si ya lo hubieran contado. Luego cuentan hacia adelante a partir de él. El último número que dicen es el total. Los niños pueden llevar la cuenta levantando un dedo o haciendo un punto por cada número mientras cuentan hacia adelante. El diagrama a continuación muestra tanto el método de los dedos como el de los puntos.

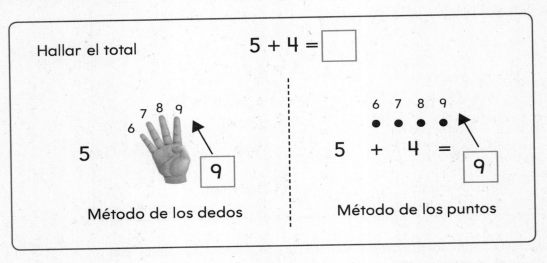

En esta unidad se les presentarán a los niños las monedas de un centavo y de cinco centavos. Aplicarán la estrategia de contar hacia adelante mientras cuentan las monedas para hallar la cantidad total de centavos.

Contar hacia adelante requiere práctica. Esto sucede en las actividades de clase y tareas. En esta unidad, su niño está aprendiendo a hallar un total desconocido. En la próxima unidad, aprenderá a usar la estrategia de contar hacia adelante para restar.

Contar hacia adelante es un método que sirve como ayuda para que los niños dominen la suma y la resta en operaciones hasta el 10. La meta es lograr que al final del año escolar sepan automáticamente la respuesta cuando el total sea 10 ó menos.

Atentamente,
El maestro de su niño

Explore Solution Methods

Name _____

Count on. Write the total.

1 5 + 2 = ☐

5   ••

2 6 + 4 = ☐

6   ••••

3 8 + 1 = ☐

8   •

4 3 + 5 = ☐

3   •••••

5 7 + 3 = ☐

7   •••

6 2 + 2 = ☐

2   ••

7 4 + 5 = ☐

4   •••••

8 9 + 1 = ☐

9   •

9 3 + 2 = ☐

3   ••

10 5 + 1 = ☐

5   •

Explore Solution Methods **61**

11 Solve.

7 + 2 = ☐

Draw or write to explain how to count on.

Draw or write a different way to solve.

12 Choose a number 1, 2, 3, 4, or 5. Count on 3 more.
Complete the equation. Draw or write to explain.

☐ + 3 = ☐

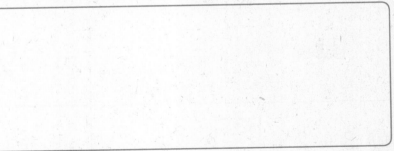

✓ **Check Understanding**

Explain if you would use counting all or
counting on to solve 5 + 3 = ☐.

Explore Solution Methods

Name _____

Count on to find the total.

① 4 + 3 = ☐   ② 6 + 4 = ☐   ③ 6 + 2 = ☐

④ 4 + 5 = ☐   ⑤ 5 + 3 = ☐   ⑥ 8 + 2 = ☐

⑦ 2 + 3 = ☐   ⑧ 7 + 3 = ☐   ⑨ 4 + 2 = ☐

Find the total number of toys.

⑩ 3 cars in the box

☐ Total

⑪ 7 boats in the box

☐ Total

⑫ 6 dolls in the box

☐ Total

⑬ 5 balls in the box

☐ Total

⑭ Write an equation that shows a total of 10. _____

Count on to find the total.

(15) $6 + 3 =$ ☐

(16) $5 + 2 =$ ☐

(17) $7 + 2 =$ ☐

(18) $7 + 3 =$ ☐

(19) $4 + 3 =$ ☐

(20) $4 + 5 =$ ☐

(21) $8 + 2 =$ ☐

(22) $5 + 2 =$ ☐

(23) $4 + 2 =$ ☐

(24) $5 + 3 =$ ☐

(25) $7 + 2 =$ ☐

(26) $7 + 3 =$ ☐

(27) $6 + 2 =$ ☐

(28) $6 + 4 =$ ☐

(29) $3 + 4 =$ ☐

PATH to FLUENCY **Add.**

(1) $7 + 0 =$ ☐

(2) $1 + 8 =$ ☐

(3) $0 + 8 =$ ☐

(4) $9 + 0 =$ ☐

(5) $7 + 1 =$ ☐

(6) $10 + 0 =$ ☐

(7) $6 + 1 =$ ☐

(8) $8 + 0 =$ ☐

(9) $8 + 1 =$ ☐

✓ **Check Understanding**

Draw dots to show how to count on

to solve $6 + 4 =$ ☐.

© Houghton Mifflin Harcourt Publishing Company

Addition Strategies: Counting On

Name _____

Underline the greater number.
Count on from that number.

1 3 + _7_ = ☐

2 4 + 5 = ☐

3 2 + 6 = ☐

4 5 + 3 = ☐

5 7 + 2 = ☐

6 3 + 6 = ☐

7 5 + 2 = ☐

8 2 + 8 = ☐

9 7 + 3 = ☐

10 6 + 3 = ☐

11 Show two ways to count on to find the total
of 6 + 3. Which is faster?

Underline the greater number.
Count on from that number.

12 $\underline{5} + 2 = \boxed{}$

13 $7 + 3 = \boxed{}$

14 $6 + 2 = \boxed{}$

15 $5 + 3 = \boxed{}$

16 $3 + 4 = \boxed{}$

17 $2 + 7 = \boxed{}$

18 $6 + 3 = \boxed{}$

19 $8 + 2 = \boxed{}$

20 $4 + 3 = \boxed{}$

21 $2 + 5 = \boxed{}$

22 $4 + 6 = \boxed{}$

23 $3 + 7 = \boxed{}$

24 How did you solve Exercise 17?

Count On from the Greater Number

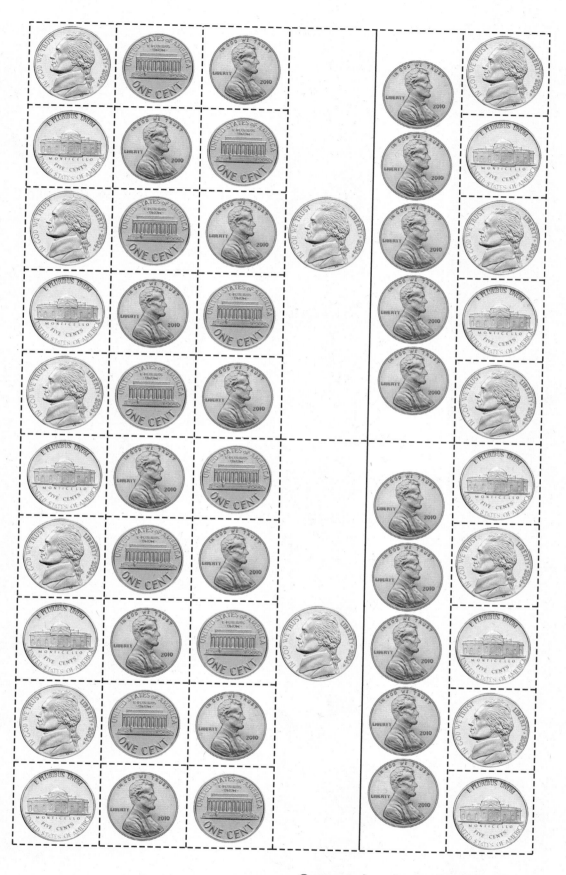

Cut on the dotted lines.
Fold on the solid lines.

Nickel Strips and Coins

Name _____

Look at the groups of **nickels** and **pennies**. Write how many **cents** in each group.

25

☐ ¢

26

☐ ¢

27

☐ ¢

28

☐ ¢

29

☐ ¢

30

☐ ¢

Count the coins. Match.

31  •

• 4¢

32  •

• 6¢

33  •

• 7¢

34  •

• 9¢

35  •

• 8¢

✓ Check Understanding

To use counting on to solve $4 + 5 = \square$,

which number would you start with? Why?

Count On from the Greater Number

$3+3=\square$ $3+4=\square$ $3+5=\square$

$3+6=\square$ $3+7=\square$ $4+3=\square$

$4+4=\square$ $4+5=\square$ $4+6=\square$

$5+3=\square$ $5+4=\square$ $5+5=\square$

$6+3=\square$ $6+4=\square$ $7+3=\square$

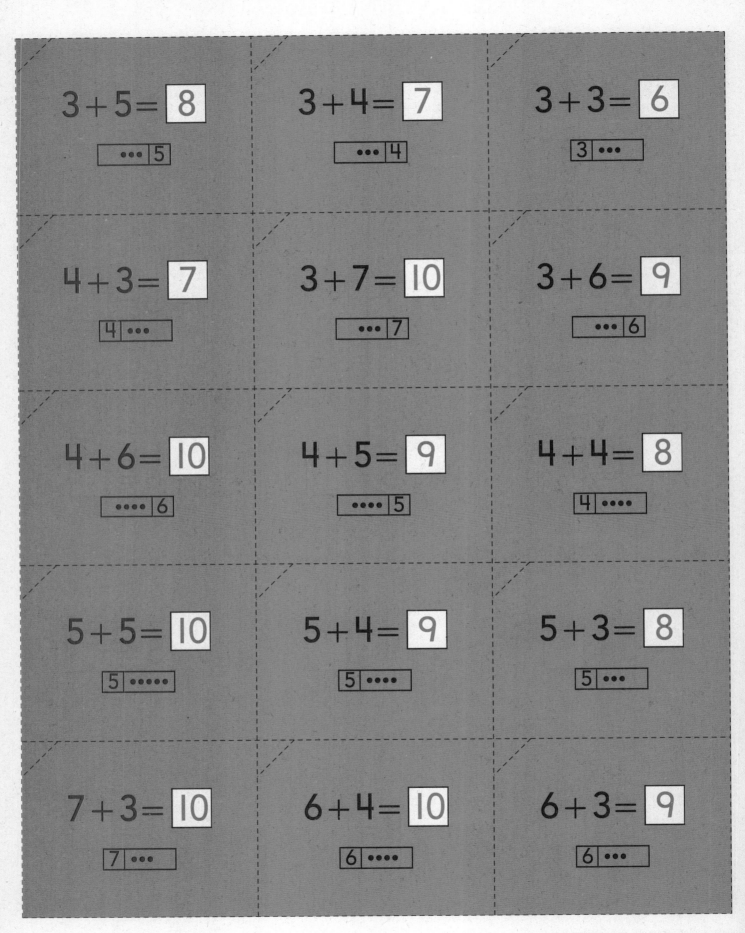

$3 + 5 = \boxed{8}$

$3 + 4 = \boxed{7}$

$3 + 3 = \boxed{6}$

$4 + 3 = \boxed{7}$

$3 + 7 = \boxed{10}$

$3 + 6 = \boxed{9}$

$4 + 6 = \boxed{10}$

$4 + 5 = \boxed{9}$

$4 + 4 = \boxed{8}$

$5 + 5 = \boxed{10}$

$5 + 4 = \boxed{9}$

$5 + 3 = \boxed{8}$

$7 + 3 = \boxed{10}$

$6 + 4 = \boxed{10}$

$6 + 3 = \boxed{9}$

Red Count-On Cards

Number Quilt 1: Unknown Totals

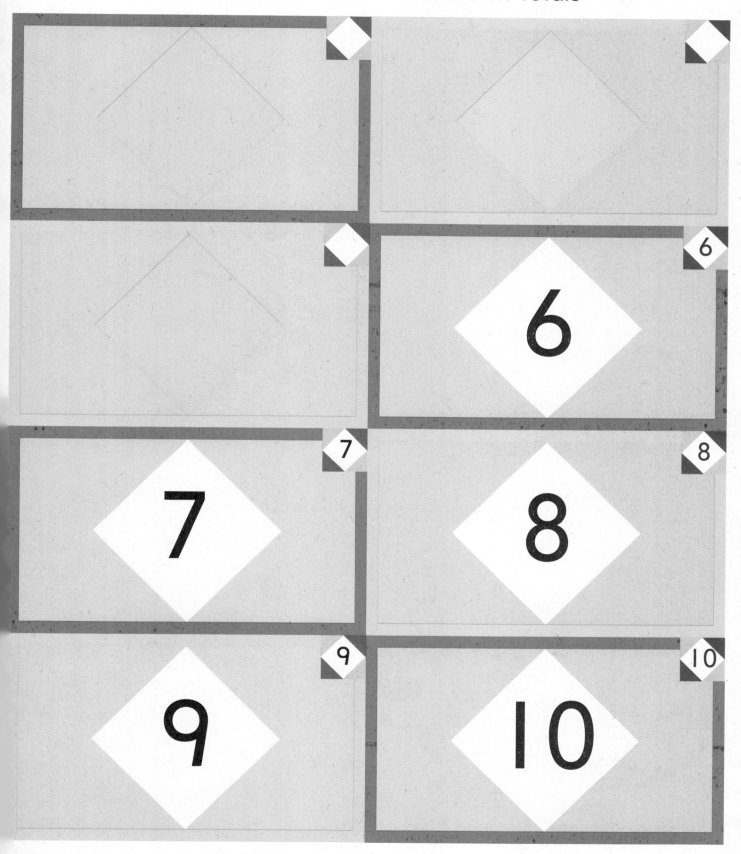

Use with Red Count-On Cards.

Name _____

Draw more to count on. Write how many in all.

 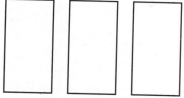

$4 + 1 = \boxed{}$

 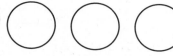 

$6 + 2 = \boxed{}$

$3 + 3 = \boxed{}$

 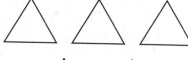 

$5 + 4 = \boxed{}$

$7 + 3 = \boxed{}$

Underline the greater number.
Count on from that number.

6 2 + <u>8</u> = ☐   **7** 5 + 4 = ☐   **8** 6 + 3 = ☐

9 7 + 3 = ☐   **10** 2 + 5 = ☐   **11** 3 + 4 = ☐

12 4 + 3 = ☐   **13** 2 + 7 = ☐   **14** 8 + 2 = ☐

15 3 + 6 = ☐   **16** 5 + 2 = ☐   **17** 6 + 2 = ☐

18 5 + 3 = ☐   **19** 4 + 5 = ☐   **20** 2 + 6 = ☐

(PATH to FLUENCY) **Add.**

1 3 + 2 = ☐   **2** 1 + 9 = ☐   **3** 7 + 0 = ☐

4 8 + 1 = ☐   **5** 0 + 9 = ☐   **6** 1 + 6 = ☐

7 8 + 0 = ☐   **8** 7 + 1 = ☐   **9** 2 + 3 = ☐

✓ **Check Understanding**

Explain how to count on to solve 6 + 3 = ☐ and
2 + 8 = ☐.

Addition Games: Unknown Totals

Name _____

Write the addition equation the model shows.

1

_____
Equation

2

_____
Equation

3

_____
Equation

4

_____
Equation

5

_____
Equation

Underline the greater addend in the equation.
Count on from that number and write the total.

6 $6 + 3 =$ ☐

| 6 | ● ● ● |

7 $2 + 5 =$ ☐

| ● ● | 5 |

8 $7 + 3 =$ ☐

| 7 | ● ● ● |

9 $5 + 3 =$ ☐

| 5 | ● ● ● |

10 $2 + 4 =$ ☐

| ● ● | 4 |

11 $4 + 5 =$ ☐

| ● ● ● ● | 5 |

12 $3 + 7 =$ ☐

| ● ● ● | 7 |

13 $6 + 2 =$ ☐

| 6 | ● ● |

14 $4 + 6 =$ ☐

| ● ● ● ● | 6 |

15 $7 + 2 =$ ☐

| 7 | ● ● |

✓ **Check Understanding**

Draw circles to show counting on to solve
$4 + 3 =$ ☐ and $2 + 7 =$ ☐.

Practice Counting On

Count on to find the total.

1 3 + 2 = ☐

2 Write how many cents.

    ¢

Underline the greater number.
Count on from that number.

3 4 + 5 = ☐

4 6 + 3 = ☐

5 Draw more to count on.
Write how many in all.

◯◯◯◯◯

5 + 2 = ☐

Name _____ Date _____

Add.

1 5 + 0 = ☐

2 0 + 6 = ☐

3 0 + 8 = ☐

4 9 + 0 = ☐

5 0 + 10 = ☐

6 9 + 1 = ☐

7 1 + 3 = ☐

8 2 + 1 = ☐

9 2 + 3 = ☐

10 1 + 5 = ☐

11 4 + 0 = ☐

12 7 + 1 = ☐

13 3 + 2 = ☐

14 1 + 9 = ☐

15 8 + 1 = ☐

Name _____

Solve. Write how many are left.

1 There are 8 apples.

$8 - 5 =$ ☐

Then 5 are eaten.

---

2 There are 9 flowers.

$9 - 4 =$ ☐

Then 4 are picked.

---

3 There are 6 dolphins.

$6 - 3 =$ ☐

Then 3 swim away.

---

4 There are 10 balloons.

$10 - 6 =$ ☐

Then 6 pop.

---

5 You have 7 balls. You lose 2 balls. How many balls are left? Solve. Show your work.

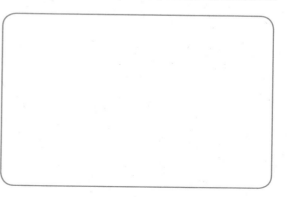

Solve. Write how many are left.

6　　　There are 10 balloons.

$10 - 4 = \boxed{}$

Then 4 pop.

7　　　There are 8 apples.

$8 - 6 = \boxed{}$

Then 6 are eaten.

---

8 Look at Puzzled Penguin's work.

There were 7 flowers.

Then 3 were picked.

$7 - 3 = \boxed{3}$

Am I correct?

Help Puzzled Penguin.

✔ **Check Understanding**
Draw circles to solve
$8 - 2 = \boxed{}$.

　　　　Represent Subtraction

© Houghton Mifflin Harcourt Publishing Company

Name _____

VOCABULARY
subtract

Subtract and write the equation.

1

Subtract 5

⟨○○○○○ ○○○○⟩

_____
Equation

2   Subtract 4

⟨○○○○○ ○○○○○⟩

_____
Equation

3   Subtract 3

⟨○○○○○ ○○⟩

_____
Equation

4   Subtract 8

⟨○○○○○ ○○○○○⟩

_____
Equation

5   Subtract 5

⟨○○○○○ ○○○⟩

_____
Equation

6   Subtract 7

⟨○○○○○ ○○○○○⟩

_____
Equation

7   Subtract 6

⟨○○○○○ ○○○○⟩

_____
Equation

Subtract and write the equation.

8   Subtract 5

_____
Equation
_____

9   Subtract 3

_____
Equation
_____

10   Subtract 6

_____
Equation
_____

11   Subtract 4

_____
Equation
_____

12   Subtract 2

_____
Equation
_____

13 There are 6 toy trucks on the
table. 4 trucks roll off. How
many toy trucks are there now?
Use a circle drawing to solve.
Then write the equation.

 Check Understanding
Make a circle drawing to show $10 - 7 = 3$.

Subtraction with Drawings and Equations

Name _____

Use the picture to solve the equation.

1 ⓞⓞⓞⓞⓞ ⦿⦿⦿⦿

$9 - 6 =$ ☐

2 ⓞⓞⓞⓞⓞ ⦿⦿⦿

$8 - 5 =$ ☐

3 ⓞⓞⓞⓞ

$4 - 4 =$ ☐

4 ⓞⓞⓞⓞⓞ ⦿⦿

$7 - 3 =$ ☐

5 ⓞⓞⓞⓞⓞ ⦿

$6 - 5 =$ ☐

6 ⓞⓞⓞⓞⓞ

$5 - 4 =$ ☐

7 ⓞⓞⓞⓞⓞ ⦿⦿⦿⦿⦿

$10 - 6 =$ ☐

8 ⓞⓞⓞⓞⓞ ⦿⦿⦿⦿

$9 - 3 =$ ☐

9 ⓞⓞⓞⓞⓞ ⦿⦿

$7 - 6 =$ ☐

10 ⓞⓞⓞⓞⓞ ⦿⦿⦿⦿⦿

$10 - 2 =$ ☐

11 ⓞⓞⓞⓞⓞ ⦿⦿⦿

$8 - 4 =$ ☐

12 ⓞⓞⓞⓞⓞ ⦿

$6 - 2 =$ ☐

Use the picture to solve the equation.

13

$$5 - 3 = \boxed{}$$

14

$$7 - 4 = \boxed{}$$

15

$$9 - 5 = \boxed{}$$

16

$$6 - 4 = \boxed{}$$

17

$$10 - 3 = \boxed{}$$

18

$$8 - 6 = \boxed{}$$

19 Make a circle drawing for the equation $6 - 2 = \boxed{}$. Then find the answer.

PATH to FLUENCY Subtract.

1 $2 - 1 = \boxed{}$ **2** $6 - 0 = \boxed{}$ **3** $1 - 0 = \boxed{}$

4 $4 - 1 = \boxed{}$ **5** $3 - 1 = \boxed{}$ **6** $10 - 0 = \boxed{}$

 Check Understanding

Listen to the story. Write and solve the equation for the story.

© Houghton Mifflin Harcourt Publishing Company

Practice with Subtraction

Name _____

Write the equation for the story problem. Draw circles to prove if the equation is true or false.

1 There are 8 people at the party.
Then 2 people leave. Now there are
6 people at the party.

_____ Equation

2 There are 6 cups on the table.
Tim puts 3 cups in the dishwasher.
Now there are 2 cups on the table.

_____ Equation

3 There are 7 birds in the tree. 4 fly away.
Now there are 4 birds in the tree.

_____ Equation

Generate Subtraction Problems **87**

Circle if the equation is true or false.
Draw to explain.

4 $9 - 4 = 7 - 1$

true   false

5 $6 - 3 = 8 - 5$

true   false

6 $4 - 1 = 5 - 2$

true   false

7 $7 - 2 = 9 - 4$

true   false

8 $3 - 1 = 4 - 1$

true   false

9 $6 - 3 = 8 - 6$

true   false

✓ **Check Understanding**

Make a circle drawing to show $9 - 6 = \boxed{}$.

© Houghton Mifflin Harcourt Publishing Company

Generate Subtraction Problems

Write how many are left.

Use the picture to help you.

1 There are 7 fish.

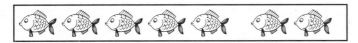

$7 - 3 = \boxed{}$

Then 3 swim away.

2 There are 10 snails.

Then 5 crawl away.

$10 - 5 = \boxed{}$

Use the picture to solve the equation.

3

$7 - 5 = \boxed{}$

Subtract and write the equation.

4

Subtract 4

_____
Equation

5

Subtract 6

_____
Equation

Name _____ Date _____

PATH to FLUENCY

Subtract.

1. $1 - 0 =$ ☐

2. $3 - 1 =$ ☐

3. $2 - 0 =$ ☐

4. $4 - 1 =$ ☐

5. $6 - 0 =$ ☐

6. $5 - 1 =$ ☐

7. $7 - 0 =$ ☐

8. $8 - 1 =$ ☐

9. $9 - 1 =$ ☐

10. $8 - 0 =$ ☐

11. $9 - 0 =$ ☐

12. $7 - 1 =$ ☐

13. $10 - 0 =$ ☐

14. $6 - 1 =$ ☐

15. $10 - 1 =$ ☐

Name _____

Relate addition and subtraction.

1

Addition	Subtraction
5 cats are here.	8 cats are here.
3 cats come.	5 cats run away.
How many cats in all?	How many cats are left?
$5 + 3 =$ ●●●●● | ○○○	$8 - 5 =$ ●●●●● ○○○
$5 + 3 = \square$	$8 - 5 = \square$
$5 + 3 = \square$	$8 - 5 = \square$
Total Unknown	Partner Unknown
	$5 + \square = 8$

Use addition to solve subtraction.

2 $4 + 4 = 8$, so I know $8 - 4 = \square$.

3 $6 + 3 = 9$, so I know $9 - 6 = \square$.

4 $7 + 3 = 10$, so I know $10 - 7 = \square$.

5 $5 + 4 = 9$, so I know $9 - 5 = \square$.

6 $3 + 3 = 6$, so I know $6 - 3 = \square$.

VOCABULARY
vertical form

Equations	Vertical Forms
$5 + 3 = 8$	$\begin{array}{r} 5 \\ + 3 \\ \hline 8 \end{array}$ $\qquad$ $\begin{array}{r} 8 \\ - 5 \\ \hline 3 \end{array}$
$8 - 5 = 3$	

Solve the **vertical form**. Use any method.

7 $\quad \begin{array}{r} 6 \\ + 4 \\ \hline \end{array}$ $\qquad$ **8** $\quad \begin{array}{r} 7 \\ + 2 \\ \hline \end{array}$ $\qquad$ **9** $\quad \begin{array}{r} 1 \\ + 6 \\ \hline \end{array}$ $\qquad$ **10** $\quad \begin{array}{r} 2 \\ + 6 \\ \hline \end{array}$ $\qquad$ **11** $\quad \begin{array}{r} 3 \\ + 7 \\ \hline \end{array}$

Solve the vertical form. Think about addition.

12 $\quad \begin{array}{r} 10 \\ - 8 \\ \hline \end{array}$ $\qquad$ **13** $\quad \begin{array}{r} 9 \\ - 5 \\ \hline \end{array}$ $\qquad$ **14** $\quad \begin{array}{r} 7 \\ - 1 \\ \hline \end{array}$ $\qquad$ **15** $\quad \begin{array}{r} 8 \\ - 3 \\ \hline \end{array}$ $\qquad$ **16** $\quad \begin{array}{r} 10 \\ - 5 \\ \hline \end{array}$

PATH to FLUENCY Subtract.

1 $4 - 0 = \boxed{}$ $\qquad$ **2** $6 - 1 = \boxed{}$ $\qquad$ **3** $4 - 2 = \boxed{}$

4 $9 - 1 = \boxed{}$ $\qquad$ **5** $5 - 2 = \boxed{}$ $\qquad$ **6** $8 - 0 = \boxed{}$

7 $3 - 2 = \boxed{}$ $\qquad$ **8** $9 - 0 = \boxed{}$ $\qquad$ **9** $7 - 1 = \boxed{}$

✓ **Check Understanding**

Write the related subtraction equation for
$5 + 4 = 9$. Write the vertical form.

Write and solve equations and vertical forms.

1 There are 3 pink flowers and 4 yellow flowers in the garden. How many flowers are there in all?

_____
Equation

2 Olivia made 4 clay animals. She made 1 green clay animal. How many clay animals are not green?

_____
Equation

3 There are 6 turtles in the water and 2 turtles crawl out of the water. How many turtles are in the water now?

_____
Equation

Solve.

4 Use the picture to write a story problem.

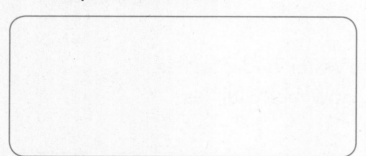

_____

- -

_____

- -

_____

- -

_____

5 Write and solve equations and vertical forms
for the problem created.

_____
Equation

 Check Understanding

Solve $7 - 3 = \square$. Write the vertical form.

Mixed Practice with Equations

Name _____

Darya and her family go to the animal park.

Use the picture to solve the equation.

1 Darya sees 5 lions. Then she sees 3 more lions.

How many lions does she see in all? $5 + 3 = \boxed{}$

---

2 Nick sees 9 crocodiles in the water.

Then 2 crocodiles climb out.

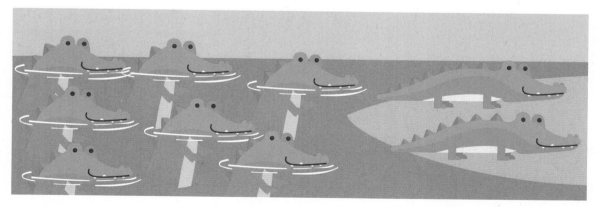

How many crocodiles are in the water now? $9 - 2 = \boxed{}$

Use the picture to solve the equation.

3 Ray sees 1 cheetah in a tree and 7 lions under a tree.

How many wild cats does he see? $1 + 7 = \boxed{}$

---

4 Sophie sees 8 baboons and 2 mandrills.

How many monkeys does she see? $8 + 2 = \boxed{}$

Focus on Problem Solving

Use addition to solve subtraction.

1 $5 + 3 = 8$, so I know $8 - 3 = \boxed{}$.

2 $6 + 4 = 10$, so I know $10 - 4 = \boxed{}$.

Solve the vertical form.
Think about addition.

3
$$\begin{array}{r} 6 \\ -\ 2 \\ \hline \end{array}$$

4
$$\begin{array}{r} 8 \\ -\ 1 \\ \hline \end{array}$$

5
$$\begin{array}{r} 9 \\ -\ 7 \\ \hline \end{array}$$

Name _____   Date _____

PATH to
FLUENCY

Subtract.

1 1 − 1 = ☐   **2** 2 − 0 = ☐   **3** 2 − 1 = ☐

4 4 − 1 = ☐   **5** 3 − 1 = ☐   **6** 5 − 0 = ☐

7 3 − 2 = ☐   **8** 5 − 1 = ☐   **9** 6 − 0 = ☐

10 7 − 0 = ☐   **11** 4 − 2 = ☐   **12** 6 − 1 = ☐

13 8 − 1 = ☐   **14** 9 − 0 = ☐   **15** 5 − 2 = ☐

Write the partners and the total.

 1

Total ⬜

2

Total

---

3 **Does the equation match the circle drawing?**
Choose Yes or No.

$3 + 2 = 5$

○ Yes   ○ No

$5 + 2 = 7$

○ Yes   ○ No

$6 + 3 = 9$

○ Yes   ○ No

Ring the total number of toys in the group.

4 7 dolls in the box

7
9
0	Total

---

5 Write how many cents.

     ¢

---

6 Ring a number to show the cars in the box. Write the total.

4
5
6

☐ Total

7 Solve. Match the story or circle drawing to the equation.

There are 8 apples.

 •

• $9 - 3 = 6$

Then 3 are eaten.

There are 7 flowers.

 •

• $10 - 6 = 4$

Then 5 are picked.

Subtract 3

   •

• $7 - 5 = 2$

Subtract 6

   •

• $8 - 3 = 5$

---

8 Make a circle drawing

for the equation $6 - 4 = \boxed{}$.

Then find the answer.

9 Write the subtraction equation below the addition equation that helps you solve it.

$10 - 2 = 8$	$8 - 5 = 3$	$9 - 4 = 5$
$3 + 5 = 8$	$5 + 4 = 9$	$8 + 2 = 10$
_____	_____	_____

---

10 Write an equation for the story. Make a
Proof Drawing to show that the equation is true.
Write the vertical form.

> There are 7 flowers in the vase.
>
> Lily puts 2 more flowers in the vase.
>
> Now there are 9 flowers.

How Many?

1 Take some red cubes.
Write the number of red cubes. _____

2 Take some blue cubes.
Write the number of blue cubes. _____

3 Draw to show the red cubes and blue cubes.

4 Write an equation that shows how many cubes in all.

_____ + _____ = _____

5 Tell how you added the cubes.

_____

_____

6 Write a subtraction equation.
Make a Proof Drawing to solve it.

_____ − _____ = _____

7 Tell how you subtracted the circles.

_____

_____

8 **Part A**

Write an addition story.

_____

_____

Part B

Write an equation to show your addition story.
Make a Proof Drawing of your addition story.

_____ + _____ = _____

Tell how you solved your addition story.

_____

9 **Part A**

Look at the numbers you used in your addition story.
Use the same numbers to write a subtraction story.

_____

_____

_____

Part B

Write an equation to show your subtraction story.
Make a Proof Drawing of your subtraction story.

_____ − _____ = _____

Tell how you solved your subtraction story.

Dear Family:

Your child has started a new unit on story problems. Because most children this age are learning to read, your child may need help reading the story problems. Offer help when it is needed, but do not give the answer.

To solve story problems, children first need to know which number is unknown. Is it the total or one of the parts? This program helps children focus on this important issue by using "Math Mountains." In a Math Mountain, the total sits at the top and the parts (or partners) sit at the bottom of the mountain. Children can quickly see the relationship between the partners and the total when they look at the mountain.

6

4 + 2

Math Mountain

Math Mountains are especially helpful in showing children how to find an unknown partner, as in the following problem: *I see 9 horses. 5 are black, and the others are white. How many horses are white?*

Children can find the answer by drawing the mountain to see which number is unknown. Then they count on from the partner they know to the total. In this way, they can find the partner they don't know.

Math Mountain with
Unknown Partner

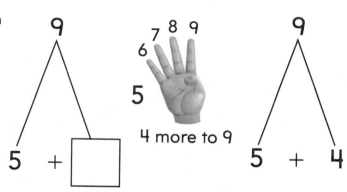

9

5 + ☐

6 7 8 9

5

4 more to 9

9

5 + 4

If you have any questions, please contact me.

Sincerely,
Your child's teacher

Estimada familia:

Su niño ha empezado una nueva unidad donde aprenderá cómo resolver problemas matemáticos. Como la mayoría de los niños a esta edad aún están aprendiendo a leer, es probable que su niño necesite ayuda para leer los problemas. Ofrezca ayuda cuando haga falta, pero no dé la respuesta.

Para resolver problemas, los niños primero deben hallar el número desconocido. ¿Es el total o una de las partes? Este programa los ayuda a concentrarse en este punto importante usando "Montañas matemáticas". En una montaña matemática el total está en la cima y las partes están al pie de la montaña. Al ver la montaña, los niños pueden ver rápidamente la relación entre las partes y el total.

$$6$$
$$4 + 2$$

Montaña matemática

Las montañas matemáticas son especialmente útiles para mostrar a los niños cómo hallar una parte desconocida, como en el problema siguiente: *Veo 9 caballos. 5 son negros y los demás son blancos. ¿Cuántos caballos son blancos?*

Los niños pueden hallar la respuesta dibujando la montaña para saber cuál es el número desconocido. Luego, cuentan hacia adelante a partir de la parte que conocen para hallar el total. De esta manera, pueden hallar la parte desconocida.

Montaña matemática con parte desconocida

$$9$$
$$5 + \square$$

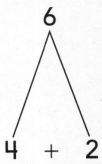

$$5$$
4 más hasta 9

$$9$$
$$5 + 4$$

Si tiene alguna pregunta, por favor comuníquese conmigo.

Atentamente,
El maestro de su niño

subtraction
story problem

8 flies are on a log.
6 are eaten by a frog.
How many flies are left?

Name _____

Find the unknown partner.

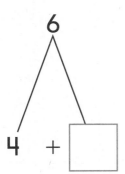

1
6
4 + ☐

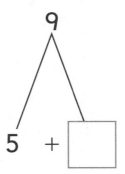

2
9
5 + ☐

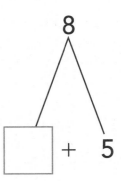

3
8
☐ + 5

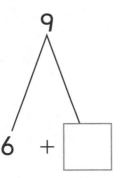

4
9
6 + ☐

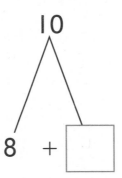

5
10
8 + ☐

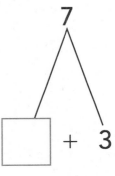

6
7
☐ + 3

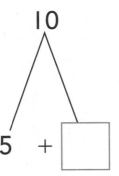

7
10
5 + ☐

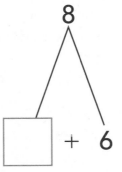

8
8
☐ + 6

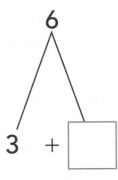

9
6
3 + ☐

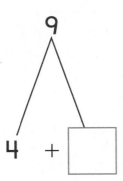

10
9
4 + ☐

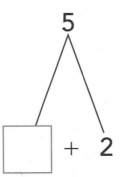

11
5
☐ + 2

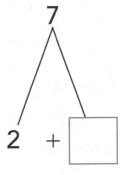

12
7
2 + ☐

Explore Unknowns **107**

⓭ Make three different Math Mountains with a total of 10.

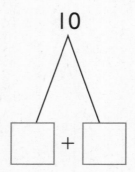   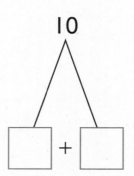   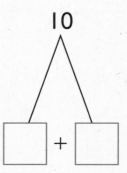

⓮ Make three different Math Mountains with a total of 8.

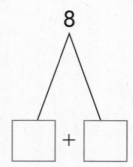   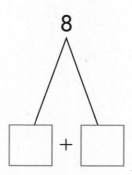   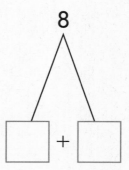

⓯ Make three different Math Mountains with a total of 7.

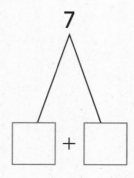   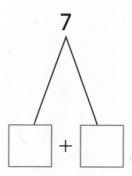   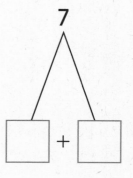

✓ Check Understanding

Draw a Math Mountain with a total of 8 and the partner 5. Count on to find the unknown partner.

Explore Unknowns

Name _____

Solve the story problem.

Show your work. Use drawings, numbers, or words.

1. We see 9 fish.
   5 are big. The others are small.
   How many fish are small?

   ▢ _____
       label

   fish

2. 8 boys are riding bikes.
   6 ride fast. The rest ride slow.
   How many boys ride slow?

   ▢ _____
       label

   bike

3. Ana has 2 hats.
   Then she gets more.
   Now she has 5.
   How many hats does she get?

   ▢ _____
       label

   hat

4. Why is it important to write a
   label in the answer?

   _____

   _____

Solve the story problem. Use cubes to help.

5 Raja has 6 peaches. He wants to put some on each of two plates. How many can he put on each plate? Show 4 answers.

$6 = \boxed{} + \boxed{}$

$6 = \boxed{} + \boxed{}$

$6 = \boxed{} + \boxed{}$

$6 = \boxed{} + \boxed{}$

✔ **Check Understanding**

Kelly has 5 cubes. He gives some to Maria and some to Jake. How many cubes can he give to each person? Find 3 answers.

© Houghton Mifflin Harcourt Publishing Company

Problems with Unknown Partners

Name _____

Count on to find the unknown partner.

1. $3 + \boxed{} = 6$ 　 2. $7 + \boxed{} = 10$ 　 3. $2 + \boxed{} = 6$

4. $7 + \boxed{} = 9$ 　 5. $4 + \boxed{} = 8$ 　 6. $5 + \boxed{} = 8$

Count on to solve.

7. 6 letters total

How many letters are in the box? $\boxed{}$ _____

label

8. 10 footprints total

How many footprints are under water? $\boxed{}$ _____

label

9 Look at Puzzled Penguin's work.

2 + ☐ = 8

2 + ☐10☐ = 8

Am I correct?

---

10 Help Puzzled Penguin.

2 + ☐ = 8

PATH to FLUENCY Add.

1 4 + 4 = ☐ **2** 3 + 7 = ☐ **3** 3 + 3 = ☐

---

4 8 + 2 = ☐ **5** 2 + 2 = ☐ **6** 6 + 4 = ☐

---

7 1 + 1 = ☐ **8** 1 + 9 = ☐ **9** 5 + 5 = ☐

---

10 7 + 3 = ☐ **11** 2 + 8 = ☐ **12** 4 + 6 = ☐

✔ **Check Understanding**

Explain how to count on using dots to

solve the equation 6 + ☐ = 10.

Solve Equations with Unknown Partners

$3 + \boxed{} = 6$

$3 + \boxed{} = 7$

$3 + \boxed{} = 8$

$3 + \boxed{} = 9$

$3 + \boxed{} = 10$

$4 + \boxed{} = 7$

$4 + \boxed{} = 8$

$4 + \boxed{} = 9$

$4 + \boxed{} = 10$

$5 + \boxed{} = 8$

$5 + \boxed{} = 9$

$5 + \boxed{} = 10$

$6 + \boxed{} = 9$

$6 + \boxed{} = 10$

$7 + \boxed{} = 10$

3 + [5] = 8

[3][•••••]

3 + [4] = 7

[3][••••]

3 + [3] = 6

[3][•••]

4 + [3] = 7

[4][•••]

3 + [7] = 10

[3][•• ••]

3 + [6] = 9

[3][•••••]

4 + [6] = 10

[4][•••••]

4 + [5] = 9

[4][•••••]

4 + [4] = 8

[4][••••]

5 + [5] = 10

[5][•••••]

5 + [4] = 9

[5][••••]

5 + [3] = 8

[5][•••]

7 + [3] = 10

[7][•••]

6 + [4] = 10

[6][••••]

6 + [3] = 9

[6][•••]

Yellow Count-On Cards

Number Quilt 2: Unknown Partners

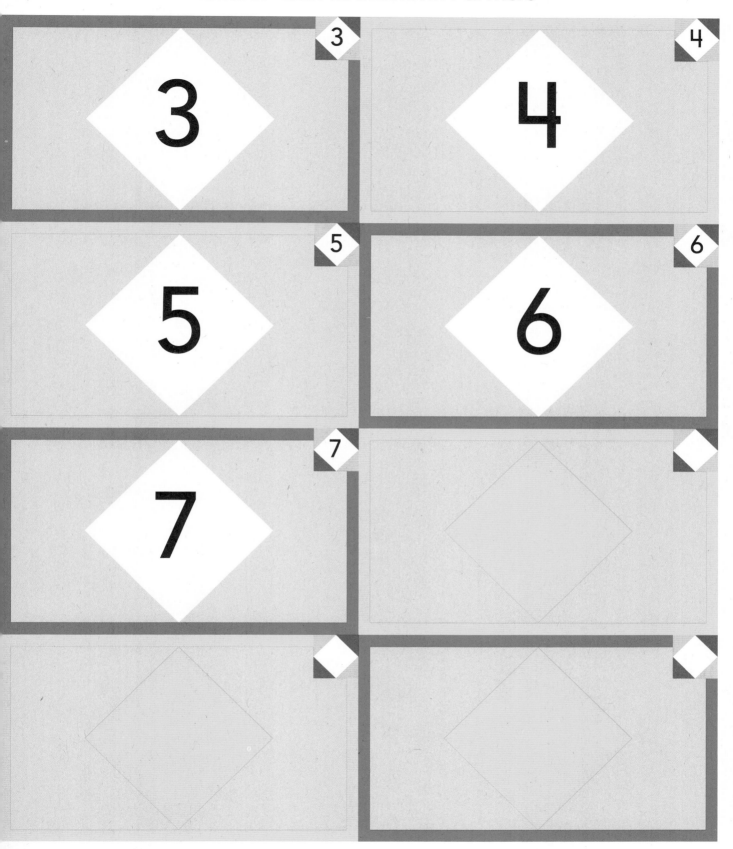

Use with the Yellow or Orange Count-On Cards.

Number Quilt 2

Name _____

Solve the story problem.

Show your work. Use drawings, numbers, or words.

1 Sam has 4 balloons.
Then he gets some more.
Now he has 9.
How many balloons does he get?

balloon

[ ] _____
label

2 There are 8 crayons on the table.
There are 5 red crayons.
The others are green.
How many crayons are green?

table

[ ] _____
label

3 Rabia sees 10 eagles.
There are 3 in a tree.
The rest are flying.
How many eagles are flying?

eagle

[ ] _____
label

Solve the story problem.

Show your work. Use drawings, numbers, or words.

4 Maddox has 3 toy trains.
Then he gets more.
Now he has 7.
How many trains does he get?

train

☐ _____
label

5 We pick 10 apples from the trees.
6 are green. Some are red.
How many apples are red?

tree

☐ _____
label

6 Milena wants to put 8 balls
in a box. She wants to have
soccer balls and footballs.
How many of each ball could
she use? Show two answers.

soccer ball

☐ soccer balls and ☐ footballs

or ☐ soccer balls and ☐ footballs

 Check Understanding
Write the unknown partner. $4 + \boxed{} = 10$

Addition Game: Unknown Partners

Draw a **Math Mountain**, and write an equation to represent the story.

1. There are 8 cows in the field. There are 6 brown cows. The rest are black. How many cows are black?

_____
Equation

2. There are 5 kittens sleeping. Some more join them. Now there are 9 kittens sleeping. How many kittens join?

_____
Equation

3. Jenny has 7 flowers. She wants to put some flowers in a red vase and a pink vase. How many flowers can she put in each vase?

_____
Equation

Draw a Math Mountain for the equation.

4 $6 + \square = 10$

5 $7 + \square = 10$

6 $5 + \square = 10$

7 $9 + \square = 10$

8 $4 + \square = 10$

9 $2 + \square = 10$

 Check Understanding

Draw a Math Mountain that matches the equation $7 + \square = 9$.

© Houghton Mifflin Harcourt Publishing Company

Practice with Unknown Partners

Count on to find the unknown partner.

1 $2 + \boxed{} = 5$ | **2** $4 + \boxed{} = 7$ | **3** $5 + \boxed{} = 9$

Count on to solve.

4 7 pencils total

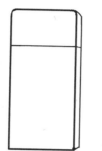 

How many pencils are in the box?

$\boxed{}$ _____
label

5 10 pennies total

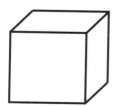

How many pennies are in the box?

$\boxed{}$ _____
label

Name _____ Date _____

Add.

1 1 + 1 = ☐   **2** 2 + 8 = ☐   **3** 8 + 2 = ☐

4 3 + 7 = ☐   **5** 2 + 2 = ☐   **6** 1 + 9 = ☐

7 0 + 10 = ☐   **8** 4 + 6 = ☐   **9** 3 + 3 = ☐

10 9 + 1 = ☐   **11** 4 + 4 = ☐   **12** 6 + 4 = ☐

13 5 + 5 = ☐   **14** 10 + 0 = ☐   **15** 7 + 3 = ☐

VOCABULARY
subtraction story problem

Solve the **subtraction story problem**. Show your work. Use drawings, numbers, or words.

1 8 flies are on a log.
   A frog eats 6 of them.
   How many flies are left?

frog

☐ _____
        label

2 I find 7 shells by the sea.
   Then I lose 3 of them.
   How many shells do I
   have now?

shell

☐ _____
        label

3 I draw 10 houses.
   Then I erase 5 of them.
   How many houses are left?

house

☐ _____
        label

4 Write a subtraction story problem.

_____

- - - - - - - - - - - - - - - - - - - -

_____

- - - - - - - - - - - - - - - - - - - -

_____

- - - - - - - - - - - - - - - - - - - -

_____

5 Write an equation to solve the story problem.
Use a box for the unknown number.

PATH to FLUENCY **Subtract.**

1 $6 - 5 = \boxed{}$ **2** $2 - 1 = \boxed{}$ **3** $8 - 7 = \boxed{}$

4 $10 - 9 = \boxed{}$ **5** $5 - 4 = \boxed{}$ **6** $3 - 2 = \boxed{}$

✓ **Check Understanding**

Listen to the subtraction story. Write an equation
to solve. Use a box for the unknown number.

       Subtraction Strategies

6 − 3 = ☐

7 − 3 = ☐

8 − 3 = ☐

9 − 3 = ☐

10 − 3 = ☐

7 − 4 = ☐

8 − 4 = ☐

9 − 4 = ☐

10 − 4 = ☐

8 − 5 = ☐

9 − 5 = ☐

10 − 5 = ☐

9 − 6 = ☐

10 − 6 = ☐

10 − 7 = ☐

8 − 3 = 5

3 | ·····

7 − 3 = 4

3 | ····

6 − 3 = 3

3 | ···

7 − 4 = 3

4 | ···

10 − 3 = 7

3 | :::·

9 − 3 = 6

3 | :····

10 − 4 = 6

4 | :····

9 − 4 = 5

4 | ·····

8 − 4 = 4

4 | ····

10 − 5 = 5

5 | ·····

9 − 5 = 4

5 | ····

8 − 5 = 3

5 | ···

10 − 7 = 3

7 | ···

10 − 6 = 4

6 | ····

9 − 6 = 3

6 | ···

Orange Count-On Cards

Name _____

Solve. Make a drawing, and write an equation.

1. There are 9 stickers on the sheet. John uses 6 stickers. How many stickers are left?

label

Equation

2. Cody sees 7 bees on flowers. Then 3 bees fly away. How many bees are there now?

label

Equation

3. The tomato plant has 5 tomatoes. Marvin picks 2 tomatoes. How many tomatoes are left?

label

Equation

Count on to find the partner.

4 $6 - 3 =$ ☐

| 3 | ● ● ● |

5 $7 - 5 =$ ☐

| 5 | ● ● |

6 $7 - 3 =$ ☐

| 3 | ● ● ● ● |

7 $5 - 3 =$ ☐

| 3 | ● ● |

8 $9 - 5 =$ ☐

| 5 | ● ● ● ● |

9 $8 - 4 =$ ☐

| 4 | ● ● ● ● |

10 $10 - 7 =$ ☐

| 7 | ● ● ● |

11 $9 - 6 =$ ☐

| 6 | ● ● ● |

✓ **Check Understanding**

Explain how to solve the subtraction

problem $9 - 4 =$ ☐.

Subtraction Stories and Games

Name _____

Solve and discuss.

1 We see 10 dogs.
Then 7 run away.
How many are left?

[   ] _____
            label

_____   _____
Equation   Equation

2 We see 9 dogs.
There are 5 not barking.
The rest are barking.
How many are barking?

[   ] _____
            label

_____   _____
Equation   Equation

3 Discuss the methods you used to solve the problems.
How are they alike and different?

Solve the story problem.

4 There are 8 apples. 6 apples are eaten.
How many apples are there now?

apple

☐ _____
      label

5 There are 10 birds in the tree.
6 are singing. The rest are not singing.
How many birds are not singing?

tree

☐ _____
      label

6 Liam has 8 carrots. He eats 4 carrots.
How many carrots are left?

carrot

☐ _____
      label

✓ **Check Understanding**
Solve the problem. Write the equation.
We see 9 bunnies in the grass.
3 are hopping. The rest are not hopping.
How many bunnies are not hopping?

bunny

☐ _____   Equation
      label

Practice with Subtraction Stories

Subtract.

1 $6 - 3 = \boxed{}$

2 $7 - 2 = \boxed{}$

3 $10 - 4 = \boxed{}$

Solve the story problem.

Show your work.

4 Corey has 9 grapes.
He eats 5 of them.
How many grapes are left?

$\boxed{}$ _____
label

---

5 There are 8 kittens.
6 kittens are black.
The rest are white.
How many kittens are white?

$\boxed{}$ _____
label

Name _____   Date _____

Subtract.

1 $2 - 1 =$ ☐   **2** $4 - 3 =$ ☐   **3** $3 - 2 =$ ☐

4 $7 - 6 =$ ☐   **5** $6 - 5 =$ ☐   **6** $5 - 4 =$ ☐

7 $9 - 8 =$ ☐   **8** $8 - 7 =$ ☐   **9** $10 - 9 =$ ☐

10 $4 - 3 =$ ☐   **11** $6 - 5 =$ ☐   **12** $2 - 1 =$ ☐

13 $5 - 4 =$ ☐   **14** $10 - 9 =$ ☐   **15** $7 - 6 =$ ☐

Name _____

Solve and discuss.

1 There are 4 cats. Then
3 more cats join them.
How many cats are there now?

$4 + 3 = \boxed{}$

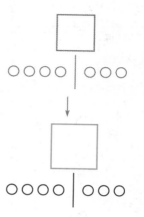
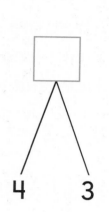

2 There are 6 cats.
Some more cats join them.
Now there are 8 cats.
How many cats join?

$6 + \boxed{} = 8$

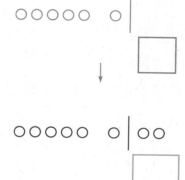
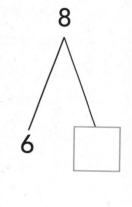

3 There are some cats.
Then 4 more cats join them.
Now there are 9 cats.
How many cats are there
at the start?

$\boxed{} + 4 = 9$

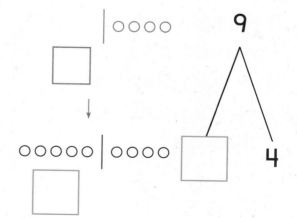

Solve and discuss.

4 There are 7 cats. Then
3 cats walk away.
How many cats are left?

$7 - 3 = \boxed{}$

$3 + \boxed{} = 7$

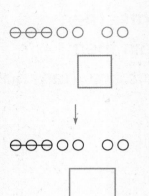

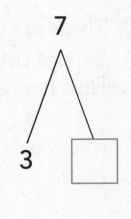

---

5 There are 8 cats.
Some cats walk away.
There are 6 cats left.
How many cats walk away?

$8 - \boxed{} = 6$

$6 + \boxed{} = 8$

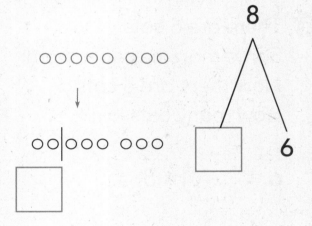

---

6 There are some cats.
4 cats walk away.
Now there are 5 cats.
How many cats are there
at the start?

$\boxed{} - 4 = 5$

$5 + 4 = \boxed{}$

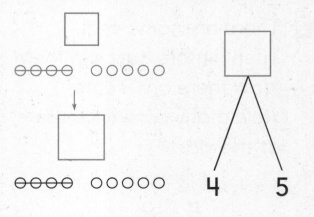

Relate Addition and Subtraction Situations

Name _____

Solve the story problem.

Show your work. Use drawings, numbers, or words.

7 There are 10 kittens. There are 7 playing.
The rest are sleeping.
How many are sleeping?

kitten

◻ _____
label

8 Emma has 5 beads. She gets some more
beads. Now she has 9 beads. How many
beads does she get?

bead

◻ _____
label

9 There are 8 boys at the park. Some boys go
home. Now 3 boys are left. How many boys
go home?

boy

◻ _____
label

10 Some horses are in the barn. Then 3 more
horses go in. Now 7 horses are in the barn.
How many are there at the start?

barn

◻ _____
label

Relate Addition and Subtraction Situations **135**

Solve the story problem.

Show your work. Use drawings, numbers, or words.

11 Dad picks some flowers. He puts 2 in the red vase and the other 5 in the blue vase. How many does he pick?

flower

◻ _____
　　　label

12 Meg has some cherries. She eats 6. There are 4 left. How many did she have at first?

cherry

◻ _____
　　　label

13 There are 5 puppies. Then 3 more puppies come. How many puppies are there now?

puppy

◻ _____
　　　label

 Check Understanding

Listen to the story problem. Draw a picture and write both a subtraction and an addition equation to solve the story problem.

　　Relate Addition and Subtraction Situations

Solve.

1 Sam scores 4 points. Julio scores 3 points. How many points do they score in all?

Sam ____   Julio ____   Together ☐

2 Sam scores 4 points. Julio also scores some points. In all they score 7 points. How many points does Julio score?

Sam ____   Julio ☐

Together ____

3 Sam scores some points. Then Julio scores 3 points. In all they score 7 points. How many points does Sam score?

Sam ☐

Julio ____

Together ____

Solve the story problem.

Show your work. Use drawings, numbers, or words.

4 8 frogs are in the pond. Some hop away.
2 are left. How many frogs hop away?

pond

☐ _____
label

5 Ivan has some balls. He gives 4 to friends.
He has 3 left. How many did he have before?

ball

☐ _____
label

6 There are 7 flowers. Sam picks 2.
How many flowers are left?

flower

☐ _____
label

PATH to FLUENCY **Subtract.**

1 $2 - 2 =$ ☐   **2** $4 - 2 =$ ☐   **3** $4 - 4 =$ ☐

✓ **Check Understanding**
Listen to the story problem.
Draw a Math Mountain or write
an equation to solve the problem.

Solve Mixed Problems

Number Quilt 3: Any Unknown

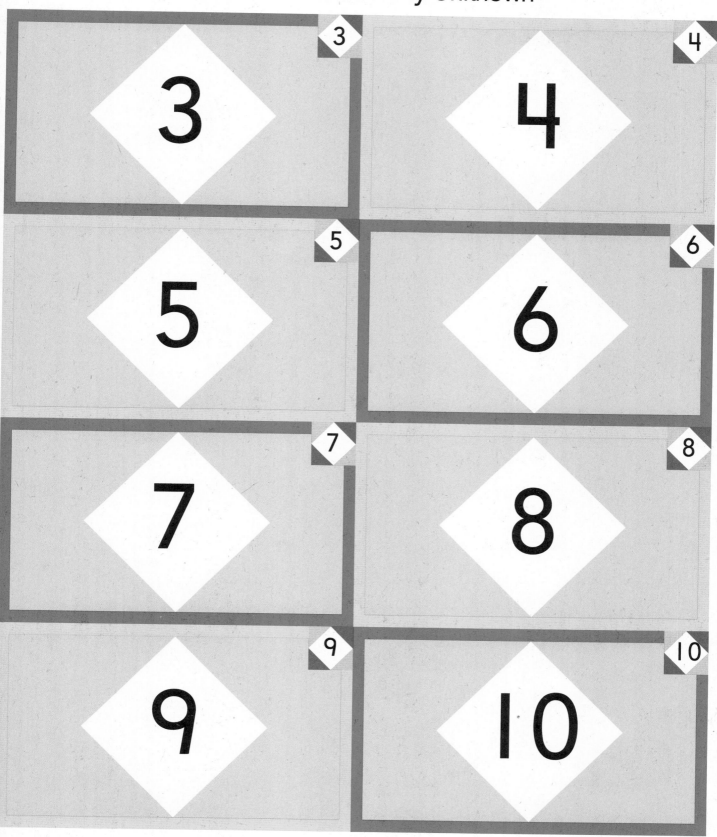

Use with any of the Count-On Cards.

Number Quilt 3

Name _____

Solve the story problem.

1 There are 4 owls in the tree. Then some more owls come. Now there are 6 owls in the tree. How many owls come?

owl

[ ] _____
        label

2 Some children are on the bus. 5 more get on the bus. Now there are 8. How many children are on the bus before?

bus

[ ] _____
        label

3 There are 7 plants in the garden. There are 2 carrot plants. The rest are onions. How many plants are onions?

onion

[ ] _____
        label

4 Some lizards are on a log. Then 3 lizards leave. Now there are 7 lizards. How many lizards are there to start?

lizard

[ ] _____
        label

Solve.

5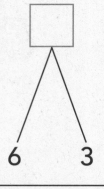

6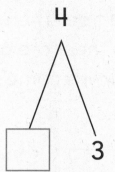

7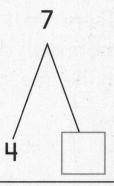

8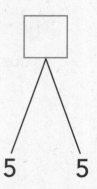

9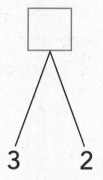

10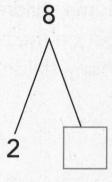

11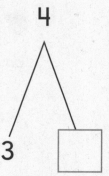

12

13

14 $\boxed{} + 8 = 10$ **15** $4 + \boxed{} = 6$ **16** $10 - \boxed{} = 2$

 Check Understanding

Solve. Draw to show how you solved the equation.

$\boxed{} - 4 = 6$

Practice with Mixed Problems

Name _____

Write the equation to solve.

1 There are 7 balls in the box. Jabar puts some more balls in the box. Now there are 10 balls in the box. How many balls does Jabar put in the box?

  □ = □

Jabar puts □ balls in the box.

2 There were 8 baseballs in the bucket. Leslie takes some baseballs from the bucket. Now there are 6 baseballs in the bucket. How many baseballs does Leslie take?

   = □

Leslie takes baseballs.

3 Use the picture to write a story problem.
Write and solve the equation.

label

Find the unknown partner or total.
Watch the signs.

1 $6 - 5 = \boxed{}$

2 $8 + 2 = \boxed{}$

3 $7 - \boxed{} = 1$

Solve the story problem.   **Show your work.**

4 Kyle catches 8 frogs.
He lets some frogs go.
Now Kyle has 2 frogs.
How many frogs did he let go?

$\boxed{}$ _____
            label

---

5 Some birds are in a tree. Then 4 birds fly away.
Now there are 5 birds. How many birds
are in the tree at the start?

$\boxed{}$ _____
            label

Name _____   Date _____

PATH to
FLUENCY

Subtract.

1 2 − 1 = ☐   **2** 3 − 3 = ☐   **3** 1 − 1 = ☐

4 2 − 2 = ☐   **5** 4 − 2 = ☐   **6** 5 − 5 = ☐

7 7 − 7 = ☐   **8** 6 − 6 = ☐   **9** 6 − 3 = ☐

10 8 − 8 = ☐   **11** 8 − 4 = ☐   **12** 9 − 9 = ☐

13 10 − 10 = ☐   **14** 10 − 5 = ☐   **15** 4 − 4 = ☐

1 Match each set of partners to a total.

6 + 2 = _____ •

9 − 3 = _____ •

3 + 7 = _____ •

8 − 3 = _____ •

•5

•10

•8

•6

Make three different Math Mountains with a total of 6.

2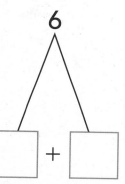

3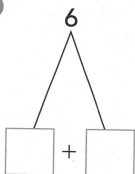

4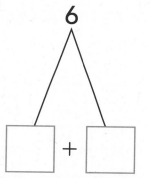

5 Count on to solve.

8 rakes total

How many rakes are in the shed?

  _____

label

Solve the story problem.

6 Maisy has 5 balloons. She gets some more balloons. Now she has 9 balloons. How many balloons does Maisy get?

balloon

◻ _____
   label

_____

7 Han picks 5 apples.
Then he picks 3 more.
How many apples does Han pick?

apple

◻ _____
   label

_____

8 Avery has 7 baseballs. Then he gets some more. Now Avery has 10 baseballs. How many baseballs does he get?

ball

◻ _____
   label

_____

Complete the equations.
Use the numbers on the tiles.

9 $10 - \boxed{} = 2$

10 $4 + \boxed{} = 8$

11 $3 + \boxed{} = 9$

12 $8 - \boxed{} = 3$

© Houghton Mifflin Harcourt Publishing Company

Ring the number that makes the sentence true.

13 Lila has 10 books. She gives 4 books away.

book

Now Lila has
| 4 |
| 6 |
| 10 |
books.

14 Use the picture to write a story problem.
Write and solve the equation.

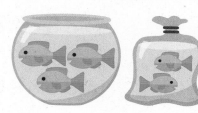

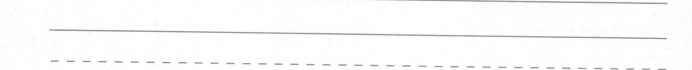

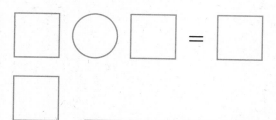

label

Solve the story problem.

15 Marty sees 8 birds at a feeder.
There are red birds and blue birds.
How many of each color bird can Marty see?
Show three correct answers.

bird

☐ red birds and ☐ blue birds

or ☐ red birds and ☐ blue birds

or ☐ red birds and ☐ blue birds

---

16 Read the story problem. Write a subtraction
and an addition equation for the story.
Draw a Math Mountain to match.

There are 7 leaves on the branch.
Then 3 leaves fall off.
How many leaves are on the branch now?

Hide and Seek

Some children are playing hide and seek.

Choose a number from 1–10 for each ☐ .
Use each number only once.

1 10 children are playing. ☐ go and hide.
How many are left?

☐ children

2 ☐ children are hiding. ☐ more children
hide. How many children are hiding?

☐ children

3 Write equations for Problems 1 and 2.

☐ ◯ ☐ = ☐ | ☐ ◯ ☐ = ☐

4 Show you know which partners and total to write in
each equation. Use drawings, numbers, or words.

Soccer

Some children are playing soccer.
Choose a number from 1–10. Use each number only once.

5 **Part A** 10 children play soccer. ☐ players leave.

How many are left? ☐ children

Part B Draw a picture to tell the story.

Write an equation for the story. ☐ ◯ ☐ = ☐

6 **Part A** 4 children play soccer. ☐ players join.

How many in all? ☐ children

Part B Draw a picture to tell the story.

Write an equation for the story. ☐ ◯ ☐ = ☐

Dear Family:

Your child is learning about place value and numbers to 100. In this program, children begin by counting tens: 10, 20, 30, 40, and so on. They use a 10 × 10 Grid to help them "see" the relationship between the tens digit in a decade number and the number of tens it has.

10 20 30 40

40 is 4 tens.

Soon, children will link 2-digit numbers to tens and extra ones. They will learn that a 2-digit number, such as 46, is made up of tens and ones, such as 40 and 6. Next, children will use what they know about adding 1-digit numbers to add 2-digit numbers.

$$3 + 4 = 7, \text{ so } 30 + 40 = 70.$$

Finally, they will learn to regroup and count on to find a total. For example:

$$19 + 5 = \boxed{24}$$

$$\overset{20}{(19)} \; \circ \circ \circ \circ \circ \; 24$$

Right now, your child may enjoy counting by tens for you. He or she may also enjoy using household items to make groups of ten and extra ones, and then telling you the total number.

Sincerely,
Your child's teacher

Estimada familia:

Su niño está aprendiendo sobre valor posicional y los números hasta 100. En este programa, los niños empiezan contando decenas: 10, 20, 30, 40, etc. Usan una cuadrícula de 10 por 10 como ayuda para "ver" la relación entre el dígito de las decenas en el número que termina en cero y el número de decenas que tiene.

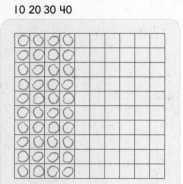

10 20 30 40

40 es 4 decenas.

En poco tiempo, los niños harán la conexión entre números de 2 dígitos y decenas más otras unidades. Aprenderán que un número de 2 dígitos, tal como 46, consta de decenas y unidades, como 40 y 6. Luego, los niños usarán lo que saben de la suma de números de 1 dígito para sumar números de 2 dígitos.

3 + 4 = 7, por lo tanto 30 + 40 = 70.

Finalmente, aprenderán a reagrupar y contar hacia adelante para hallar el total. Por ejemplo:

$$19 + 5 = \boxed{24}$$

20
(19) ○ ○ ○ ○ ○ 24

Por lo pronto, tal vez a su niño le guste contar en decenas para Ud. También puede gustarle usar objetos del hogar para formar grupos de diez más otras unidades y luego decir el número total.

Atentamente,
El maestro de su niño

Introduction to Tens Groupings

compare

doubles
minus 2

dime

doubles
plus 1

doubles
minus 1

doubles
plus 2

7 + 7 = 14, so
7 + 5 = 12, 2 less than 14.

11 is less than 12.
11 < 12
12 is greater than 11.
12 > 11

6 + 6 = 12, so
6 + 7 = 13, 1 more than 12.

front   back

10 cents or 10¢

6 + 6 = 12, so
6 + 8 = 14, 2 more than 12.

7 + 7 = 14, so
7 + 6 = 13, 1 less than 14.

number word

quarter

tens

12
twelve ← **number word**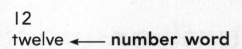

front   back

25 cents or 25¢

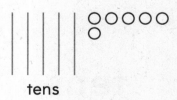

tens

56 has 5 **tens**.

Name _____

How many circles? Count by **tens**.

VOCABULARY
tens

  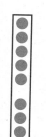   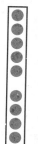  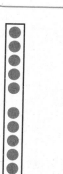

___ ___ ___ ___ ___ ___ ___ ___

Total

Add 1 ten.

 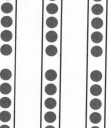 +

 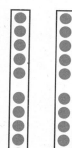  +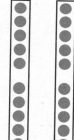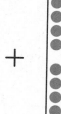

Equation _____   Equation _____

 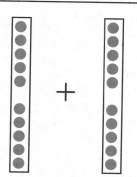

 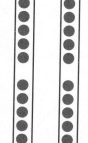 +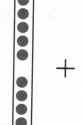

Equation _____   Equation _____

Add 10.

6 50 + 10 = ☐

7 10 + 10 = ☐

8 30 + 10 = ☐

9 80 + 10 = ☐

10 70 + 10 = ☐

11 60 + 10 = ☐

12 40 + 10 = ☐

13 90 + 10 = ☐

Write the numbers.

14 20 = _____ tens _____ ones

15 80 = _____ tens _____ ones

16 50 = _____ tens _____ ones

17 10 = _____ ten _____ ones

18 Draw tens to solve.
Write the unknown number.

☐ + 10 = 30

✓ **Check Understanding**
How are counting tens and
adding tens the same?

Introduction to Tens Groupings

Name _____

Solve. Write an equation to show
one ten and extra ones.

---

1 Choi has 10 pencils in a pack and
4 extra pencils. How many pencils
does he have in all?

pencil

[ ] + [ ] = [ ]

[ ] pencils

---

2 There are 10 cups in a box and
7 extra cups. How many cups
are there altogether?

cup

[ ] + [ ] = [ ]

[ ] cups

---

3 Ginger has a tray of 10 plants and
2 extra plants. How many plants
are there in all?

plant

[ ] + [ ] = [ ]

[ ] plants

---

4 Abe has a pail of 10 brushes
and 8 extra brushes. How many
brushes are there in all?

paintbrush

[ ] + [ ] = [ ]

[ ] brushes

© Houghton Mifflin Harcourt Publishing Company

Explore Teen Numbers **157**

Draw circles in the grid to show
the teen number. Write the equation.

5 Model 16

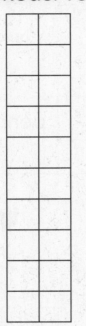

____ + ____ = ____

6 Model 13

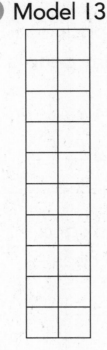

____ + ____ = ____

7 Model 11

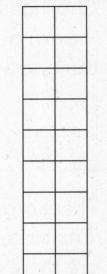

____ + ____ = ____

8 There is a set of 10 books on a shelf
and 5 extra books. How many books
are there altogether?

Show the teen number in two different ways.

 Check Understanding

Explain what a teen number is.

Explore Teen Numbers

Dear Family:

To help children "see" the tens and ones in 2-digit numbers, the *Math Expressions* program uses special drawings of 10-sticks to show tens, and circles to show ones. These images help children learn place value. Below are the numbers 27 and 52 shown with 10-sticks and circles:

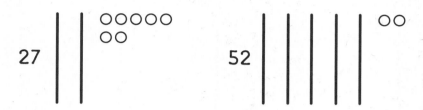

10-sticks and circles will also be used later to help children solve addition problems that require regrouping (sometimes called "carrying"). When there are enough circles to make a new ten, they are circled and then added like a 10-stick. The problem below shows 38 + 5:

Step 1: Show the two numbers with 10-sticks and circles.

Step 2: Group the ones to make a new ten. Count by tens and ones.

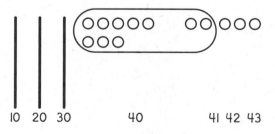

Right now, your child is just beginning to show teen numbers with 10-sticks and circles. Soon your child will be able to draw 10-sticks and circles for any 2-digit number.

In this unit, children will also use coins to help them understand place value, find equivalent values between coins, and solve coin story problems. As they complete their homework, they may use real or play coins to help them.

Sincerely,
Your child's teacher

Estimada familia:

Para ayudar a los niños a "ver" las decenas y las unidades en los números de 2 dígitos, el programa *Math Expressions* usa dibujos especiales de palitos de decenas para mostrar las decenas, y círculos para mostrar las unidades. Estas imágenes ayudan a los niños a aprender el valor posicional. Abajo se muestran los números 27 y 52 con palitos de decenas y círculos:

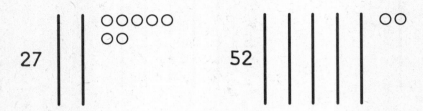

Más adelante, los palitos de decenas y los círculos también se usarán para ayudar a los niños a resolver problemas de suma que requieren reagrupar (que a veces se llama "llevar"). Cuando hay suficientes círculos para formar una nueva decena, se encierran en un círculo y se suman como si fueran un palito de decena. El siguiente problema muestra 38 + 5:

Paso 1: Mostrar los dos números con palitos de decenas y círculos.

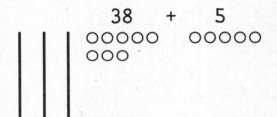

Paso 2: Agrupar las unidades para formar una nueva decena. Contar en decenas y unidades.

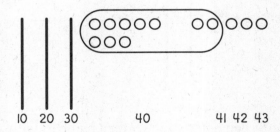

Su niño está comenzando a mostrar los números de 11 a 19 con palitos de decenas y círculos. Pronto, podrá dibujar palitos de decenas y círculos para cualquier número de 2 dígitos.

En esta unidad los niños también usarán monedas que les servirán para comprender el valor posicional, hallar los valores equivalentes entre monedas y resolver problemas de monedas. Al completar su tarea, pueden usar monedas reales o de juego para ayudarlos.

Atentamente,
El maestro de su niño

Name _____

Write the teen number for each model.

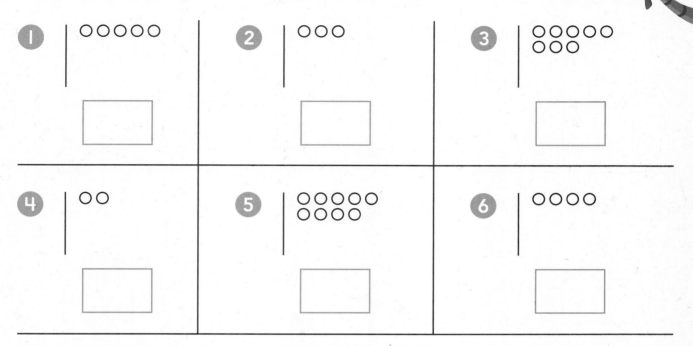

Draw a stick for 10 and circles for ones to represent the teen number.

7 Ben buys a package of 10 erasers. He already has 2 erasers. How many erasers does Ben have now?

8 Olivia has 16 bottles of water. A box holds 10. Draw a stick and circles to show how many boxes she can fill and how many bottles will be left over.

Represent and Compare Teen Numbers **161**

Write the number. Compare the numbers. Use =, <, or >.

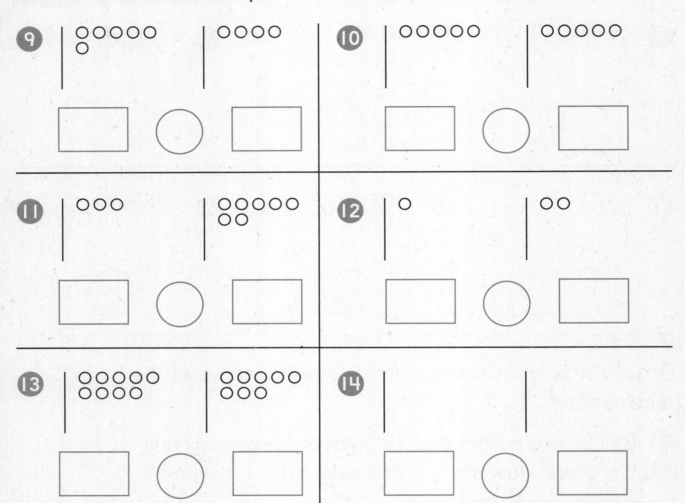

15 Compare the numbers 16 and 12 two different ways. Draw to explain.

✓ Check Understanding

Draw to explain why 15 is greater than 11.

Name _____

1 Look at what Puzzled Penguin wrote.

$7 + 8 = 10 + \boxed{3}$

$7 + 8 = \boxed{13}$

Am I correct?

2 Help Puzzled Penguin.

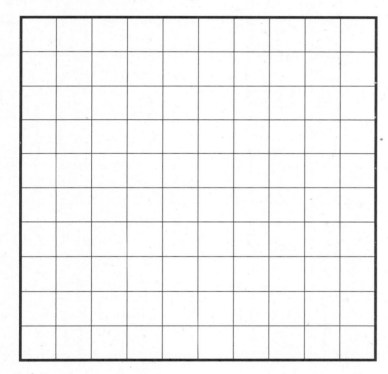

$7 + 8 = 10 + \boxed{}$

$7 + 8 = \boxed{}$

Find the total. Then make a ten.

3 7 + 4 = ⬚

10 + ⬚ = ⬚

4 8 + 8 = ⬚

10 + ⬚ = ⬚

5 8 + 4 = ⬚

10 + ⬚ = ⬚

6 9 + 6 = ⬚

10 + ⬚ = ⬚

7 8 + 6 = ⬚

10 + ⬚ = ⬚

8 5 + 7 = ⬚

10 + ⬚ = ⬚

9 5 + 8 = ⬚

10 + ⬚ = ⬚

10 2 + 9 = ⬚

10 + ⬚ = ⬚

11 Write two equations that show different partners for 13. Use 10 in one equation.

_____

_____

✔ **Check Understanding**

How can 10 + 4 help you solve 9 + 5?

Visualize Teen Addition

$5 + 7 = \boxed{}$

$6 + 7 = \boxed{}$

$9 + 9 = \boxed{}$

$8 + 7 = \boxed{}$

$9 + 7 = \boxed{}$

$3 + 8 = \boxed{}$

$4 + 8 = \boxed{}$

$5 + 8 = \boxed{}$

$6 + 8 = \boxed{}$

$7 + 8 = \boxed{}$

$8 + 8 = \boxed{}$

$9 + 8 = \boxed{}$

$3 + 9 = \boxed{}$

$4 + 9 = \boxed{}$

$5 + 9 = \boxed{}$

$9 + 9 = 18$

9 | •   • • • •
       • • • •
9 + 1 + 8

$6 + 7 = 13$

7 | • • •   • • •
7 + 3 + 3

$5 + 7 = 12$

7 | • • •   • •
7 + 3 + 2

$3 + 8 = 11$

8 | • •   •
8 + 2 + 1

$9 + 7 = 16$

9 | •   • • •
       • • •
9 + 1 + 6

$8 + 7 = 15$

8 | • •   • • • • •
8 + 2 + 5

$6 + 8 = 14$

8 | • •   • • • •
8 + 2 + 4

$5 + 8 = 13$

8 | • •   • • •
8 + 2 + 3

$4 + 8 = 12$

8 | • •   • •
8 + 2 + 2

$9 + 8 = 17$

9 | •   • • • • •
       • •
9 + 1 + 7

$8 + 8 = 16$

8 | • •   • • •
       • • •
8 + 2 + 6

$7 + 8 = 15$

8 | • •   • • • • •
8 + 2 + 5

$5 + 9 = 14$

9 | •   • • • •
9 + 1 + 4

$4 + 9 = 13$

9 | •   • • •
9 + 1 + 3

$3 + 9 = 12$

9 | •   • •
9 + 1 + 2

Green Make-a-Ten Cards

$6 + 9 = \boxed{}$

$7 + 9 = \boxed{}$

$7 + 4 = \boxed{}$

$8 + 4 = \boxed{}$

$9 + 4 = \boxed{}$

$6 + 5 = \boxed{}$

$7 + 5 = \boxed{}$

$8 + 5 = \boxed{}$

$9 + 5 = \boxed{}$

$5 + 6 = \boxed{}$

$8 + 9 = \boxed{}$

$7 + 6 = \boxed{}$

$8 + 6 = \boxed{}$

$9 + 6 = \boxed{}$

$4 + 7 = \boxed{}$

7 + 4 = 11

7 ••• •
7 + 3 + 1

7 + 9 = 16

9 • ••••
9 + 1 + 6

6 + 9 = 15

9 • •••••
9 + 1 + 5

6 + 5 = 11

6 •••• •
6 + 4 + 1

9 + 4 = 13

9 • •••
9 + 1 + 3

8 + 4 = 12

8 •• ••
8 + 2 + 2

9 + 5 = 14

9 • ••••
9 + 1 + 4

8 + 5 = 13

8 •• •••
8 + 2 + 3

7 + 5 = 12

7 ••• ••
7 + 3 + 2

7 + 6 = 13

7 ••• •••
7 + 3 + 3

8 + 9 = 17

9 • •••••••
9 + 1 + 7

5 + 6 = 11

6 •••• •
6 + 4 + 1

4 + 7 = 11

7 ••• •
7 + 3 + 1

9 + 6 = 15

9 • •••••
9 + 1 + 5

8 + 6 = 14

8 •• ••••
8 + 2 + 4

Green Make-a-Ten Cards

Name _____

Find the teen total.

1 5 + 9 = ☐

2 7 + 5 = ☐

3 7 + 4 = ☐

4 9 + 6 = ☐

5 9 + 8 = ☐

6 9 + 9 = ☐

7 3 + 9 = ☐

8 7 + 8 = ☐

9 9 + 4 = ☐

10 6 + 5 = ☐

11 8 + 8 = ☐

12 8 + 4 = ☐

13 7 + 6 = ☐

14 9 + 7 = ☐

15 Write an equation with a teen total. Draw or explain how making a ten can help you solve your equation.

_____

Teen Addition Strategies **169**

Find the total.

16 $10 + 9 =$ ☐

17 $9 + 10 =$ ☐

18 $6 + 4 =$ ☐

19 $10 + 3 =$ ☐

20 $10 + 8 =$ ☐

21 $3 + 10 =$ ☐

22 $1 + 9 =$ ☐

23 $10 + 10 =$ ☐

24 Draw or write to explain how you solved Exercise 23.

✓ **Check Understanding**

Explain how to use the Make a Ten strategy to solve $8 + 6$?

Teen Addition Strategies

Name _____

Use doubles to find the total.

1 $5 + 5 =$ ⬚ 2 $6 + 6 =$ ⬚ 3 $7 + 7 =$ ⬚

4 $8 + 8 =$ ⬚ 5 $9 + 9 =$ ⬚ 6 $10 + 10 =$ ⬚

Use **doubles plus 1** or **doubles minus 1** to find the total.

7 $4 + 4 = 8$
$4 + 5 = 8 +$ ___ = ___

8 $8 + 8 = 16$
$8 + 7 = 16 -$ ___ = ___

9 $5 + 6 =$ ⬚ 10 $9 + 8 =$ ⬚ 11 $6 + 7 =$ ⬚

Use **doubles plus 2** or **doubles minus 2** to find the total.

12 $4 + 4 = 8$
$4 + 6 = 8 +$ ___ = ___

13 $8 + 8 = 16$
$8 + 6 = 16 -$ ___ = ___

14 $7 + 5 =$ ⬚ 15 $7 + 9 =$ ⬚ 16 $6 + 8 =$ ⬚

Use a double to find the total.

17 8
   + 7

18 10
   + 8

19 5
   + 7

20 6
   + 5

21 8
   + 9

22 7
   + 8

23 7
   + 5

24 7
   + 6

25 Write the double you used to solve Exercise 23.

_____

PATH to FLUENCY Subtract.

1 6
  − 5

2 9
  − 2

3 7
  − 3

4 8
  − 2

5 10
  − 1

6 9
  − 4

7 8
  − 5

8 10
  − 8

 Check Understanding

Write a doubles plus 1 equation for 6 + 6.

_____

Investigate Doubles

Find the total. Then make a ten.

1. $7 + 5 =$ ☐

   $10 +$ ☐ $=$ ☐

2. $2 + 9 =$ ☐

   $10 +$ ☐ $=$ ☐

Use doubles or doubles plus 1 to find the total.

3. $6 + 6 =$ ☐

4. $9 + 8 =$ ☐

5. $8 + 7 =$ ☐

Name _____   Date _____

Subtract.

1
6
− 2
___

2
8
− 1
___

3
7
− 0
___

4
8
− 4
___

5
7
− 3
___

6
6
− 3
___

7
9
− 4
___

8
6
− 5
___

9
7
− 2
___

10
10
− 5
___

11
9
− 6
___

12
10
− 2
___

13
9
− 7
___

14
10
− 9
___

15
8
− 5
___

Name _____

Write the number.

1

2

3

4

5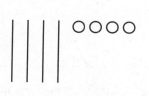

6

7

8

9

10

11

12

Draw 10-sticks and circles. Write the equation.

13   32

[ ] + [ ] = [ ]

14   68

[ ] + [ ] = [ ]

15   93

[ ] + [ ] = [ ]

16   77

[ ] + [ ] = [ ]

Draw 10-sticks and circles. Write the number.

17   4 tens 8 ones

[ ]

18   8 tens 3 ones

[ ]

 Check Understanding

Draw 10-sticks and circles to show 63.
Write the number of tens and ones.

     Understand Tens and Ones

Name _____

VOCABULARY
number word

1 one	11 eleven	10 ten
2 two	12 twelve	20 twenty
3 three	13 thirteen	30 thirty
4 four	14 fourteen	40 forty
5 five	15 fifteen	50 fifty
6 six	16 sixteen	60 sixty
7 seven	17 seventeen	70 seventy
8 eight	18 eighteen	80 eighty
9 nine	19 nineteen	90 ninety
10 ten	20 twenty	

Write the number.

1 five _____   fifteen _____   fifty _____

2 three _____   thirteen _____   thirty _____

3 two _____   twelve _____   twenty _____

4 sixty _____   sixteen _____   six _____

5 eighteen _____   eighty _____   eight _____

Write the **number word**.

6 4 _____   14 _____   40 _____

7 9 _____   19 _____   90 _____

8 2 _____   12 _____   20 _____

9 1 _____   10 _____   11 _____

Integrate Tens and Ones **177**

1 one	11 eleven	10 ten
2 two	12 twelve	20 twenty
3 three	13 thirteen	30 thirty
4 four	14 fourteen	40 forty
5 five	15 fifteen	50 fifty
6 six	16 sixteen	60 sixty
7 seven	17 seventeen	70 seventy
8 eight	18 eighteen	80 eighty
9 nine	19 nineteen	90 ninety
10 ten	20 twenty	

Write the number word.

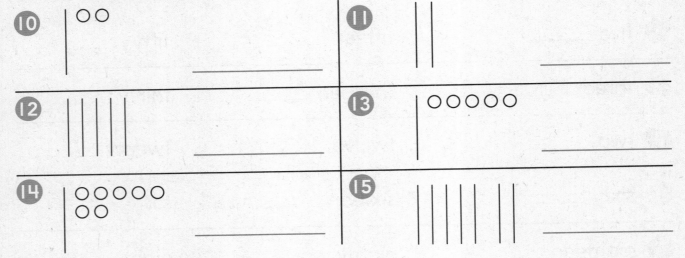

10 _____ **11** _____

12 _____ **13** _____

14 _____ **15** _____

16 Write the numbers 1–20.

1									
									20

17 Write the decade numbers 10–90.

10	20							

Integrate Tens and Ones

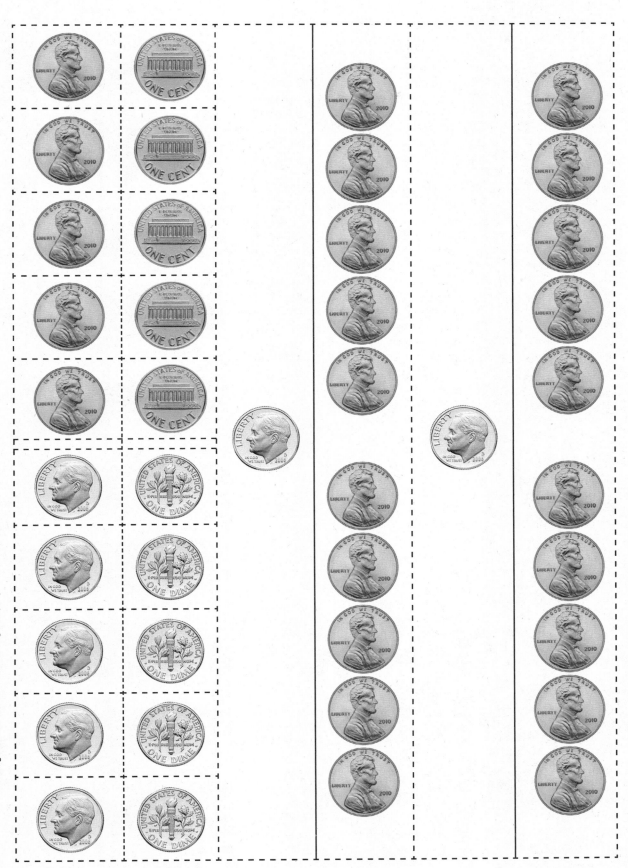

Dime Strips, Dimes, and Pennies

Dime Strips, Dimes, and Pennies

Name _____

Look at the **dimes** and pennies.

VOCABULARY
dime

Ring 46 cents.

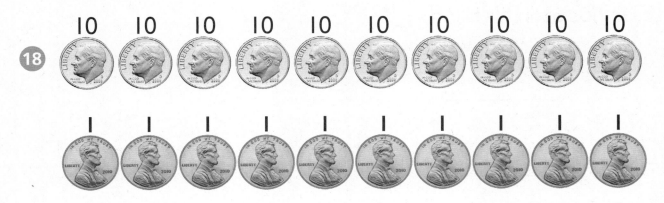

Ring 83 cents.

How many cents?

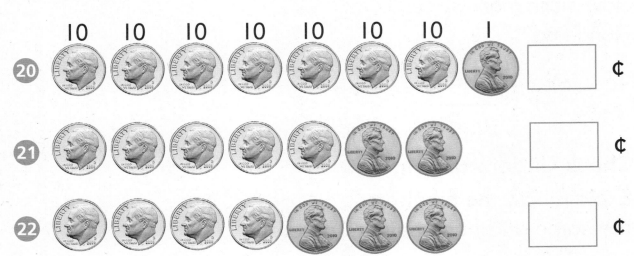

20 [ ] ¢

21 [ ] ¢

22 [ ] ¢

Integrate Tens and Ones **181**

Draw dimes and pennies to solve the equation.

23 Lucas has 7¢ in his pocket.
He has 6¢ in his hand.
How much money does
Lucas have?

$7¢ + 6¢ = \boxed{}$ ¢

---

24 Alma has 8¢ in her bank.
Her mom gives her 8¢.
How much money does
Alma have?

$8¢ + 8¢ = \boxed{}$ ¢

---

25 Fiona finds 9¢ in her coat.
She finds 6¢ on her desk.
How much money does
Fiona find?

$9¢ + 6¢ = \boxed{}$ ¢

✓ **Check Understanding**

Explain how the numbers 2, 12, and 20 are
the same and how they are different.

Integrate Tens and Ones

Draw 10-sticks and circles.
Write the total.

1 [ ] = 50 + 3

2 [ ] = 70 + 6

3 [ ] = 20 + 9

4 [ ] = 40 + 2

5 [ ] = 30 + 7

6 [ ] = 10 + 8

7 [ ] = 90 + 1

8 [ ] = 50 + 5

Draw 10-sticks and circles to add.
Write the total.

9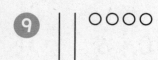

$24 + 3 =$ ☐

10 || ⚪⚪⚪⚪⚪ ⚪⚪

$27 + 6 =$ ☐

11

$41 + 5 =$ ☐

12 |||||| ⚪⚪⚪⚪⚪ ⚪⚪⚪⚪

$79 + 5 =$ ☐

13

$67 + 2 =$ ☐

14 |||||| ⚪⚪⚪⚪

$54 + 4 =$ ☐

15

$65 + 6 =$ ☐

16 ||| ⚪⚪⚪

$33 + 7 =$ ☐

✓ **Check Understanding**
Explain how to add $29 + 3$.

Practice Grouping Ones into Tens

Each box has 10 muffins. How many muffins are there?

1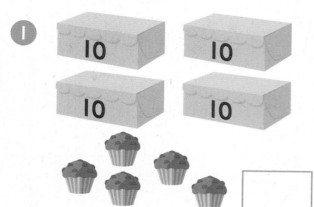

2

3

4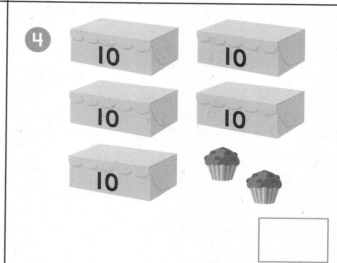

5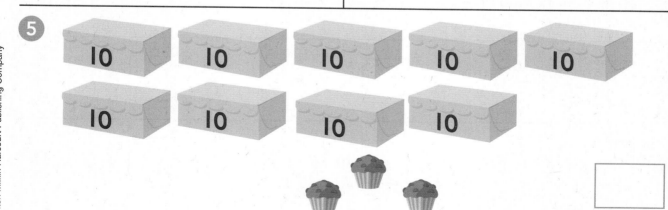

6 How are 23 and 32 the same?
How are they different?

PATH to FLUENCY **Add.**

1 3 + 3 = ☐   **2** 4 + 5 = ☐   **3** 1 + 5 = ☐

4 3 + 7 = ☐   **5** 8 + 0 = ☐   **6** 2 + 5 = ☐

7 ☐ = 5 + 2   **8** ☐ = 7 + 1   **9** ☐ = 5 + 5

10 ☐ = 1 + 6   **11** ☐ = 7 + 3   **12** ☐ = 5 + 3

PATH to FLUENCY **Find the unknown number.**

13 2 + ☐ = 9   **14** 6 + ☐ = 10   **15** 4 + ☐ = 7

16 8 + ☐ = 10   **17** 3 + ☐ = 8   **18** 1 + ☐ = 10

19 ☐ + 3 = 9   **20** ☐ + 6 = 8   **21** ☐ + 8 = 9

22 ☐ + 6 = 6   **23** ☐ + 4 = 7   **24** ☐ + 2 = 9

✓ **Check Understanding**

Explain how to use tens and ones to find 43 + 6.

Add with Groups of Ten

1	2	10	20
1	2	1 0	2 0

3	4	30	40
3	4	3 0	4 0

5	6	50	60
5	6	5 0	6 0

7	8	70	80
7	8	7 0	8 0

9	90	100
9	9 0	1 0 0

Secret Code Cards

Name _____

Write the number of tens and ones.
Write the number.

1

___ tens ___ ones

2

___ tens ___ ones

3

___ tens ___ ones

4

___ tens ___ ones

5

___ tens ___ ones

6

___ tens ___ ones

7

___ tens ___ ones

8

___ tens ___ ones

Practice with Tens and Ones **189**

Draw 10-sticks and circles.
Write the number of tens and ones.

9 75

_____ tens _____ ones

10 90

_____ tens _____ ones

11 41

_____ tens _____ ones

12 59

_____ tens _____ ones

13 26

_____ tens _____ ones

14 88

_____ tens _____ ones

✓ **Check Understanding**

Draw 10-sticks and circles for a 2-digit
number that has 7 tens and another
2-digit number that has 7 ones.

Practice with Tens and Ones

Name _____

Compare the numbers. Write >, <, or =.

VOCABULARY
compare

1

30 ◯ 25

2

23 ◯ 28

3 70 ◯ 80   **4** 60 ◯ 59   **5** 76 ◯ 67

6 24 ◯ 84   **7** 37 ◯ 37   **8** 48 ◯ 50

9 56 ◯ 56   **10** 17 ◯ 42   **11** 99 ◯ 33

Compare the numbers two ways.
Write the numbers.

12 Compare 53 and 54.

◯
____ ____

◯
____ ____

13 Compare 80 and 79.

◯
____ ____

◯
____ ____

14 Compare 49 and 94.

◯
____ ____

◯
____ ____

15 Compare 36 and 32.

◯
____ ____

◯
____ ____

Write to compare the numbers.

16 Compare 39 and 40.

_____ ◯ _____

17 Compare 86 and 68.

_____ ◯ _____

18 Compare 95 and 91.

_____ ◯ _____

19 Compare 72 and 72.

_____ ◯ _____

20 Compare 20 and 10.

_____ ◯ _____

21 Compare 60 and 16.

_____ ◯ _____

22 Look at what Puzzled Penguin wrote.

29 ◯> 36

Am I correct?

23 Help Puzzled Penguin.

29 ◯ 36

✔ **Check Understanding**
Compare 26 and 62.   _____ ◯ _____

Use Place Value to Compare Numbers

Write the numbers.

_____ tens _____ ones = _____

_____ tens _____ ones = _____

Compare the numbers. Write >, <, or =.

3

4

5 20 ⭕ 20

PATH to
FLUENCY

Find the unknown partner or total.

1 $3 + 3 = \boxed{}$　　　**2** $2 + 4 = \boxed{}$　　　**3** $5 + 3 = \boxed{}$

4 $3 + 4 = \boxed{}$　　　**5** $8 + 1 = \boxed{}$　　　**6** $2 + 5 = \boxed{}$

7 $4 + \boxed{} = 6$　　　**8** $7 + \boxed{} = 9$　　　**9** $1 + \boxed{} = 7$

10 $4 + \boxed{} = 8$　　　　　**11** $8 + \boxed{} = 10$

12 $3 + \boxed{} = 10$　　　　　**13** $\boxed{} + 3 = 9$

14 $\boxed{} + 5 = 8$　　　　　**15** $\boxed{} + 4 = 10$

Name _____

Write the totals.

1   $4 + 4 =$ ☐

     $40 + 40 =$ ☐

2   $6 + 3 =$ ☐

     $60 + 30 =$ ☐

3   $2 + 3 =$ ☐

     $20 + 30 =$ ☐

4   $1 + 7 =$ ☐

     $10 + 70 =$ ☐

5   $5 + 2 =$ ☐

     $50 + 20 =$ ☐

6   $3 + 3 =$ ☐

     $30 + 30 =$ ☐

7   $7 + 2 =$ ☐

     $70 + 20 =$ ☐

8   $2 + 2 =$ ☐

     $20 + 20 =$ ☐

9   Use 10-sticks and circles to solve.

$4 + 5 =$ ☐ $40 + 50 =$ ☐

Explain how the totals are different.

_____

- -

_____

- -

_____

Complete the equation.
Draw a 10-stick or a circle to solve for the total.

10 14

[ ] + 1 = [ ]

11 16

[ ] + 10 = [ ]

12 13

[ ] + 1 = [ ]

13 23

[ ] + 1 = [ ]

14 39

[ ] + 10 = [ ]

15 42

[ ] + 10 = [ ]

16 57

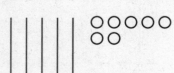

[ ] + 1 = [ ]

✓ **Check Understanding**
Explain if the total of
58 + 10 will be 59 or 68.

Add Tens or Ones

Name _____

Solve.

1 3 + 6 = _____

30 + 60 = _____

30 + 6 = _____

2 4 + 5 = _____

40 + 50 = _____

40 + 5 = _____

3 2 + 4 = _____

20 + 40 = _____

20 + 4 = _____

4 5 + 2 = _____

50 + 20 = _____

50 + 2 = _____

5 7 + 2 = _____

70 + 20 = _____

70 + 2 = _____

6 4 + 1 = _____

40 + 10 = _____

40 + 1 = _____

7 3 + 2 = _____

30 + 20 = _____

30 + 2 = _____

8 1 + 8 = _____

10 + 80 = _____

10 + 8 = _____

Complete the set of equations to follow the
same rules as each set above. Then solve.

9 3 + 5 = _____

30 + _____ = _____

30 + _____ = _____

10 4 + 3 = _____

40 + _____ = _____

40 + _____ = _____

Mixed Addition with Tens and Ones **197**

Find the unknown numbers to complete
the set of equations.

11 $2 +$ _____ $= 5$

$20 + 30 =$ _____

$20 +$ _____ $= 23$

12 $4 +$ _____ $= 8$

_____ $+ 40 = 80$

$40 + 4 =$ _____

13 _____ $+ 2 = 6$

$40 +$ _____ $= 60$

_____ $+ 2 = 42$

14 _____ $+ 7 = 8$

$10 +$ _____ $= 80$

$10 + 7 =$ _____

15 Look at what Puzzled Penguin wrote.

$50 + 4 =$ $\boxed{90}$

Am I correct?

16 Help Puzzled Penguin.

$50 + 4 =$ $\boxed{}$

✓ **Check Understanding**

Write tens, ones, or both to add the numbers.

$40 + 30$ adding _____ $40 + 3$ adding _____

Mixed Addition with Tens and Ones

Here is a riddle.

> I like to hop,
> but my ears are small.
> I have four legs, but I stand tall.
> I have a pocket,
> but I cannot buy.
> Guess my name. Who am I?

Find the total. Use any method.

1 $46 + 5 =$ ☐ O   2 $40 + 2 =$ ☐ O

3 $12 + 7 =$ ☐ K   4 $29 + 5 =$ ☐ R

5 $64 + 6 =$ ☐ A   6 $20 + 9 =$ ☐ A

7 $27 + 5 =$ ☐ G   8 $89 + 2 =$ ☐ N

Who am I? Write the letter for each total.

___ ___ ___ ___ ___ ___ ___ ___
19   70   91   32   29   34   42   51

PATH to FLUENCY Add.

1 4 + 5 = ☐   **2** 0 + 7 = ☐   **3** 7 + 3 = ☐

4 1 + 6 = ☐   **5** 6 + 2 = ☐   **6** 4 + 2 = ☐

7 ☐ = 7 + 1   **8** ☐ = 3 + 6   **9** ☐ = 7 + 2

10 ☐ = 6 + 4   **11** ☐ = 2 + 4   **12** ☐ = 4 + 3

PATH to FLUENCY Find the unknown number.

13 1 + ☐ = 8   **14** 3 + ☐ = 7   **15** 5 + ☐ = 8

16 8 + ☐ = 10   **17** 4 + ☐ = 8   **18** 9 + ☐ = 9

19 ☐ + 1 = 6   **20** ☐ + 4 = 9   **21** ☐ + 7 = 10

22 ☐ + 8 = 9   **23** ☐ + 5 = 8   **24** ☐ + 8 = 10

✓ **Check Understanding**

Explain how to count on to find 28 + 3.

Counting On Strategy: 2-Digit Numbers

Use this sandwich sheet when you play
The Sandwich Game.

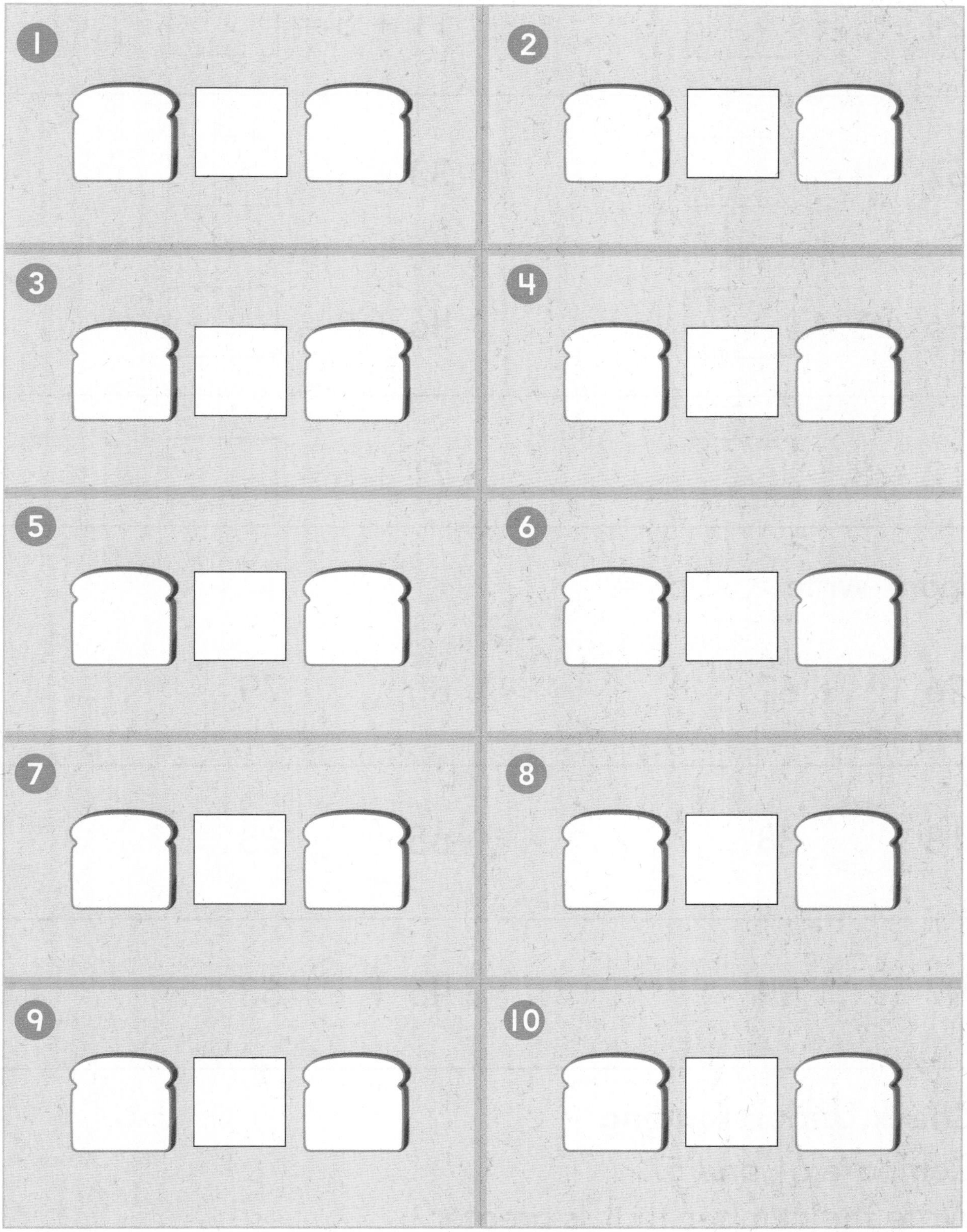

1

2

3

4

5

6

7

8

9

10

Find the total. Use any method.

⑪ 29 + 3 = ☐   ⑫ 11 + 8 = ☐

⑬ 67 + 4 = ☐   ⑭ 33 + 9 = ☐

⑮ 96 + 3 = ☐   ⑯ 46 + 4 = ☐

⑰ 12 + 8 = ☐   ⑱ 71 + 5 = ☐

Compare. Write >, <, or =.

⑲ 26 ◯ 62   ⑳ 80 ◯ 79

㉑ 18 ◯ 38   ㉒ 65 ◯ 65

㉓ 97 ◯ 94   ㉔ 45 ◯ 53

✓ **Check Understanding**
Compare 61 and 57.
Write the number that is greater. _____

Practice with 2-Digit Numbers

Write the number.

 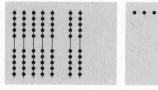

 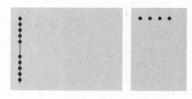

Draw 10-sticks and circles to show the number.

5   50 2 5 2

6   90 7 9 7

7    60 5 6 5

8    80 9 8 9

Draw 10-sticks and circles to count on.
Write the total.

9 Count on 4.

○○○○○
○○○ ○

10 Count on 3.

| ○

11 Count on 6.

| ○○○○○
○○○○ ○

12 Count on 2.

||| ○○○○○
○○○ ○

13 Count on 5.

||||| ○○○○○
○○○○ ○

14 Count on 4.

||||| || ○○○○○
○

15 Count on 6.

||||| ||| ○○○○○

16 Count on 4.

||||| ||| ○○○○

✓ **Check Understanding**

Write the total for 38 + 4.

2-Digit Addition Games

Name _____

Linda and her family go to a show.

1 10 cars can park in each row.

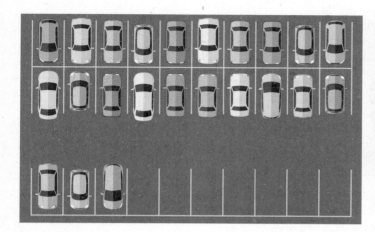

How many cars are there?

_____ tens _____ ones = _____ cars

2 10 people can sit in each row.

How many people are there?

_____ tens _____ ones = _____ people

Show tickets were sold on Friday,
Saturday, and Sunday.

3 Write the number of tickets sold each day.

Friday	
	_____ tens _____ ones = _____ tickets
Saturday	
	_____ tens _____ ones = _____ tickets
Sunday	
	_____ tens _____ ones = _____ tickets

Compare the number of tickets sold.
Use >, <, or =.

4 Friday   Saturday

   ☐   ◯   ☐

5 Friday   Sunday

   ☐   ◯   ☐

6 Saturday   Sunday

   ☐   ◯   ☐

7 Sunday   Saturday

   ☐   ◯   ☐

     Focus on Problem Solving

Name _____

Date _____

Add.

1 20 + 50 = ☐

2 60 + 3 = ☐

Find the total.

3 44 + 3 = ☐

4 72 + 9 = ☐

Solve the story problem.   **Show your work.**

5 Cindy has 56 stamps.
She buys 4 more stamps.
How many stamps does she have now?

☐ _____
              label

Name _____   Date _____

Find the unknown partner or total.

1 $5 + 2 =$ ☐   2 $1 + 5 =$ ☐   3 $2 + 4 =$ ☐

4 $5 + 4 =$ ☐   5 $2 + 6 =$ ☐   6 $5 + 5 =$ ☐

7 $1 +$ ☐ $= 7$ 8 $4 +$ ☐ $= 6$ 9 $0 +$ ☐ $= 8$

10 $6 +$ ☐ $= 9$ 11 $2 +$ ☐ $= 8$

12 $9 +$ ☐ $= 10$ 13 ☐ $+ 3 = 6$

14 ☐ $+ 0 = 9$ 15 ☐ $+ 7 = 8$

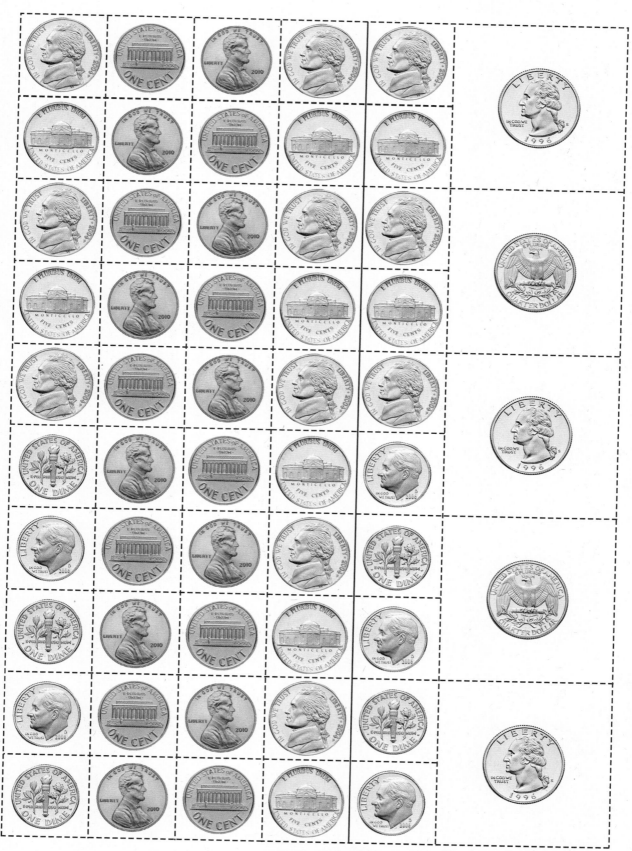

Cut on the dotted lines.

Coins

Name _____

VOCABULARY
quarter

Match the dime, nickel, and **quarter**
to the same amount in pennies.
Write the amount in cents.

  •   • 5 pennies ¢

  •   • 25 pennies ¢

 •   • 10 pennies ¢

Draw coins to show 10¢.

④ Use pennies.

_____

⑤ Use nickels.

_____

⑥ Use dimes.

_____

⑦ Use nickels and pennies.

Show the price with sticks and circles.
Then write how many of each coin.

17¢

Dimes _____   Pennies _____

62¢

Dimes _____   Pennies _____

44¢

Dimes _____   Pennies _____

✓ Check Understanding

Write how many cents each coin is worth.

_____   _____   _____   _____

Pennies, Nickels, Dimes, and Quarters

Name _____

Ring the correct coin.

1 I am worth the same as
two nickels.
What am I?

2 You need 10 of me to
make a dime.
What am I?

3 I am worth the same as
two dimes and one nickel.
What am I?

Solve the story problems.
Write the amount using ¢.

**Show your work. Use drawings,
numbers, or words.**

4 Jana has 1 dime, 2 nickels,
and 3 pennies. How many
cents does Jana have?

_____

5 Brooke has 2 dimes, 3 nickels,
and 2 pennies. How many
cents does Brooke have?

_____

Solve the story problems.
Write the amount using ¢.

Show your work. Use drawings, numbers, or words.

6 José bought an apple for 2 dimes, 1 nickel, and 2 pennies. How many cents did he pay?

_____

7 Lexi bought a pencil for 3 dimes, 1 nickel, and 4 pennies. How many cents did she pay?

_____

8 Mia has 3 dimes, 3 nickels, and 3 pennies on her desk. How many cents does she have?

_____

9 Chaz has 5 dimes, 4 nickels, and 3 pennies in his pocket. How many cents does he have?

_____

✓ Check Understanding

Ty has 2 dimes and 3 pennies. How many cents does Ty have? _____

Coin Stories

For questions 1 and 2, draw coins to show 25¢.

1 Use dimes and pennies.

2 Use nickels.

_____

Solve the story problems.

3 Javed buys a banana with 2 dimes,
1 nickel, and 5 pennies. How many
cents does he pay?

_____

_____

4 Marita has 5 pennies and 2 nickels.
How many cents does Marita have?

_____

_____

5 Sam exchanges 15 pennies for nickels
and dimes. Which coins should he
get in return?

_____

Find the unknown partner or total.

1. $4 + 2 = \boxed{}$ 2. $1 + 4 = \boxed{}$ 3. $2 + 3 = \boxed{}$

4. $5 + 5 = \boxed{}$ 5. $2 + 7 = \boxed{}$ 6. $4 + 5 = \boxed{}$

7. $0 + \boxed{} = 6$ 8. $3 + \boxed{} = 5$ 9. $0 + \boxed{} = 9$

10. $5 + \boxed{} = 8$ 11. $1 + \boxed{} = 7$

12. $8 + \boxed{} = 10$ 13. $\boxed{} + 4 = 8$

14. $\boxed{} + 0 = 10$ 15. $\boxed{} + 5 = 6$

1 Does the number match the picture?
Choose Yes or No.

50   ○ Yes   ○ No

| ○ ○ ○

31   ○ Yes   ○ No

Draw 10-sticks and circles.
Write the number of tens and ones.

2   32

□ tens □ ones = 32

3   64

□ tens □ ones = 64

Use the words on the tiles to name each number.

| seventy | seven | seventeen |

4 17 _____

5 70 _____

6 7 _____

7 Add 1 ten.

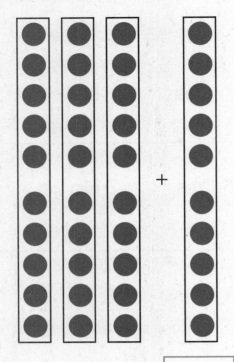

$30 + 10 =$ [ ]

8 How many paper clips?

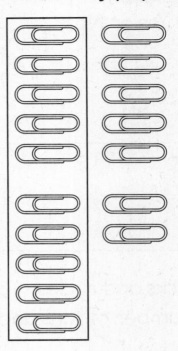

[ ]

9 Draw a picture for the problem.
Write an equation to solve.

There are 10 birds in one tree.
There are 7 birds in another tree.
How many birds are there?

[ ] _____
label

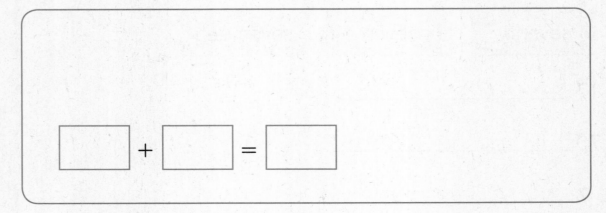

[ ] + [ ] = [ ]

10 How many muffins are there?

○ 22
○ 25
○ 42
○ 62

11 Show 47¢ with sticks and circles.
Then write how many of each coin.

Dimes _____ Pennies _____

Solve the story problem.

12 Kimi has 8 red apples and
5 green apples. How many
apples does she have?

apple

[ ] _____
         label

13 Shonda finds 2 dimes, 3 nickels, and 3 pennies.
How many cents does she find?

[ ] _____
         label

Ring >, <, or = to compare the numbers.

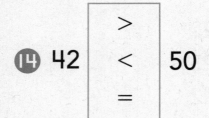

⑭ 42 | > < = | 50

⑮ 34 | > < = | 33

Find the unknown numbers to complete
the set of equations.

⑯ 3 + _____ = 7

30 + 40 = _____

30 + _____ = 34

⑰ _____ + 7 = 9

20 + _____ = 90

20 + 7 = _____

⑱ Write a number from 10 to 40.
Add 1 ten. Write the new number.
Draw and write to compare the numbers.

Snack Time

It is snack time at sports camp. Each team gets these drinks.

Water	Milk	Orange Juice	Apple Juice
13 bottles	11 cartons	9 boxes	7 boxes

① Does each team get more bottles of water or more

cartons of milk? _____

Draw or write to tell how you know.

② Draw 10-sticks and circles to show
the number of water bottles.

③ Each team has 20 children. Does a team get enough juice

boxes for everyone? _____

Draw or write to tell how you know.

Snack Time (continued)

Use the drink chart on page 221 for Problem 4.

4 **Part A**
The Red team has 20 children.
They choose two kinds of drinks.
Show how many they might
choose of each.

Kind of Drink	How many?

Draw or write to tell how you know there
are 20 drinks.

Part B
The Blue team has 20 children.
No children want milk.
Show how they might choose
other drinks.
(Choose at least one of each).

Kind of Drink	How many?

Draw or write to tell how you know there
are 20 drinks.

Addition and Subtraction Problem Types

	Result Unknown	Change Unknown	Start Unknown
Add To	Six children are playing tag in the yard. Three more children come to play. How many children are playing in the yard now? *Situation and Solution Equation*[1]: $6 + 3 = \square$	Six children are playing tag in the yard. Some more children come to play. Now there are 9 children in the yard. How many children came to play? *Situation Equation:* $6 + \square = 9$ *Solution Equation:* $9 - 6 = \square$	Some children are playing tag in the yard. Three more children come to play. Now there are 9 children in the yard. How many children were in the yard at first? *Situation Equation:* $\square + 3 = 9$ *Solution Equation:* $9 - 3 = \square$
Take From	Jake has 10 trading cards. He gives 3 to his brother. How many trading cards does he have left? *Situation and Solution Equation:* $10 - 3 = \square$	Jake has 10 trading cards. He gives some to his brother. Now Jake has 7 trading cards left. How many cards does he give to his brother? *Situation Equation:* $10 - \square = 7$ *Solution Equation:* $10 - 7 = \square$	Jake has some trading cards. He gives 3 to his brother. Now Jake has 7 trading cards left. How many cards does he start with? *Situation Equation:* $\square - 3 = 7$ *Solution Equation:* $7 + 3 = \square$

[1]A situation equation represents the structure (action) in the problem situation. A solution equation shows the operation used to find the answer.

Problem Types

Addition and Subtraction Problem Types (continued)

	Total Unknown	Addend Unknown	Other Addend Unknown
Put Together/ Take Apart	There are 9 red roses and 4 yellow roses in a vase. How many roses are in the vase? *Math Drawing²:* □ ／＼ 9　4 *Situation and Solution Equation:* $9 + 4 = □$	Thirteen roses are in the vase. 9 are red and the rest are yellow. How many roses are yellow? *Math Drawing:* 13 ／＼ 9　□ *Situation Equation:* $13 = 9 + □$ *Solution Equation:* $13 - 9 = □$	Thirteen roses are in the vase. Some are red and 4 are yellow. How many are red? *Math Drawing:* 13 ／＼ □　4 *Situation Equation:* $13 = □ + 4$ *Solution Equation:* $13 - 4 = □$

Both Addends Unknown is a productive extension of this basic situation, especially for small numbers less than or equal to 10. Such take apart situations can be used to show all the decompositions of a given number. The associated equations, which have the total on the left of the equal sign, help children understand that the = sign does not always mean makes or results in but always does mean is the same number as.

Both Addends Unknown

Ana has 13 roses. How many can she put in her red vase and how many in her blue vase?

Math Drawing:

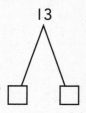

Situation Equation:
$13 = □ + □$

²These math drawings are called Math Mountains in Grades 1–3 and break-apart drawings in Grades 4 and 5.

Addition and Subtraction Problem Types (continued)

Compare[3]	Difference Unknown	Bigger Unknown	Smaller Unknown
	Aki has 8 apples. Sofia has 14 apples. How many **more** apples does Sofia have than Aki? Aki has 8 apples. Sofia has 14 apples. How many **fewer** apples does Aki have than Sofia? *Math Drawing:* S [14] A [8] (?) *Situation Equation:* $8 + \square = 14$ *Solution Equation:* $14 - 8 = \square$	**Leading Language** Aki has 8 apples. Sofia has 6 more apples than Aki. How many apples does Sofia have? **Misleading Language** Aki has 8 apples. Aki has 6 fewer apples than Sofia. How many apples does Sofia have? *Math Drawing:* S [?] A [8] (6) *Situation and Solution Equation:* $8 + 6 = \square$	**Leading Language** Sofia has 14 apples. Aki has 6 fewer apples than Sofia. How many apples does Aki have? **Misleading Language** Sofia has 14 apples. Sofia has 6 more apples than Aki. How many apples does Aki have? *Math Drawing:* S [14] A [?] (6) *Situation Equation:* $\square + 6 = 14$ *Solution Equation:* $14 - 6 = \square$

[3]A comparison sentence can always be said in two ways. One way uses *more*, and the other uses *fewer* or *less*. Misleading language suggests the wrong operation. For example, it says *Aki has 6 fewer apples than Sofia*, but you have to add 6 to Aki's 8 apples to get 14 apples.

5-group*

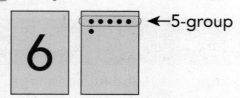

←5-group

10-group

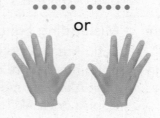

or

10-stick*

| | | | OO You can show 32 with three **10-sticks** and two ones.

A

add

$$3 + 2 = 5$$

addend

$$5 + 4 = 9 \qquad 5 + 4 + 8 = 17$$

↑ ↑   ↑ ↑ ↑

addends   addends
(partners)

addition story problem

There are 5 ducks.
Then 3 more come.
How many ducks are there now?

B

bar graph

Vegetables We Like						
Carrots						
Corn						
Peppers						

0 1 2 3 4 5 6

break-apart*

You can **break apart** the number 4.

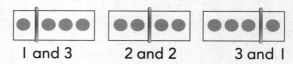

1 and 3   2 and 2   3 and 1

1 and 3, 2 and 2, and 3 and 1 are
break-aparts of 4.

C

cents (¢)

The number of cents is the value of
a coin or a set of coins.

7 cents

circle

*A classroom research-based term developed for *Math Expressions*

circle drawing*

$$3 + 4$$
○○○|○○○○
7

$$9 - 5$$
⊖⊖⊖⊖⊖|○○○○
4

clock

analog
clock

digital
clock

column

1	11	21	31	41	51	61	71	81	91
2	12	22	32	42	52	62	72	82	92
3	13	23	33	43	53	63	73	83	93
4	14	24	34	44	54	64	74	84	94
5	15	25	35	45	55	65	75	85	95
6	16	26	36	46	56	66	76	86	96
7	17	27	37	47	57	67	77	87	97
8	18	28	38	48	58	68	78	88	98
9	19	29	39	49	59	69	79	89	99
10	20	30	40	50	60	70	80	90	100

compare

You can **compare** numbers.

11 is less than 12.

$$11 < 12$$

12 is greater than 11.

$$12 > 11$$

You can **compare** objects by length.

The crayon is shorter than the pencil.
The pencil is longer than the crayon.

comparison bars*

Joe has 6 roses. Sasha has 9 roses.
How many more roses does Sasha have
than Joe?

S [9]   comparison
J [6] (?)   bars

cone

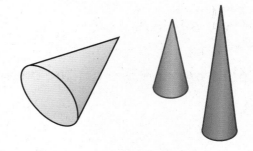

*A classroom research-based term developed for *Math Expressions*

Glossary

corner

count

count all

$5 + 4 = \boxed{9}$

1 2 3 4 5   6 7 8 9

count on

$5 + 4 = \boxed{9}$

$5 + \boxed{4} = 9$

$9 - 5 = \boxed{4}$

5 6 7 8 9

Count on from 5 to get the answer.

cube

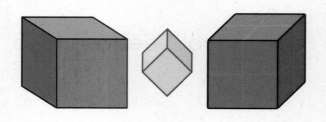

cylinder

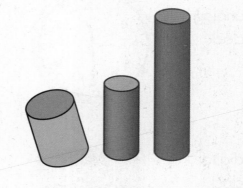

D

data

Colors in the Bag									
Red	○	○	○						
Yellow	○	○	○	○	○	○	○	○	
Blue	○	○	○	○	○	○			

The **data** show how many of each color.

decade numbers

10, 20, 30, 40, 50, 60, 70, 80, 90

*A classroom research-based term developed for *Math Expressions*

difference

$$11 - 3 = 8$$

$$\begin{array}{r} 11 \\ -\ 3 \\ \hline 8 \end{array}$$

difference → 8

digit

15 is a 2-**digit** number.

The I in 15 means I ten.

The 5 in 15 means 5 ones.

dime

front   back

10 cents or 10¢

dot array

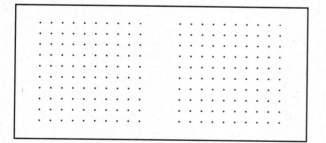

doubles

$$4 + 4 = 8$$

Both partners are the same.
They are doubles.

doubles minus I

7 + 7 = 14, so

7 + 6 = 13, I less than 14.

doubles minus 2

7 + 7 = 14, so

7 + 5 = 12, 2 less than 14.

doubles plus I

6 + 6 = 12, so

6 + 7 = 13, I more than 12.

doubles plus 2

6 + 6 = 12, so

6 + 8 = 14, 2 more than 12.

E

edge

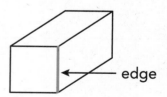

edge

equal shares

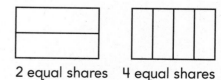

2 equal shares   4 equal shares

These show **equal shares.**

Glossary

equal to (=)

$$4 + 4 = 8$$

4 plus 4 is **equal to** 8.

equation

$$4 + 3 = 7 \qquad 7 = 4 + 3$$

$$9 - 5 = 4 \qquad 4 = 9 - 5$$

F

face

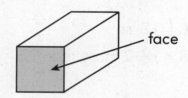

face

fewer

Eggs Laid This Month

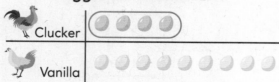

Clucker laid **fewer** eggs than Vanilla.

fewest

Eggs Laid This Month

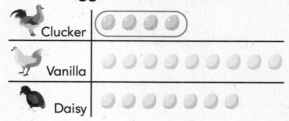

Clucker laid the **fewest** eggs.

fourth of

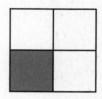

One **fourth of** the shape is shaded.

fourths

 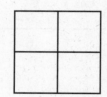

1 whole   4 **fourths**, or
                   4 quarters

G

greater than (>)

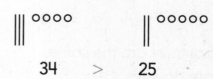

34   >   25

34 is **greater than** 25.

grid

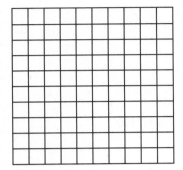

halves

1 whole   2 **halves**

growing pattern

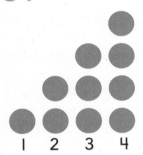

1   2   3   4

hexagon

H

half-hour

A **half-hour** is 30 minutes.

hour

hour hand

An **hour** is 60 minutes.

hour hand

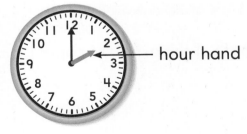

hour hand

half of

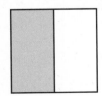

One **half of** the shape is shaded.

Glossary

hundred

1	11	21	31	41	51	61	71	81	91
2	12	22	32	42	52	62	72	82	92
3	13	23	33	43	53	63	73	83	93
4	14	24	34	44	54	64	74	84	94
5	15	25	35	45	55	65	75	85	95
6	16	26	36	46	56	66	76	86	96
7	17	27	37	47	57	67	77	87	97
8	18	28	38	48	58	68	78	88	98
9	19	29	39	49	59	69	79	89	99
10	20	30	40	50	60	70	80	90	100

or

K

known partner*

$5 + \boxed{} = 7$

5 is the **known partner**.

L

length

The **length** of this pencil is 6 paper clips.

less than (<)

45   <   46

45 is **less than** 46.

longer

The pencil is **longer** than the crayon.

longest

The pencil is the **longest**.

M

make a ten

$8 + 6 = \boxed{}$

⑧ ○○ ○○○○

$10 + 4 = 14$,
so $8 + 6 = 14$.

*A classroom research-based term developed for *Math Expressions*

Math Mountain*

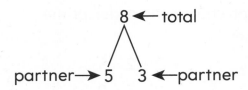

8 ← total

partner → 5   3 ← partner

measure

You can use paper clips to **measure** the length of the pencil.

minus (—)

$$8 - 3 = 5$$

$$\begin{array}{r} 8 \\ -3 \\ \hline 5 \end{array}$$

8 **minus** 3 equals 5.

minute

There are 60 **minutes** in an hour.

more

Eggs Laid This Month

Vanilla laid **more** eggs than Clucker.

most

Eggs Laid This Month

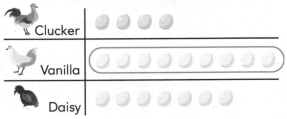

Vanilla laid the **most** eggs.

N

New Group Above Method*

$$\begin{array}{r} \overset{1}{5}6 \\ + 28 \\ \hline 84 \end{array}$$

6 + 8 = 14
The 1 new ten in 14 goes up to the tens place.

New Group Below Method*

$$\begin{array}{r} 56 \\ + 28 \\ \hline 84 \end{array}$$

6 + 8 = 14
The 1 new ten in 14 goes below in the tens place.

*A classroom research-based term developed for *Math Expressions*

nickel

front   back

5 cents or 5¢

not equal to (≠)

6 ≠ 8

6 is **not equal to** 8.

number line

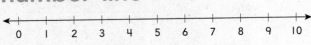

number word

12

twelve ← number word

ones

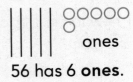

ones

56 has 6 **ones**.

order

You can change the **order** of the partners.

$$7 + 2 = 9$$
$$2 + 7 = 9$$

You can **order** objects by length.

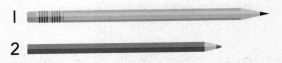

partner*

$$5 = 2 + 3$$

2 and 3 are **partners** of 5.
2 and 3 are 5-**partners**.

partner house*

9
5 + 4
6 + 3
3 + 6
4 + 5
7 + 2
8 + 1
2 + 7
1 + 8

*A classroom research-based term developed for *Math Expressions*

partner train*

4-train

3 + 1   2 + 2   1 + 3

pattern

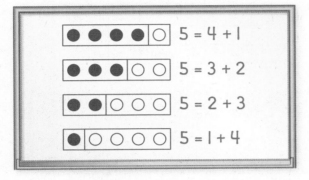

- 5 = 4 + 1
- 5 = 3 + 2
- 5 = 2 + 3
- 5 = 1 + 4

The partners of a number show a **pattern**.

penny

front   back

1 cent or 1¢

plus (+)

$$3 + 2 = 5 \qquad \begin{array}{r} 3 \\ + 2 \\ \hline 5 \end{array}$$

3 **plus** 2 equals 5.

Proof Drawing*

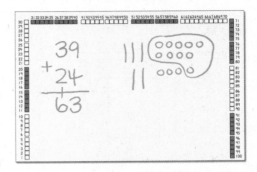

$$\begin{array}{r} 39 \\ + 24 \\ \hline 63 \end{array}$$

Q

quarter

front   back

25 cents or 25¢

quarter of

One **quarter of** the shape is shaded.

quarters

       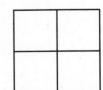

1 whole   4 **quarters**, or 4 fourths

*A classroom research-based term developed for *Math Expressions*

Glossary

R

rectangle

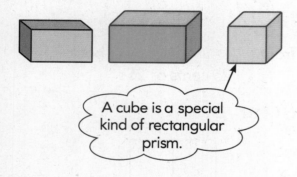

A square is a special kind of rectangle.

rectangular prism

A cube is a special kind of rectangular prism.

repeating pattern

row

1	11	21	31	41	51	61	71	81	91
2	12	22	32	42	52	62	72	82	92
3	13	23	33	43	53	63	73	83	93
4	14	24	34	44	54	64	74	84	94
5	15	25	35	45	55	65	75	85	95
6	16	26	36	46	56	66	76	86	96
7	17	27	37	47	57	67	77	87	97
8	18	28	38	48	58	68	78	88	98
9	19	29	39	49	59	69	79	89	99
10	20	30	40	50	60	70	80	90	100

S

shapes

2-dimensional   3-dimensional

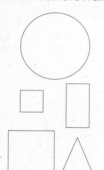

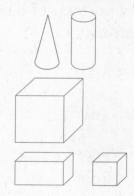

shorter

The crayon is **shorter** than the pencil.

*A classroom research-based term developed for *Math Expressions*

shortest

The paper clip is the **shortest**.

Show All Totals Method*

$$
\begin{array}{r}
25 \\
+\ 48 \\
\hline
60 \\
13 \\
\hline
73
\end{array}
$$

shrinking pattern

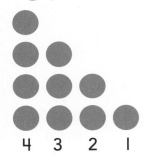

4   3   2   1

side

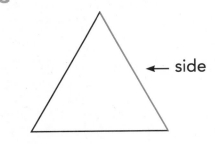

← side

sort

You can **sort** the animals into groups.

sphere

square

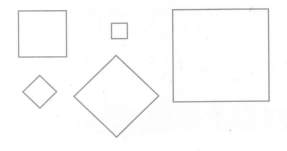

square corner

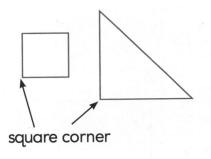

square corner

sticks and circles*

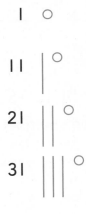

*A classroom research-based term developed for *Math Expressions*

subtract

$8 - 3 = 5$

subtraction story problem

8 flies are on a log.
6 are eaten by a frog.
How many flies are left?

switch the partners*

 7 + 2

 2 + 7

T

tally mark

Vegetables	Tally Marks	Number
Carrots	|||||	5
Corn	||||	4
Peppers	|||| ||	7

teen number

11 12 13 14 15 16 17 18 19

teen numbers

teen total*

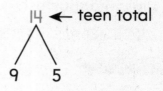

tens

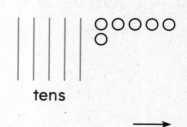

tens

56 has 5 **tens**.

total

$4 + 3 = 7$

total

$$\begin{array}{r} 4 \\ + 3 \\ \hline 7 \end{array}$$

trapezoid

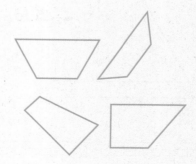

*A classroom research-based term developed for *Math Expressions*

triangle

U
---

unknown partner*

$$4 + \boxed{} = 7$$

unknown total*

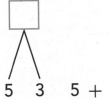

$$5 + 3 = \boxed{}$$

V
---

vertex

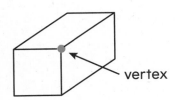

vertex

vertical form

$$\begin{array}{r} 6 \\ + 3 \\ \hline 9 \end{array} \qquad \begin{array}{r} 9 \\ - 3 \\ \hline 6 \end{array}$$

Z
---

zero

There are **zero** apples on the plate.

*A classroom research-based term developed for *Math Expressions*

Mathematical Standards

<table>
<tr><td colspan="3">1.ARO Algebraic Reasoning and Operations</td></tr>
<tr>
<td>1.ARO.1</td>
<td>Solve addition and subtraction word problems that involve adding to, putting together, taking from, taking apart, and comparing and have unknown quantities in all positions; represent problems using words, objects, drawings, length-based models (connecting cubes), numerals, number lines, as well as equations with a symbol for the unknown quantity.</td>
<td>Unit 1 Lessons 2, 3, 4, 5, 6, 7, 8;
Unit 2 Lessons 1, 2, 3, 4, 6, 8, 10, 11, 12, 13, 14, 15, 16;
Unit 3 Lessons 2, 3, 4, 5, 6, 7, 8, 9, 10, 11, 12;
Unit 4 Lesson 5;
Unit 5 Lessons 1, 2, 3, 4, 5, 11;
Unit 6 Lessons 1, 2, 3, 4, 5, 6, 7, 8, 9</td>
</tr>
<tr>
<td>1.ARO.2</td>
<td>Solve addition word problems that involve three addends with a sum less than or equal to 20; represent a problem using objects or pictures or other methods, and equations that have a symbol for the unknown quantity.</td>
<td>Unit 5 Lessons 6, 11;
Unit 6 Lessons 1, 4, 5, 9</td>
</tr>
<tr>
<td>1.ARO.3</td>
<td>Add and subtract applying the properties of operations.</td>
<td>Unit 1 Lessons 3, 4, 5, 6, 7, 8, 9;
Unit 2 Lessons 7, 8, 9, 13;
Unit 3 Lesson 5;
Unit 4 Lessons 5, 10;
Unit 5 Lessons 4, 6</td>
</tr>
<tr>
<td>1.ARO.4</td>
<td>Understand that a subtraction problem can be thought of as an unknown addend situation.</td>
<td>Unit 3 Lessons 6, 7, 8, 9, 10, 12;
Unit 5 Lessons 2, 5, 10</td>
</tr>
<tr>
<td>1.ARO.5</td>
<td>Recognize the relationship between addition/subtraction and counting and understand that counting strategies can be used to add and subtract.</td>
<td>Unit 1 Lessons 1, 2, 3, 4, 9;
Unit 2 Lessons 5, 6, 7, 8, 9;
Unit 3 Lessons 1, 3, 4, 6, 7, 11;
Unit 4 Lessons 1, 4, 5, 7, 15, 16, 17;
Unit 5 Lessons 1, 2, 4</td>
</tr>
</table>

1.ARO.6	Fluently add and subtract through 10. Know how to add and subtract through 20 using strategies such as: for addition, *count on; make a ten* (example: $7 + 5 = 7 + 3 + 2$, so $7 + 3 + 2 = 10 + 2$, and $10 + 2 = 12$); *make an easier equal sum* (example: $9 + 6 = ?$, think $9 + 1 + 5 = 10 + 5$, so $10 + 5 = 15$; for subtraction, *decompose a number to get ten* (example: $17 - 8 = 17 - 7 - 1$, think $17 - 7 = 10$ and $10 - 1 = 9$); *use a related addition to subtract* (example: if you know $5 + 6 = 11$, then you can find $11 - 5 = 6$).	Unit 1 Lessons 3, 4, 5, 6, 7, 8, 9; Unit 2 Lessons 1, 2, 3, 5, 6, 7, 8, 9, 10, 11, 12, 13, 14, 15, 16; Unit 3 Lessons 1, 3, 4, 5, 6, 7, 10, 12; Unit 4 Lessons 4, 5, 6, 10, 15; Unit 5 Lessons 1, 2, 3, 4, 5, 10, 11; Unit 6 Lessons 3, 8; Unit 7 Lessons 5, 8, 13; Unit 8 Lesson 5
1.ARO.7	Know the meaning of the equal sign; decide whether or not an equation that involves addition or subtraction is true or false.	Unit 2 Lessons 3, 4, 11, 12, 13, 16; Unit 3 Lesson 12; Unit 5 Lesson 11
1.ARO.8	Find the unknown number in an addition or subtraction equation (examples: $9 + ? = 12$; $8 = ? - 5$; $7 + 2 = ?$).	Unit 1 Lessons 3, 4, 5, 6, 7, 8; Unit 2 Lessons 5, 6, 7, 8, 9, 10, 12, 13, 14, 16; Unit 3 Lessons 3, 4, 5, 6, 7, 8, 9, 11, 12; Unit 4 Lessons 4, 5, 6, 10, 13, 14, 15, 16; Unit 5 Lessons 1, 2, 3, 4, 5, 10; Unit 6 Lessons 6, 7
1.ARO.9	Create simple patterns using objects, pictures, numbers and rules. Identify possible rules to complete or extend patterns. Patterns may be repeating, growing or shrinking. Calculators can be used to create and explore patterns.	Unit 1 Lessons 10, 11; Unit 5 Lesson 9

1.PVO Place Value and Operations

1.PVO.1	Count, with or without objects, forward and backward to 120, starting at any number less than 120. For the number sequence to 120, read and write the corresponding numerals; represent a group of objects with a written numeral, addition and subtraction, pictures, tally marks, number lines and manipulatives, such as bundles of sticks and base 10 blocks. Skip count by 2s, 5s, and 10s.	Unit 4 Lessons 1, 2, 7, 8, 9, 10, 11, 15, 16, 18; Unit 5 Lessons 7, 8, 9; Unit 6 Lessons 4, 5

Mathematical Standards

1.PVO.2	For a two-digit number, understand that the digit to the right represents ones and the digit to the left represents tens.	Unit 4 Lessons 1, 2, 3, 4, 7, 8, 9, 10, 11, 12, 13, 14, 16, 17, 18; Unit 5 Lessons 7, 8, 9; Unit 8 Lesson 1
1.PVO.2.a	Understand that 10 can be thought of as a group of ten ones named *ten*.	Unit 4 Lessons 1, 2, 3, 4, 9, 10, 16, 18; Unit 5 Lessons 8, 10; Unit 8 Lesson 1
1.PVO.2.b	Understand that the numbers 11 through 19 are made up of one ten and one through nine ones.	Unit 4 Lessons 2, 3, 4, 5, 8, 10; Unit 5 Lesson 8
1.PVO.2.c	Know that the decade numbers 10 through 90 represent one through nine tens and zero ones.	Unit 4 Lessons 1, 7, 8, 9, 13, 14, 18; Unit 5 Lesson 10; Unit 8 Lesson 1
1.PVO.3	Apply place value concepts to compare two 2-digit numbers using the symbols >, <, and =.	Unit 4 Lessons 3, 12, 16, 18; Unit 8 Lesson 6
1.PVO.4	Add numbers through 100, such as a two-digit number and a one-digit number or a two-digit number and a multiple of ten. Understand that groups of objects or drawings and strategies can be used to find sums (examples of strategies: *relationship between addition and subtraction, place value, properties of operations*) and explain how the strategy and recorded result are related. Know that to add two-digit numbers, ones are added to ones and tens are added to tens and in some instances, ten ones will result in making one ten.	Unit 4 Lessons 9, 10, 11, 13, 14, 15, 16, 17, 18; Unit 5 Lessons 9, 10, 11; Unit 8 Lessons 1, 2, 3, 4, 5, 6
1.PVO.5	Use mental math to find a number that is 10 more or 10 less than any given two-digit number (without using counting) and explain the reasoning used to find the result.	Unit 5 Lessons 8, 9
1.PVO.6	For numbers 10 through 90, subtract multiples of 10 resulting in differences of 0 through 80. Use groups of objects or pictures and strategies to subtract. Strategies can include place value concepts, the relationship between addition and subtraction, and properties of operations. Explain how the strategy and recorded result are related.	Unit 5 Lessons 9, 10, 11; Unit 8 Lesson 6

1.MDA Measurement and Data Analysis

1.MDA.1	Compare to order three items by length. Compare the lengths of two items using a third item (indirect comparison).	Unit 7 Lessons 12, 14
1.MDA.2	Determine the length of an object by placing as many same-size smaller units end-to-end as needed along the span of the object ensuring no gaps or overlaps. Understand that length of the object is the number of same-size units that were used. (Note: The number of "length-units" should not extend beyond the end of the object being measured.)	Unit 7 Lessons 13, 14
1.MDA.3	Use analog and digital clocks to express time orally and in written form in hours and half-hours.	Unit 7 Lessons 1, 2, 3, 4, 5, 14
1.MDA.4	Organize, represent, and interpret data with up to three categories using picture graphs, bar graphs, and tally charts. Ask questions and provide answers about how many in all comprise the data and how many are in each category. Compare the number in one category to that in another category.	Unit 6 Lessons 1, 2, 3, 4, 5, 9
1.MDA.5	Recognize and identify coins (penny, nickel, dime, and quarter) and their value and use the ¢ (cent) symbol appropriately.	Unit 2 Lesson 7; Unit 4, Lessons 8, 19, 20
1.MDA.6	Know the comparative values of all U.S. coins (e.g. a dime is of greater value than a nickel). Find equivalent values (e.g., a nickel is equivalent to 5 pennies.) Solve problems and use the values of the coins in the solutions of the problems.	Unit 2 Lesson 7; Unit 4 Lessons 8, 19, 20
1.MDA.7	Explore dimes and pennies as they relate to place value concepts.	Unit 4 Lessons 8, 19, 20

1.GSR Geometry and Spatial Reasoning

1.GSR.1	Understand the difference between defining attributes of a figure (examples: a square has 4 sides of equal length and 4 vertices) and non-defining attributes (examples: size, color, position). Using concrete materials and paper and pencil, build and draw geometric figures according to their defining attributes.	Unit 7 Lessons 6, 7, 8, 9, 10
1.GSR.2	Create composite geometric figures by putting together two-dimensional figures (triangles, squares, rectangles, trapezoids, half-circles, and quarter-circles) or three-dimensional figures (cubes, rectangular prisms, cylinders, and cones), then form a new figure from the composite figure.	Unit 7 Lessons 9, 10, 11
1.GSR.3	Separate rectangles and circles into two or four equal shares, and use the words *halves, fourths,* and *quarters,* and the phrases *half of, fourth of,* and *quarter of* to identify the equal-size shares. Use the terms "two of" or " four of" to describe the number of equal shares in the whole. Understand that when a figure is separated into more equal shares, the size of the shares is smaller.	Unit 7 Lessons 8, 9, 14

Mathematical Processes and Practices

MPP1

Problem Solving

Unit 1 Lessons 2, 3, 4, 6, 8, 9, 10, 11
Unit 2 Lessons 1, 2, 3, 4, 6, 7, 8, 9, 10, 13, 14, 16
Unit 3 Lessons 1, 2, 3, 4, 6, 7, 8, 9, 10, 11, 12
Unit 4 Lessons 2, 3, 5, 10, 18, 19, 20
Unit 5 Lessons 1, 2, 3, 4, 5, 6, 9, 11
Unit 6 Lessons 1, 2, 4, 5, 6, 7, 8, 9
Unit 7 Lessons 8, 12, 14
Unit 8 Lessons 1, 3, 4, 6

MPP2

Abstract and Quantitative Reasoning

Unit 1 Lessons 3, 4, 5, 6, 7, 8, 9
Unit 2 Lessons 1, 2, 3, 4, 6, 10, 11, 12, 13, 15, 16
Unit 3 Lessons 3, 5, 6, 12
Unit 4 Lessons 1, 3, 4, 6, 7, 8, 9, 10, 11, 12, 14, 15, 16, 17, 18, 19
Unit 5 Lessons 1, 2, 3, 4, 5, 9, 10, 11
Unit 6 Lessons 1, 2, 3, 5, 6, 8, 9
Unit 7 Lessons 8, 9, 14
Unit 8 Lessons 1, 2, 3, 4, 5, 6

MPP3

Use and Evaluate Logical Reasoning

Unit 1 Lessons 1, 2, 3, 4, 5, 6, 7, 8, 9, 10
Unit 2 Lessons 1, 2, 3, 4, 6, 7, 8, 9, 10, 11, 12, 13, 14, 16
Unit 3 Lessons 2, 3, 4, 6, 7, 8, 9, 10, 11, 12
Unit 4 Lessons 1, 2, 3, 4, 5, 6, 7, 8, 9, 10, 11, 12, 13, 14, 15, 16, 17, 18, 19, 20
Unit 5 Lessons 1, 2, 3, 4, 5, 6, 7, 8, 9, 10, 11
Unit 6 Lessons 1, 2, 3, 4, 5, 6, 7, 8, 9
Unit 7 Lessons 1, 2, 3, 4, 5, 6, 7, 8, 9, 10, 11, 12, 13, 14
Unit 8 Lessons 1, 2, 3, 4, 5, 6

MPP4

Mathematical Modeling

Unit 1 Lessons 2, 3, 9
Unit 2 Lessons 1, 2, 6, 10, 13, 16
Unit 3 Lessons 1, 2, 5, 6, 7, 8, 9, 10, 11, 12
Unit 4 Lessons 2, 3, 4, 5, 10, 18, 19, 20
Unit 5 Lessons 1, 2, 3, 4, 6, 8, 9, 11
Unit 6 Lessons 2, 3, 4, 5, 6, 7, 8, 9
Unit 7 Lessons 3, 8, 12, 14
Unit 8 Lessons 1, 2, 3, 6

MPP5

Use Mathematical Tools

Unit 1 Lessons 1, 2, 3, 4, 5, 6, 7, 8, 9
Unit 2 Lessons 5, 6, 7, 8, 16
Unit 3 Lessons 1, 2, 3, 4, 7, 11
Unit 4 Lessons 1, 2, 3, 4, 5, 6, 7, 8, 9, 10, 11, 12, 13, 14, 16, 17, 18, 19
Unit 5 Lessons 1, 2, 6, 7, 8, 9, 10, 11
Unit 6 Lessons 3, 4, 5, 8, 9
Unit 7 Lessons 1, 2, 5, 6, 7, 8, 9, 10, 11, 12, 13, 14
Unit 8 Lessons 2, 3, 6

MPP6

Use Precise Mathematical Language

Unit 1 Lessons 1, 2, 3, 4, 5, 6, 7, 8, 9, 10
Unit 2 Lessons 1, 3, 4, 5, 6, 7, 8, 9, 10, 11, 12, 13, 14, 16
Unit 3 Lessons 1, 2, 3, 4, 5, 6, 7, 8, 9, 10, 11, 12
Unit 4 Lessons 1, 2, 3, 4, 5, 6, 7, 8, 9, 10, 11, 12, 13, 14, 15, 16, 17, 18, 19, 20
Unit 5 Lessons 1, 2, 3, 4, 5, 6, 7, 8, 9, 10, 11
Unit 6 Lessons 1, 2, 3, 4, 5, 6, 7, 8, 9
Unit 7 Lessons 1, 2, 3, 4, 5, 6, 7, 8, 9, 10, 11, 12, 13, 14
Unit 8 Lessons 1, 2, 3, 4, 5, 6

MPP7

See Structure

Unit 1 Lessons 1, 2, 3, 4, 5, 6, 7, 8, 9, 10, 11
Unit 2 Lessons 13, 14, 16
Unit 3 Lessons 1, 3, 9, 12
Unit 4 Lessons 1, 2, 3, 5, 6, 7, 8, 9, 10, 13, 17, 18, 19
Unit 5 Lessons 1, 2, 3, 5, 6, 7, 8, 9, 10, 11
Unit 6 Lessons 6, 8, 9
Unit 7 Lessons 1, 2, 3, 4, 5, 6, 7, 9, 10, 11, 14
Unit 8 Lessons 2, 6

MPP8

Generalize

Unit 1 Lessons 1, 2, 3, 4, 5, 6, 7, 8, 9
Unit 2 Lessons 6, 7, 8, 11, 14, 16
Unit 3 Lessons 8, 9, 12
Unit 4 Lessons 1, 2, 5, 6, 7, 9, 10, 12, 13, 14, 15, 17, 18
Unit 5 Lessons 1, 2, 4, 5, 6, 7, 8, 9, 10, 11
Unit 6 Lessons 1, 6, 7, 9
Unit 7 Lessons 3, 6, 7, 8, 9, 10, 12, 14
Unit 8 Lessons 1, 2, 4, 6

Index

© Houghton Mifflin Harcourt Publishing Company

Index

Illustrator: Josh Brill

Did you ever try to use shapes to draw animals like the frog on the cover?

Over the last 10 years Josh has been using geometric shapes to design his animals. His aim is to keep the animal drawings simple and use color to make them appealing.

Add some color to the frog Josh drew. Then try drawing a cat or dog or some other animal using the shapes below.

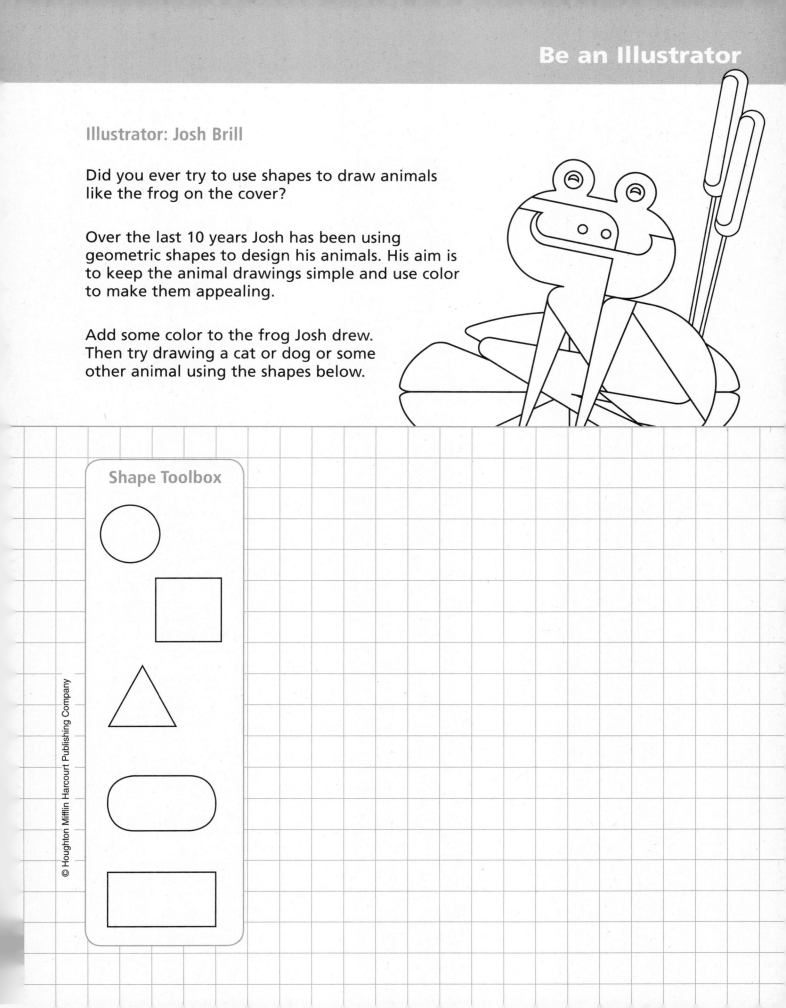

Shape Toolbox